*Fort Hood: The First Fifty Years*

# FORT HOOD

*The first fifty years*

by
Odie B. Faulk
& Laura E. Faulk

The Frank W. Mayborn Foundation
Temple Texas • 1990

Dedicated to
**FRANK W. MAYBORN**
who had the vision to see what could be

# Contents

# Preface

IN August of 1970, when he was Chief of Staff of III Corps, General Robert M. Shoemaker described Fort Hood as "an ideal place to be given big jobs." Thirty years earlier when Frank W. Mayborn, publisher of the *Temple Daily Telegram*, was trying to convince the Army to locate an Army camp in Bell and Coryell counties, he told General Richard Donovan, commander of the 4th Army in San Antonio, that the site he was recommending was ideal for training soldiers. At the start of the final decade of the 20th century, as Fort Hood approaches its fiftieth birthday, the current commander, Lieutenant General Richard Graves, echoes the same sentiments when he refers to Fort Hood as one of the best places in the world for preparing soldiers for combat.

And Fort Hood, throughout its years of service as the largest armor post in the free world, has been an economic bonanza for Central Texas, just as Frank Mayborn envisioned it would be when he worked so hard to convince the Army that the site he proposed was the best place for the military reservation. In 1989 Fort Hood had the largest single payroll in the state of Texas, injecting some $1 billion a year into the local economy. Other than the noise from cannon fire and helicopter flights, Fort Hood has been a non-polluting industry responsible for the presence in Central Texas of some 150,000 soldiers, military dependents, and retirees. It truly has become an economic colossus, the engine which has fueled much of the growth in Central Texas.

As world conditions change at the start of the 1990s, no one can foretell what the military needs of the nation will be as the Cold War appears to be ending and historic alignments in Europe change. However, until we arrive at that blessed time of peace, when the world will beat its swords into plowshares and there is no need for armed forces, Fort Hood will remain for the United States Army, as the sign at its gate proclaims, "The Great Place."

Initially a camp for training Tank Destroyers and evaluating their weapons, Fort Hood evolved into an Infantry Replacement Training facility and then, after World War II ended, a home for Armor, at one time or another serving as headquarters for the 1st, 2nd, and 4th Armored Divisions and the 1st Cavalry Division. The goal at Fort Hood from the 1950s to the end of the 1980s, as described in May of 1978 by Lieutenant General Marvin D. Fuller, has been "how quick we can get out of here to reinforce NATO." In addition, Fort Hood also has been a place for constant training of Armor as well as testing new weapons and ideas, new methods of organization, and new contingency plans.

It was our purpose, in writing this book, to trace the founding of Fort Hood and its history subsequent to that time, showing its contributions to the United States Army and its economic and social impact on Central Texas.

In our work we incurred a great obligation to the Frank W. Mayborn Foundation and to its President, Sue Mayborn. She made available to us her husband's papers and the transcripts of his recollections relative to Fort Hood; these were invaluable in their insights about every phase of the post's existence. These cover such major events as getting the post located in Texas, getting it made permanent, civilian-military relations, attempts at expanding the size of the reservation, and many other facets of its history, including Mayborn's first-hand recollections of going through basic training at the fort as a private, then attending officers' candidate school there and the Tank Destroyer combat courses. After World War II, Mayborn was a friend and confidant to almost every post commander and served on the Fort Hood Civilian Advisory Committee for years. Our work would have been far more difficult without access to the Mayborn files. In addition, we thank Mrs. Mayborn for allowing us full use of the morgue files on Fort Hood at the *Temple Daily Telegram* as well as the Fort Hood anniversary issues of that paper and the *Killeen Daily Herald*; these likewise were of tremendous help to us in our research.

We also acknowledge our debt to Lieutenant General Richard Graves, the present commanding general of III Corps and Fort Hood, for giving us access to the files kept by the historical branch of his command and for extending us many courtesies at the post. His staff gave generously of their time to check facts and locate documents. Moreover, we thank all the general officers who granted us access to their memories of the post by allowing us to interview them. In addition, we acknowledge the assistance of public librarians in Killeen, Temple, and Waco, of librarians at Central Texas College, Temple Junior College, Baylor University, and the Texas Collection and the W.R. Poage Legislative Library Center at Baylor. In Washington, D.C., we were given tremendous help at the Center for Military History and at the Washington National Records Center of the National Archives and Records Administration. To all who assisted, we are deeply grateful for making our work easier.

Odie B. Faulk
Laura E. Faulk

*Chapter One*

# Land and People

WHEN Anglo-Texan settlers first began to move into the 340 square miles that would come to be Fort Hood, this during the days of the Republic, the region was still largely the way the Creator had fashioned it. It was not a place of mountains purple in their majesty nor was it a plain covered with a waving and tossing sea of grass. It was not a desert of magnificent vistas nor yet a forest of trees towering up to reach the sky.

Rather this land–the western portion of present Bell County and the southeastern part of Coryell County–is a transition zone. To the west is the southern edge of the High Plains, to the east the Black and Grand Prairies. It is a limestone plain susceptible to gullying by erosion, a land of rugged bluffs and sharp slopes, upthrusts that the early settlers, if Spanish in descent, called "mesas" or "mesitas," and if from portions of the Old South referred to as "knobs" or "mountains." Today it is called the Limestone Hill Country, a place of ridges, hills, and escarpments seemingly designed to torture the soldiers and equipment in training there.

That portion of Coryell and Bell counties that would come to be Fort Hood is drained by Cowhouse and Owl creeks and their numerous tributaries, all of whose water flow into the Leon River, itself eventually to become part of the Little River. Generally the average rainfall is some thirty inches a year, but this falls so unevenly that prior to the construction of dams in the area the region was subject to periodic flooding when spring and fall clouds opened in sudden outbursts.

The open areas of Fort Hood are covered by sedge grass as tall as wheat, grass that grows so abundant in a climate so mild that cattle can usually find grazing all year. Along the banks of Cowhouse, Owl, and the other creeks are dense thickets of cane and stately groves of cottonwood, elm, hackberry, ash, and giant pecans. Higher up on the limestone caprock of the knobs and mesas are juniper thickets sprinkled about with cedar brakes and numerous live oak trees along with green prickly pear cacti and a few mesquite.[1]

For uncounted centuries this was the home of diverse and numerous wildlife: turkeys and mud hens and prairie chickens, deer and pronghorn antelope and wolves, catamounts and cougars and pumas, black bears and bison and wild hogs, along with rabbits, raccoons, and opossums. There were rattlesnakes of several types, water moccasins, and coral snakes as well as several nonpoisonous varieties of snakes. There were black widow spiders, scorpions, centipedes, flies, gnats, chiggers, ticks, wasps, bees, and stinging lizards. In fact, almost every poisonous reptile and insect known in the United States, save the gila monster of southwestern deserts, could be found in this area. Many soldiers training at Fort Hood would swear that the Creator populated the area with every stinging and biting variety of animal and insect.

The creeks and rivers of this region also abounded with mud and blue and channel catfish, bass, trout, and perch. And also it boasted flowers of a hundred stunning varieties, butterflies so beautiful they seemed to be flowers on the wing, and birds of multicolored hue whose songs were like the music of heaven itself.[2]

Sharing this land with its plant, animal, and insect life were bands of nomadic Native Americans, moving about as nature and their own whims dictated. Securing a livelihood in the region was not difficult even for their technology, and they hunted and gathered and fished to provide a rich diet for themselves. So many Indians once camped here temporarily or made more permanent homes in the area that in Coryell County archaeologists have unearthed one of the greatest collections of aboriginal stone artifacts ever assembled in the New World.[3]

The first accounts of these prehistoric residents of the region were written by Spanish explorers and settlers who began moving north into this region after Mexico was conquered by the sons of Castile and Leon. No Spanish missions or forts or civil settlements were erected in the area, however, and the land continued to be the domain of the Indian lords of the plains. In 1821 ownership of the region passed from Spain to Mexico, and it was during the Mexican era that Sterling

Robertson, an American, secured a contract to settle colonists from the United States in Central Texas, some of whom actually located in what now is Bell County. Then in 1835-1836 came the Texas Revolution and Republic, and on December 20, 1836, the First Congress created giant Milam County in Central Texas.[4] As a hardy few pioneers moved into old Milam County, they began a lengthy war with the Lipan Apaches, Tonkawas, Comanches, Kiowas, Huecos (or Wacos) and other Indians who had a previous claim to the region.

One of those who died in that long war of a thousand skirmishes for ownership of Central Texas was James Coryell, an adventuresome and "likable young fellow" who came to Texas in the 1820s from his native Ohio in search of inexpensive land. In 1831 he was wounded by Indians when he accompanied James Bowie in search of a rumored lost silver mine on the San Saba River. Four years later he was surveying a headright granted him along the creek that would come to bear his name, and it was in that area the following year that he joined the Rangers to defend the area against Indians. In 1837, while out with a group of men cutting down a bee tree and eating honey, he came into a fierce fight with Indian warriors and was killed and scalped.[5]

Only the hardy few ventured into this region during the days when the Lone Star flag of the Republic flew overhead. Nor did many more migrate there in the immediate aftermath of Statehood (on December 29, 1845) and the two years of the war with Mexico that followed. Once that conflict was settled by the Treaty of Guadalupe Hidalgo in early 1848, settlers did begin moving westward once again in Texas, and they were vocal in their demands that the federal government extend them protection from Native American nomads. It was for this reason that Fort Gates was established on October 26, 1849, on the north bank of the Leon River some five miles above the mouth of Coryell Creek. Stationed at the post, named in honor of Major C.R. Gates, were two companies of the 8th Infantry. Lumber for building had to be hauled 85 miles from a mill at Bastrop, Texas. Four officers' quarters were erected; these were of frame construction and covered with oak clapboard. The other buildings–the hospital, store room, shops, stables, and barracks, seventeen structures in all–were made with upright posts sharpened and driven into the ground and chinked with clay. A short distance away was a trading post operated by R.G.

scene just after the robbery and killing to give chase to the outlaws, who made good their escape by holing up in a cave in the hills of what now is Coryell County.

Later when one of the outlaws became ill, another of their number rode to the little settlement at Fort Gates (near the present Gatesville) and persuaded the town doctor to tend the sick man. The doctor was blindfolded outside town and taken for a ride that he estimated to be 10 miles. Inside the cave his blindfold was removed, and he was ordered to tend the sick man. After he had done his chore as a doctor, he was shown what in the retelling became "stacks and stacks of gold bullion" in the cave and was told to take what he wanted. The good doctor said he would take only a nominal fee, then was blindfolded once again and returned to town. No one, neither bandits nor doctor, ever found the cave again, and its contents supposedly are still in that cave waiting to be found.[11]

Another story told by old-timers in Central Texas, equally in the grand tradition of the Hollywood Western, concerned a payroll bound for Fort Gates along the old military road running to the post. As in the previous story, dastardly outlaws laid in wait and ambushed the wagon containing the gold, killing the paymaster and his military escort, and then they buried their treasure somewhere along the road between the fort and the place where it crossed the Bosque River (near the present town of Clifton). For reasons never fully explained, the outlaws in this case, like those who took gold from the Forty-Niners, never returned to retrieve their treasure. Somewhere out in the hills of what now is the military reservation of Fort Hood, the gold supposedly waits for a lucky soldier on maneuvers to find it.[12]

Moreover, there is a story that Bell or Coryell County may be the location of a silver mine that once belonged to Jim Bowie. According to this tale, Bowie, who would gain some measure of immortality at the Alamo in company with Davy Crockett and William Barret Travis, earlier had become a blood brother to Lipan Apaches who showed him a productive silver mine worked for hundreds of years by Indians, then by Spaniards and Mexicans. However, this mine and its underground treasure room, reported to contain millions in gold and silver bullion and coins, was sealed off about 1830, and no one has found it since.[13]

In addition, legend holds that just a few miles away, in adjoining

Williamson County, the treasure of the great Aztec king, Montezuma, may be buried. This consists of millions in gold and silver hurried north so that the Spanish conqueror, Hernan Cortez, and his followers could not lay hands on it.

Finally, a story concerning a possible stash of wealth on the Fort Hood reservation surfaced in 1974 when a bulldozer, working at a remote corner of the post, unearthed a slab of limestone caught in the roots of a long-dead live oak tree. This proved to be a tombstone on which could still be read–in English–the words, "General J.P. Flores, 1805, Spanish War." Jim P. Shirah, secretary and supervisor of excavation for the Fort Hood Archaeological Society, wrote to the chief of the Army Center of Military History, Historical Services Division, in Washington asking for help in identifying the mysterious General Flores, previously totally unknown in Texas history and for whom no record survived in Spanish records. Shirah commented that this accidental discovery had set off "rumors of gold hoards and buried treasure, and even wilder nonsense," while a newspaper account quoted several people who speculated that Flores had been in the area with gold coins belonging to the Aaron Burr Conspiracy. These rumors gradually died when no gold or any records of General Flores could be found.[14]

In addition to tales of lost mines, buried treasure, and hidden loot, there are many stories about the days when Bell and Coryell counties were traversed by several leading outlaws of Western fact and legend–John Wesley Hardin, who was reported to have more than 40 notches on his pistols; Bill Longley, who only killed about half as many men as Hardin; and Sam Bass, whose career in bank and train robbing was ended a few miles to the south at Round Rock. Jesse and Frank James along with the Younger boys passed through the region on their way to scenes of nefarious activity, and these outlaws, like Indians and Spaniards, were reported to have buried some of their ill-gotten loot along Owl and Cowhouse creeks in Bell and Coryell counties.[15]

Most of those who settled in this area never set out in search of lost mines or buried treasure. Rather they spent their years trying to coax coins from the stubborn earth in the form of cotton or corn by way of hard, unremitting labor or else contending with cattle that seemed determined to do the opposite of what was wanted by those tending them. Because those living in the country needed someplace to buy feed and seed along with sacks of flour, coffee, and sugar as well as needles and thread and an occasional bolt of cloth or yard of ribbon, small trading centers grew in northwestern Bell County and southeastern Coryell County, communities such as Antelope, Clear Creek, Silver City, Palo Alto, New Hope, Sugar Loaf, and Brookhaven. In each there were those who dreamed that their community someday might become a great city to rival Dallas or Galveston or San Antonio in population, magnificence, and importance, but most never amounted to more than a rural school, a church or two, perhaps a country general store, and a cemetery.

Farming gradually came to dominate in the region, good bottom land going for up to $10 an acre by the end of the century, while prairie acres capable of cultivation were valued at $1 to $5 each; grazing land remained inexpensive at about $1 per acre. Land already cleared and plowed could be rented for $3 per acre per year or for one-third of the grain and one-fourth of the cotton. The increase in farming was made possible by three advances in technology: barbed wire, which made sturdy fencing relatively inexpensive; windmills, easy to drill because of better cable tool drilling rigs, which brought a stable supply of water for man and farm animals; and the railroad, which reached eastern Bell County in 1880 and ran west across Coryell County in 1882, thereby allowing easier access to market for crops and livestock.

Always there were complainers, known then as "croakers," who predicted drought and plague and falling farm prices would bring only disaster, but most of the early settlers were optimistic, believing better fortune awaited them in the near future if they plowed yet more acres and planted additional fields of wheat and cotton. Others looked at the wet-dry cycles of rainfall and argued that Central Texas, particularly the broken country of western Bell County and eastern Coryell County, should not be plowed but rather kept in its natural state as a paradise for stock raising.

Yet others thought the high bluffs, secluded valleys, and dense cane brakes of Cowhouse and other creeks in the area along the Bell-Coryell county line an ideal place for hiding horses and cattle stolen from honest ranchers. This area near Sugar Loaf Mountain and Cowhouse and Owl creeks was yet "almost a wilderness" in the 1870s.[16] Especially was rustling a problem in the era of Reconstruction (1865-1874) when lawlessness and disorder were rampant. Ranchers, farmers, and townspeople alike grew so angry at the seeming helplessness of law enforcement officials and at the conniving and slippery ways of lawyers and courts that many times they took matters into their own hands and began dispensing a rough form of justice. When caught, or even strongly suspected, rustlers were given a warning to leave the country. On the occasion of the second offense—and many times at the first if caught red-handed—they were summarily hanged on the sturdy limb of a tree without benefit of judge or jury.

In May of 1874 there was an even greater indication of outrage at the boldness of rustlers and the helplessness which honest citizens felt. Sheriff Robert B. Halley and a posse had nabbed a band of horse thieves who were operating out of cedar brakes along the Bell-Coryell county line, and eight of them were confined in one cell at the county jail in Belton along with a man from Coryell County who was awaiting trial for killing his wife. About 2:00 a.m. on the morning of May 25, when Sheriff Halley was out of town, a band of about 100 unmasked citizens came to the jail, escorted the four guards outside, and used axes and hatchets to break down the jail doors. Reportedly some of the horse thieves inside were heard to comment, "Our friends have come to release us." The infuriated mob thereupon began firing shotguns into the mass of nine bodies in the cell, continuing to shoot, as the newspaper in Waco reported, "as long as one moved a limb. They were a hard pack but their fate was certainly a horrible one. God pity the poor wretches!"[17] All nine were killed, and no one was ever found who could identify any member of the vigilante mob. For the next 20 years there was a noticeable reduction in rustling in the area around Belton, which had replaced Nolanville as the seat of Bell County.

Between the removal of the Indians in 1875 and the turn of the 20th century, the population in the region grew dramatically. Coryell County increased from 4,124 in 1870 to 21,308 in 1900,[18] while Bell County grew from 4,799 in 1860 to 45,535.[19] Temple, founded in 1880 at the arrival of the Gulf, Colorado and Santa Fe Railroad, had grown to 7,065 people at the start of the 20th century. The third-largest town in Bell County was Killeen, started in 1882 when the Gulf, Colorado and

Santa Fe arrived at that point; by 1900 the little agricultural center had 780 people, almost all of them in one way or another focusing their lives on the GC&SF depot; to it came supplies for the merchants, and from it was shipped the produce of farm and ranch.[20]

Temple seemed a booming metropolis in comparison to the communities in neighboring Coryell County. There the major city was the county seat, Gatesville, started in 1854. By 1900 it boasted 1,865 residents, thanks in large measure to the arrival in 1882 of the St. Louis Southwestern Railway, also known as the Cotton Belt System. Second in size in the county was Copperas Cove. It originally had been located some two miles away from where it eventually would grow at the site of a spring in a natural cove created by surrounding hills. The water gushing from this spring, according to some, tasted like the mineral copperas. Thus the community that grew there was named Copperas Cove. When the GC&SF Railroad built through the area in 1882, the town moved to its permanent location and slowly, ever so slowly grew. By 1900 the population stood at 475.[21]

In the first three decades of the 20th century, only Temple would grow to significant size, reaching 15,345 by 1930, then dropping one in number by 1940 to 15,344. Killeen, in those same years, would struggle to reach 1,263 residents, while Gatesville would grow to approximately 3,177 in 1940 and Coryell County to 20,226. Copperas Cove, meanwhile, was sliding slowly toward what seemed a certain death; after rising to 509 residents in 1920, it dropped to 406 in 1930 and then to 356 in 1940.[22]

The first three decades of the 20th century saw a few miles of roads paved through the region, but most were still only graded dirt lanes that twisted and turned from one tiny community to another, even making ninety-degree turns at section lines or even at quarter-section farms. Until 1932 most highways in Texas were financed by individual counties, and Bell and Coryell had too small a tax base to hard-surface anything except the most-used roads in the vicinity of towns. And after 1932 each county had to purchase the right-of-way for state and federal highways. Thus in the first three decades of the 20th century years, Bell and Coryell county roads remained little more than long, thin quagmires in which Henry Ford's Model Ts or Model As became hopelessly mired when it rained, and they would have to be extracted with teams of mules or horses. Farms were numerous and small, averaging less than 100 acres each, and tenancy was on the rise, especially in the late 1920s and during the depression years of the 1930s. Cotton had become the leading money crop, while oats and corn had far surpassed wheat in significance, but nothing produced enough income to satisfy the debts that seemed to sprout faster than weeds and Johnson grass.[23]

This was a time when the economic life in both Bell and Coryell counties revolved around farming and credit. During spring and summer, farmers making purchases would sign IOUs for what they needed and then try to settle their bills in the fall when their cotton was ginned and sold or when they rounded up cattle and delivered them to loading pens at railroad towns. This was a time of hard work and few comforts, most farm families handling less than $300 in cash money a year. In towns there was electricity and running water, and telephone lines were installed to link all the cities and some of the rural farm communities with the outside world. But in the countryside, life was still little changed from Biblical times. The labor was done largely with human and animal power, light came from lamps, and food was cooked on wood stoves. Usually at the second frost in the fall, hogs were killed and the meat salted to preserve it, while potatoes were buried in the storm cellar and fruit was sun-dried. Few farm homes had running water or indoor plumbing, and only the privileged few had a wind charger powering a radio that pulled a signal out of the air from distant Dallas, Fort Worth, or San Antonio stations.

Then came the Great Depression of 1929 and the hard times of the 1930s. Suddenly the price of cotton spiraled downward to five cents a pound–$25 for a bale of cotton–and bushels of corn and wheat brought only a few pennies each. Farmers who had borrowed to buy expensive machinery or additional land no longer could pay their banker, while sharecroppers and owners alike who had bought food and clothing on credit could not pay city merchants. The owners of grocery stores, hardware emporiums, new car dealerships, variety and department stores–like the farmers–either were ruined or driven to the brink of bankruptcy as the economy of the region suddenly switched from credit to cash. Life became extremely earnest as luxuries disappeared and necessities became dear indeed. As Frank W. Mayborn, owner of the *Temple Daily Telegram* commented about those days, "We scratched like chickens."[24]

Despite the hard times, the hard-working people of rural western Bell and eastern Coryell counties still gathered each Sunday in their community churches. There with song books and Bibles clenched in callused hands, they turned their work-lined faces heavenward and prayed–for good weather and good crops and a better future for their children. All they asked for themselves was a penny or two more a pound for their cotton or corn and, hopefully, a place in the Promised Land of their fathers when at last they mingled their dust with the good earth they worked.

So absorbed were Central Texans in their own problems during the Great Depression that few noticed the ominous news coming out of Europe. Adolph Hitler came to power in 1933 and began rearming Germany, while Benito Mussolini had his Italian soldiers invade Ethiopia. In the Far East, Japanese troops were fighting in China, and the Rising Sun of the emperor was unfurled above Mongolia. War clouds were dark and ominous by 1938, and the following year World War II began in August when German troops invaded Poland. Central Texas, like the rest of the United States, was about to be pulled out of depression by the greatest war in recorded history.

*Chapter Two*

# Creation of the Post

IN the United States of the 1930s, there were a few voices crying out that the rise of dictatorships around the world inevitably would drag the democracies into war.

However, such cries fell on pacifist ears. Intellectuals were telling fellow Americans that World War I, the Great War, had been fought not "to make the world safe for democracy," but rather to enrich munitions makers and industrialists or else that the country had been the victim of manipulation by adroit Allied propagandists. Many Americans vowed never again to be drawn into a European conflict; in fact, so many took the "Never Again" pledge that it became as fashionable as had been the temperance pledge prior to Prohibition. University students were encouraged each May Day to walk out of classes as a way of going on strike for peace, and taking the Oxford Oath, a vow never to fight in war, had almost become a campus ritual.

In 1935 Congress responded to the pacifist pressure by passing the first of a series of neutrality acts. These were intended to force the president to shun any commitment that might lead the nation into conflict. Yet from Europe and Asia came disturbing news of aggression. Roosevelt was alarmed at the actions of Hitler and Mussolini in Europe and Africa, while the Japanese warlords had invaded China and were committing acts of savage barbarism. By 1938 the president recognized a clear and present danger in the epidemic of lawlessness by the three so-called Axis powers.

However, it seemed that few beyond the president recognized any peril for the United States. America's armed forces were woefully short of everything needed to conduct a war. The National Defense Act of 1920 had reduced the Army to 280,000 men, but for years appropriations had been so low that barely half that many men were in uniform. By 1933 the United States Army had dropped in size to seventeenth in the world, and it was in desperate need of more men and new weapons; the Air Corps had planes that were outdated; and the Navy needed ships and men if it was to defend the ocean approaches to the Western Hemisphere.

An idea of how woefully inadequate the Army budget was can be seen in the type of weapons and amount of ammunition available to train officers and men during this lean period. Beverley E. Powell, a graduate of the Military Academy in 1936, was assigned to duty at Fort Sam Houston in the field artillery, and later he would tell how he and his men would go out to Camp Bullis[1] for practice in firing their weapons. The standard weapon in their unit was a French 75 millimeter piece manufactured during World War I. However, there was not sufficient ammunition for every officer to fire one 75mm shell. Therefore the barrel of a 37mm cannon, also dating from World War I, would be attached on top of the barrel of the 75mm weapon, and each officer was given one round to fire. "Half of the World War I rounds would not fire," Powell later recalled. "And if you lost a round, you paid for it personally."[2]

By the latter part of the 1930s, both Roosevelt and Congress were in agreement that the Navy needed strengthening to prevent any invasion, which would have to come by sea. Therefore in 1938 Congress passed the Naval Expansion Act, which called for doubling the amount of tonnage of American warships. And because the German Luftwaffe had so thoroughly demonstrated the effectiveness of air power in the invasion of Czechoslovakia in 1938, Roosevelt in his annual message to Congress in January 1939 recommended that $300 million be appropriated to buy military aircraft.

Yet nothing was done for the Army. The total budget for the Army, including pay, training, new weapons, research, maintenance, and construction, was $454 million that fiscal year. At the outbreak of war in Europe on September 1, 1939, as German tanks and troops swarmed across the plains of Poland, the United States Army was still woefully unprepared even to defend the boundaries of the nation from invasion, let alone carry battle to foreign shores. In July of 1939 the United States Army stood at 190,000 men. President Roosevelt on September

8 issued an executive order declaring a limited national emergency and authorized the Army to increase to a total troop strength of 227,000. This expansion did provide enough troops that the Army in April of 1940 could undertake its first maneuvers in corps size since 1918. The next month–May, 1940–there was an exercise pitting corps against corps in which several new weapons were tested along with innovations in tactics adapted to meet reported new German methods of warfare.

The Army Air Corps likewise began preparing to defend the skies of America. In July of 1940 Congress voted to increase the Air Corps to 54 air groups. Reserve and National Guard flight officers were called to active duty to man the planes that were being built, but still there were not enough pilots. Congress therefore authorized contracts with colleges and universities to give cadets instruction in ground school and primary flight training, but even that was inadequate. The next step that summer was to award contracts to civilian flight schools to give primary training. The first nine contracts went to Army Reserve officers, aging veterans of World War I, men like Bill Long in Dallas, Max Balfour in Tulsa, and Al Lodwick in Lakeland, Florida. For them the Army built runways and hangars, erected barracks, and delivered planes, all at government expense. Similarly, Congress and the president continued to be generous with the Navy, voting additional funds in 1939 and 1940 for constructing yet more capital ships of the line.

In 1940 the president and members of Congress finally became aware of the need to increase the size of the Army and to vote money for new weapons, especially after the German *Blitzkrieg* overran Denmark, Norway, and Belgium and then sliced through the fortified hills of France. Even most isolationists and pacifists conceded that America should begin arming for a war that most civilians still hoped to avoid. In fact, as events in Europe unfolded in the spring and early summer of 1940, Congress first voted to raise the Regular Army to its full strength of 280,000, then to 375,000, and finally it approved a budget of almost $3 billion, more than three times what had been voted originally for the coming fiscal year. And that summer of 1940, after France fell and British troops were evacuated from the Continent to the island fortress of England, the War Department recommended an

American Army of 1 million by October 1, 1941, and 2 million by January 1, 1942.[3]

An Army of this size meant that manpower requirements could be met only by conscription and by mobilizing the Reserves and the National Guard. All citizen-soldiers were called to national service by act of Congress on August 27, and on September 16 it passed a Selective Service Act, the first peacetime draft in history. All men between 21 and 35 had to register, and soon those whose names were called began to report for duty. There followed a storm of debate, some arguing that Roosevelt was dragging the country into an imperialists' war, others saying he was helping England fight against German aggression. This debate carried into the presidential election of 1940 in which Roosevelt won an unprecedented third term. He interpreted this as an endorsement of both his domestic and foreign policies. When Congress in March of 1941 approved the Lend-Lease Act, allowing the president to "sell, transfer, exchange, lease, lend" military equipment to any country whose defense the president deemed "vital to the defense of the United States," Commerce Secretary Jesse Jones was quoted as saying, "We're in the war; at least we are nearly in it; we're preparing for it."

Appointed Chief of Staff of the Army on September 1, 1939, the same day Germany invaded Poland, was George C. Marshall, Jr., elevated to that high post at the insistence of the aging hero of World War I, General John J. Pershing. Marshall had served on Pershing's staff in Europe in World War I. Once named Chief of Staff, Marshall quickly began to reorganize his general staff and to plan for American involvement in the war already raging in Europe. One of his innovations in the War Department was to activate a command known as General Headquarters, Field Forces, with himself heading it in addition to serving as Chief of Staff. In effect, this meant he would command both the War Department in Washington as well as troops in the field. In practice, however, he soon found the combined duties too much for one man, and he named Major General Lesley J. McNair to be the active commander of GHQ, Field Forces. McNair previously had been commandant of the Command and General Staff School. In his new post it was his job to oversee the four field armies then operating and to direct their training activities.[4]

On May 14, 1941, General McNair ordered the creation of a "planning and exploring" command in GHQ, Field Forces, to pursue research. This Planning Branch was to be part of the G-3 Section of the GHQ, War Department, and was to coordinate its activities with the National Defense Research Committee, Inventors Council, G-2, and the development people in G-4. Placed in charge of this unit, which was activated on May 15, was Lieutenant Colonel Andrew D. Bruce, a young member of the War Department General Staff.

A native of St. Louis, Bruce had grown up in the Rio Grande Valley of Texas and then had attended Texas A & M College, graduating in 1916 with a bachelor's degree in science. The following year, after the outbreak of World War I, he attended Officers' Training School at Leon Springs, then served in the 5th Machine Gun Battalion in the St. Mihiel and the Meuse-Argonne offensives. For his role in combat, he was awarded the Distinguished Service Cross, the French Legion of Honor, and the Purple Heart. In the years following the end of this conflict, he was an instructor in the Infantry School at Fort Benning, Georgia, and a professor of military science and tactics at Allen Academy in Bryan, Texas, rated by the War Department as "an honor military school." He also attended the War College, the Command and General Staff College, and the Naval War College.[5]

One of the tasks assigned the new Planning Branch was to devise innovative ways of coping with the seemingly invincible German war machine of tanks and airplanes that was sweeping across Europe, as one observer said, "like mercury spilling on a laboratory floor"; like mercury "this armored force dissolved, so to speak, the best armament Poland, France, England, Yugoslavia, and Greece could produce."[6] In short, the Planning Branch was charged with devising tactics to update the American Army's method of contending with armor and to train soldiers to use the many modern weapons denied them during the 20 years of austere budgets following the end of World War I.

For Colonel Bruce and the staff he gathered in the Planning Branch, there followed months of study in many areas. With regard to German tank warfare there were observations in the field of tanks in action as well as an examination of what had been learned in Europe. Technical people made detailed studies of German tanks showing their strong and weak points.

Prior to 1940, the commonly held military strategy for coping with tanks in Europe was to deploy antitank guns passively in cordon defense and wait for the tanks to come to them. For example, French commanders were so confident of what their antitank guns could do that one of them was quoted as saying, "At the present time, the antitank gun confronts the tank, as during the last war the machine gun confronted the infantry." The failure of this strategy became evident both in combat in the spring of 1940 in Europe, when panzer divisions easily overran the French antitank defenses, and in American maneuvers in August that year.

Therefore on September 23, 1940, WD Training Circular No. 3 dictated that American forces should place a minimum of antitank guns in passive (fixed) position and hold the remainder in reserve to be moved where needed. This change from the previous passive strategy eventually would lead to developing the aggressive tactics associated with American military efforts in World War II. And there was great need for training American troops in such tactics, for as late as the summer of 1940 few soldiers in the units charged with defense against tanks had ever seen a tank or fired their weapons at a moving target.[7] That fall of 1940 each regiment of infantry was authorized to have one antitank company consisting of eight 37-millimeter guns.

So evident was the need to find some way to stop tanks that on April 15, 1941, a month before the creation of the Planning Branch, the Operations and Training Division of the War Department General staff had hosted an antitank conference in Washington. Attending were representatives from almost every branch of the Army: cavalry, infantry, field artillery, armor, coast artillery, the War Plans Division, and GHQ itself. It had been the conclusion of this group that the best defense against tanks would be an aggressive offense, but antitank units should continue to be part of the infantry until an official armored arm was created; when that happened, armor then would take control of antitank units.[8]

So pressing was the need to find some way to stop an army of advancing tanks that another antitank conference met in Washington on May 26, 1941. Those officers in attendance recommended that antitank companies, at this time scattered in infantry regiments, be kept there, but that they should be organized into antitank battalions that would be armed with the 37-millimeter antitank gun then being manufactured in quantity. By the time the United States became involved in the war, some 2,500 of these 37-millimeter guns, which were patterned almost exactly on the German PAK 36, were deployed among the various divisions.[9]

From July 14 to 17, 1941, yet a third antitank conference, this one historic in its recommendations, was held at the Army War College in Washington, D.C. To the specialists who attended, Colonel Bruce showed the weapon he was recommending as primary for stopping tanks. This was a 75-millimeter gun mounted on a halftrack and was to be field tested during maneuvers that autumn. Bruce explained his belief that the ideal antitank weapon would be a fast-moving vehicle with a weapon packing a powerful punch, one that could be easily and quickly fired, and sufficient armored protection should be placed around it that it could not be put out of action by a machine gun. Bruce likened the ideal antitank weapon to a "cruiser" rather than a "battleship," a theme echoed by General McNair in his closing remarks:

> *...The counter-attack long has been termed the soul of defense.... There is no reason why antitank guns, supported by infantry, cannot attack tanks just as infantry, supported by artillery, has attacked infantry in the past. Certainly it is poor economy to use a $35,000 medium tank to destroy another tank when the job can be done by a gun costing a fraction as much.*

Once the proper weapon had been chosen, said General McNair, the next steps should be first, by reason and analysis, to devise a proper antitank strategy, then to test both through practical application in the field with troops. He was optimistic that such an approach would succeed, using an oft-quoted aphorism from the sport of wrestling to make his point: "There ain't no hold what can't be broke."[10]

On August 8, 1941, came a detailed memorandum from the Planning Branch calling for separate antitank battalions, 220 of them. Colonel Bruce's recommendation was based on a 55-division Army, each with an antitank battalion attached to it, another 55 battalions held at corps and field army level, and 110 battalions operating at the GHQ level. Such a concept would have meant that one-fourth of the United States

Army's ground troops would be in antitank units.

On October 18 General McNair, the Chief of Staff, acted on this recommendation by establishing an antitank center under War Department control. This new antitank center would be modeled on what had been created in 1917 when the machine gun seemed a new and insurmountable weapon. At Camp Gordon, Georgia, a Machine Gun Training Center had been established during World War I to train soldiers in the tactics to be employed against this weapon. After that war ended, the center was disbanded. In 1941 the recommendation was made to create a Tank Destroyer Training Center which, after the time of need had passed, would be disbanded. A similar recommendation was made to start an Armored School and an Anti-Aircraft Artillery School.[11]

Colonel Bruce, whose tour of duty on the General Staff of the War Department was to end on November 4, recommended three officers as possible commanders of the new Tank Destroyer Training Center. Then, his tour of duty in Washington completed, he prepared to leave for Fort Benning, Georgia, where he was to become Chief of Staff in General Walton Walker's armored division in training there. Bruce was elated at this assignment, for it meant a return to a combat division.[12] Such was not to be the case, however.

On November 27 the War Department ordered the activation of a Tank Destroyer Tactical and Firing Center on or about December 1. This called for the activation of 53 tank destroyer battalions under the direct control of this new unit, which was part of GHQ. Thereby was created what amounted to a new arm of the service whose task it would be to develop tank destroyer doctrine, equipment, and training. General McNair insisted that Colonel Bruce be named first commander of this unit, a recommendation with which the Chief of Staff, General Marshall, agreed. This order made no provision for antitank battalions in divisions, corps, or armies; rather the battalions envisioned at this time all would be under General Headquarters.

Early in December came additional clarification. All "antitank" battalions were to be renamed "tank destroyer" battalions, a name signifying their offensive rather than defensive nature. All these battalions were allotted to General Headquarters, and all old antitank units in cavalry and field artillery divisions were to be inactivated; infantry antitank battalions would be renumbered as "tank destroyer" battalions. As Colonel Bruce later recalled, "The idea was to create an aggressive way to find enemy tanks, to get into position by stealth, [to seek] and [destroy] enemy forces by fire, and to move quickly to another position for further action."[13]

The temporary location of Colonel Bruce's new command was Fort George G. Meade, Maryland. There Bruce began putting together an organization that was supposed to formulate, develop, and make recommendations to the War Department concerning tactics and training methods for tank destroyer forces, cooperate in developing new weapons, and organize and operate a Tank Destroyer Tactical and Firing Center, a Tank Destroyer Board, and a Tank Destroyer School. Bruce's first problem was to assemble a staff and educate key personnel about the methods and goals of the new organization. By the end of December 1941, he had a skeleton staff organized and was formulating plans to carry out all the tasks assigned his command, and on December 23 that year, in line with his new responsibilities, he was promoted to the rank of colonel.[14]

Simultaneously, Bruce began evaluating the various places that had been recommended as the location for a camp where tank destroyer training could take place. This would have to be a new post, for no base operated by the United States Army in December 1941 was suitable to the needs of his command. Military posts historically had reflected the size and mission of the Army. From the days of the Indian Wars, garrisons had been small, little more than "hitching post" forts as they were snidely called by some. In 1911 Chief of Staff General Leonard Wood had made a radical proposal to abolish many of these posts by consolidating them into a few larger bases, a concept alien to the wishes of congressmen who wanted federal money flowing into the pockets of their constituents. To them, even a tiny post was better than no post at all. General Wood therefore was unable to reduce the number of posts, but in 1911 he did bring together an undermanned division of 13,000 men for maneuvers in the vicinity of San Antonio; getting this many troops together in one place was considered a major accomplishment.[15]

During World War I, the size of Army posts had not increased materially, for the conscripts and volunteers of that conflict were given only basic training in the United States, then shipped overseas where they took their advanced training at large bases where they were introduced to tactics and maneuvers at division and corps levels. In midsummer of 1939 the Army had some 130 posts, most of them of battalion size–still the "hitching post" forts of the previous century. On paper the Army of 1939 had nine infantry divisions, but only the first three had divisional organization; the other six were little more than understrength brigades. In addition, the Army had two divisions of cavalry, each with only about 3,300 men, and one mechanized cavalry brigade. These units were scattered about at small posts, rarely coming together for maneuvers in division strength.[16]

When the rapid expansion of the Army began in 1940, planners in Washington suddenly discovered that a base of 40,000 and more acres was needed to train a division. In fact, some divisional camps would need as much as 100,000 acres to accommodate the needs of the troops. This triggered a hasty procurement of land for bases and construction of temporary quarters on them, so hasty that sometimes sites were chosen without surveys.

When Colonel Bruce and his staff began making plans for a Tank Destroyer Training School in December of 1941, they did not feel their needs were limited even to 100,000 acres for a camp site. Rather they recommended a post of unprecedented size–more than 500,000 acres. Bruce later would say, "My original idea was to place three to five armored divisions on the perimeter of the site with a common firing center capable of handling increased range requirements of our high-velocity guns and have a common maneuver area." He contended that a giant post such as he wanted would have been cost effective. Thereby the tanks and the men learning to destroy them would not have to be shipped to some large training ground, and the cost of the land would have been no greater than the claims filed by landowners after maneuvers were conducted on rented land. Moreover, there would have been savings on railroad transportation and wear and tear on equipment. His idea, he later recalled, "was disapproved on the grounds that it would upset the economy of the area" in which this giant post was located.[17]

On December 19, 1941, Bruce accompanied by a few of his top officers left Washington in civilian clothes to make a quiet and hurried inspection of the several sites that had been recommended as suitable to his needs. His hope was to find a site where mild weather would allow training year-round. It should have open fields, wooded areas, and slopes to allow maneuvers and firing in a variety of contours. It should be adjacent to adequate transportation facilities and have the means of communication readily available along with a water supply adequate to the needs of the command. In order to avoid congestion, it should not be close to other major military bases, and recreational facilities should be available in nearby towns.[18]

When Bruce departed Washington on his search, several towns in Texas were vying for a major new military post to be located in their vicinity. In 1940-1941, most of America had not fully recovered from the Great Depression that began in 1929. Civic leaders in communities large and small were quick to see that a military base, a flying field, an Army hospital, a munitions plant, or a civilian factory could have a significant impact on the local economy. All of these provided jobs, and the money paid these workers circulated and recirculated until cash registers all over town were jingling. Chambers of Commerce began extolling the virtues of their particular community to defense industries, and they sang the virtues of their area to Army procurement officials in Washington and at regional headquarters around the country. Yet more sophisticated civic leaders went to their congressman and senators for help in securing some post, some factory, some government facility. It can easily be argued that during the period 1940-1942 no person in the United States proved more successful in helping his community in this way than Frank W. Mayborn, publisher of the *Temple Daily Telegram* and owner-operator of radio station KTEM.

Born in Ohio in 1903, the son of a newspaperman whose work for Scripps-Howard took the family to several cities, Mayborn grew up in Evansville, Denver, Cleveland, and Dallas. After graduation from high school in 1922, he enrolled at the University of Colorado where he graduated in 1926 with a major in English and a minor in geology. Returning to Dallas, he worked for the *Dallas Morning News*, then briefly was in the oil business before he moved to Fort Worth to write advertising copy for the North Texas Traction Company, the operator of trolley cars and an interurban system. In 1929 he and his father and brothers purchased the *Temple Daily Telegram*, but only Frank would remain in this Central Texas city to operate the paper through the difficult days of the depression. It was in the midst of these hard times that in 1936 he obtained a license to build and operate radio station KTEM.[19]

During the two years preceding the outbreak of World War II, while Bruce was formulating the idea of a Tank Destroyer Training Center, this young newspaper publisher in Central Texas was trying to lift his part of the state out of the depression. As he watched events unfold in in Europe and Asia in 1939, with war beginning among the nations on the Continent and Congress voting more funds for the Army, Mayborn became determined that Temple and Bell County would be an ideal site for several types of government installations then being built in the rush to prepare the nation's defenses.

By 1940 Mayborn already had a liberal education in the labyrinthine ways of government and the methods of getting favorable treatment in Washington. In working during the 1930s to get the Brazos River Authority and the Army Corps of Engineers to build a dam on the Leon River in Bell County, as well as the location in Bell County of several New Deal programs, he had met and worked with W.R. "Bob" Poage, who represented the area in Congress, and others in the Texas delegation in Washington, D.C. Several times he had journeyed to Washington on behalf of Temple and Bell County, each time learning a little more about how to lobby in the corridors of power.

In 1939 Mayborn was elected president of the Temple Chamber of Commerce, and one of his first actions was to create an Industrial Committee to persuade businesses to locate in Temple and Central Texas. The following year, when his term as president ended, Mayborn became chairman of this group. During the remainder of 1940 Mayborn made several trips seeking new industry for Temple but without luck. However, he did begin to learn how to lobby effectively for his region, and on one trip to Washington that year he accidentally became privy to top secret military information that would have a long-range impact. He was told that the Army Air Corps needed magnesium in large quantities in order to manufacture 50-pound incendiary bombs. To make magnesium required large amounts of raw materials and low-cost electricity. Mayborn knew that the Brazos River Authority could supply electricity at four tenths of a cent per kilowatt from its dam and generator at Possum Kingdom, upstream from Central Texas. And, thanks to his training in chemistry in college, Mayborn knew that the hills around Lampasas contained 19½ percent pure magnesium that could be extracted through the electrolytic process. Therefore, he reasoned, Temple would be a good site for this facility.

He also had come to the conclusion that the Santa Fe Railroad would benefit if the plant was located in Temple and thus should be willing to help him lobby to get it. Going to Chicago, he discussed the idea with E.F. Engle, president of the Santa Fe, who agreed with him and assigned James P. "Jim" Reinhold, Los Angeles District Manager of the railroad, to work on this and other efforts. Mayborn and Reinhold then went to Washington to begin the long, hard process of knocking on doors and trying to get a hearing. In this they were helped by Congressman Poage and Texas Senators Tom Connally and Morris Sheppard.

And in Temple, Mayborn and his committee began preparing a detailed study showing why Temple and Bell County should be awarded the magnesium plant along with other defense-related industries and military installations.This study traced the history of the region, examined its population and geography and natural resources, and it covered every other topic they thought a federal defense official might conceivably consider when deciding where to locate a plant or post.[20] Unfortunately for Temple, the magnesium plant was located in Austin because cheaper electric power could be had there.[21]

In making this effort, however, Mayborn had learned more about how the system worked in Washington, and he had made additional friends there. Among those who helped him at this time was Oveta Culp Hobby, a native of Killeen who had grown up in Temple and who had married Will Hobby, former governor of Texas and publisher of the *Houston Post*. Mayborn previously had met her through his newspaper connections, and she readily agreed to help him. It was she who introduced him to Jesse Jones, the powerful director of the Reconstruction Finance Corporation (RFC).

Jones had grown up in Houston where he had become a banker, the owner of vast amounts of real estate, and the publisher of the *Houston Chronicle*. In 1932 he had been named director of the RFC and in 1933 its chairman of the board. Although not a close friend of President

Roosevelt, Jones in 1940 had been named Secretary of Commerce. Mayborn later would say that he and Jones became friends in 1940-1941 to the point where "I would tell him who I wanted to call on and get his secretary to call and get me an appointment." Yet another close friend made during this period was Senator Tom Connally of Texas. "He entertained me, and I did things for him," Mayborn later would explain.[22]

As 1940 ended and 1941 began, some members of Mayborn's Industrial Committee became discouraged and quit, but Mayborn believed that this work was vital if Temple was ever to emerge from the Great Depression. Renaming his group the War Projects Committee, he continued to travel to Washington to lobby for Central Texas, and each week he closely read a bulletin entitled *Defense*, put out in Washington by the National Defense Advisory Commission. This contained the latest news about contracts let and those to be let as well as kept track of bills in Congress affecting national defense. Mayborn understood that knowledge and influential friends were what would win the contest for industry and defense installations, and he tried to keep ahead of his competition by being knowledgeable and by making a host of influential friends.[23]

Also continuing to work to bring defense-related industries and bases to Central Texas was Jim Reinhold. Santa Fe officials had assigned him to Washington on a permanent basis, and he had company maps prepared to illustrate where war plants could be located beside Santa Fe tracks. Reinhold, thanks to some of the Santa Fe's powerful friends in the senate, was privy to inside information which he shared with Mayborn because of their friendship and their mutual desire to get plants and bases in Central Texas.

Early in February of 1941 Mayborn began hearing rumors from his various sources that the Army was interested in locating a major Army camp somewhere in Central or West Texas. He immediately contacted Congressman Poage about this rumor, saying he had heard that the War Department wanted a minimum of 20,000 acres in a rural setting to house a post that would have some 30,000 men stationed there. This base would be in West Texas, East Texas "having been ruled out for numerous reasons." Mayborn said he knew that Temple "would be unable to finance" such a post "due to the small farm units and the cost of land" in the area. However, he and the Chamber of Commerce in

Temple "would like to keep our hand in" to be considered in the future.[24]

In a story in the *Temple Daily Telegram* on February 16, headlined "Army Camp Obstacles," Mayborn declared, "The difference in the cost of farm and ranch land is Temple's number one handicap in its effort to get an army unit or defense plant located here.... Land values aren't as high as they used to be, but they are far higher than those of West Texas." At this time any community seeking an Army base was being asked to purchase the land and then donate it to the government.

Congressman Poage suggested that, if Mayborn was interested in getting an Army post in the vicinity of Temple, he should contact the commander of the Eighth Army Corps at Fort Sam Houston, Texas. The congressman said that it was at this level that the Army made its recommendations for locating posts in Texas and vicinity. Immediately Mayborn and his Defense Projects Committee prepared the case for Temple and sent a packet of information to San Antonio. Chambers of commerce in several other nearby cities, including Brownwood, San Angelo, and Valley Mills, did the same thing, as did leaders in Bosque County, just northwest of Coryell County, who were pushing for a camp to be located between the towns of Hico and Iredell.

Congressman Poage, caught between urgent requests for help in getting such a post in almost every city in his district, told everyone that he would fight to get the base in his district but that he could not favor one town over another. In a letter written later that year of 1941 to a friend, he complained:

> *If I could take a rest, or rather if I could cut down on the hours of nervous concentration each day, I think that I would soon be alright [sic], but with world conditions as they are today and with the demands that local communities are making, it just doesn't seem possible.*
>
> *...At this very moment, there are seven communities in our District that are insisting that they have the ideal location for an Army camp.... I have undertaken to present the claims of each and every community in the 11th District that sought to present a site.... I can not refuse to present briefs, or to go with the representatives of any of the communities that are interested.*

*The result is that the people from all of the communities either believe, or say they believe, that I am helping their rival. I know of no way to avoid this. It is certainly a matter of the worst kind of nervous irritation.*[25]

A congressman's road to re-election was not easy, especially in a district trying to recover from the Great Depression.

The rumor Mayborn kept hearing about the Army needing a large post in Central Texas was confirmed by A.C. Ater, general passenger agent for the Gulf, Colorado & Santa Fe Railway. On February 15, 1941, he wrote Mayborn that he had "some very confidential information": the Army was "in the market for some four or five division-size camps, and General Brees has a very tender spot in his heart for Central Texas. In fact, he very plainly stated that he thought there were great possibilities in the territory west of Temple for training areas." Army engineers already were surveying in New Mexico in the vicinity of Carlsbad and Roswell, said Ater. From there they would proceed to the West Texas towns of Post and Sweetwater. Ater commented that in his conversations with military authorities he had been told that the "essential points" concerning location were: "availability of a rail-head for movement of supplies and equipment, as well as men; water, and plenty of it; hotel facilities within a reasonable distance from the camp site; and one of the more major problems is recreation for the men."[26]

Mayborn was out of town when this letter arrived and did not see it until the end of February. At that time his response to Ater was similar to what he had written to Congressman Poage as well as to what he had written in the *Daily Telegram*: "The cost of securing 75,000 acres of land or anything like that much is prohibitive in this area with our limited means."[27] Yet on the possibility that Temple still might somehow get this base, Mayborn made several trips to San Antonio to confer with decision-makers at the Eighth Army Corps Headquarters at San Antonio.

In his effort to get an army post located near Temple, Mayborn thought he had an ally in the Waco Chamber of Commerce. This city, 35 miles to the north and far larger in size, already had secured a major Army Air Corps training facility, and leaders in that city seemingly were anxious to get a division-sized Army facility somewhere in the region–even west of Temple or south of Gatesville. However, Mayborn gradually came to believe that the Waco Chamber of Commerce was pushing for a Central Texas base closer to that city rather than south of Gatesville or west of Temple; the location Waco's leaders preferred was at Valley Mills, some twenty miles west of their city. Mayborn continued to work hard for the location south of Gatesville, firing off telegrams to congressmen and senators and making several trips to Washington.[28]

In May of 1941 Mayborn learned that business leaders in Waco had the Army leaning strongly toward locating the Central Texas post at the tiny town of Valley Mills. Urgently Mayborn wrote to Congressman Poage and Senator Tom Connally to suggest that the area west of Temple would be a superior location. Poage replied:

> *I just have your letter of [June] 4th…. I fully understand and appreciate your attitude in regard to the army camp. I have felt as you did about the location and told everyone from Waco who discussed the matter with me that I thought that they were taking a short sided viewpoint of the thing. I still think that Waco itself would have been better off had this camp been located at Gatesville…. Frankly, I did not say anything against anybody's location, but I was rather surprised that the army seemed to favor the Valley Mills location. You understand that there has been no definite location of a camp at all, but I do know that the army is definitely considering the Valley Mills location, and I think that it is quite sure that a camp will be located there.[29]*

Mayborn refused to become discouraged until a definite decision was announced and construction commenced. He kept a close eye on real estate speculation in the vicinity of Valley Mills, noting that land values were escalating because of the rumors about a post there and that if a base was located there it would take many millions of dollars to secure the land for it. To Dan McClellan at Gatesville's Chamber of Commerce Mayborn wrote on June 17, "…Your cantonment location may not be completely out of the picture if the army runs into trouble securing land in the Valley Mills area."[30] Again on July 9 Mayborn wrote the people in Gatesville urging them not to lose hope: "Colonel Patrick [who was in the chain of command making decisions about the location of new Army posts] flew into Waco day before yesterday and the citizens have taken new hope, though I understand they will have to lease the land and deliver it to the Government at $1 per acre, which I believe is an impossible task."[31]

For a time there was talk of an Army post being opened in Coryell County near the town of Oglesby. Another site recommended as suitable for a base was in northwest Coryell County with some land in adjoining Bosque County. However, in both instances the land suggested as suitable for an Army base was being farmed intensively. The people in Gatesville working to get a base near their town pointed out that the land in the area of Oglesby and north at Valley Mills was valued at $10.47 per acre while that northwest of Killeen was currently estimated to be worth $6.15 per acre.[32]

With the fight for this post intensifying in the fall of 1941, statistics such as those gathered by the people in Gatesville assumed great significance. With the Army expanding dramatically as the country prepared its defenses, the federal government began buying land for major posts, not just leasing the land for the duration of the war at $1 per acre per year, freeing communities from assuming the huge cost of acquiring the land and then making it available to the government. This change came precisely because of the reason Mayborn had stated about Temple not being able to buy 75,000 acres. No city could afford the large block of land the Army needed as home for a division. Moreover, such expensive acreage could be obtained only through condemnation proceedings and forced sale, which required millions of dollars and use of the government's right of eminent domain. Local governments did not have this power, and politicians in Austin did not want to be held responsible for using the state's power to accomplish the deed.

Quietly Mayborn continued to lobby Army officials in San Antonio and federal officials in Washington. He and his Defense Projects Committee had decided to push for a base north and west of Killeen in Bell and Coryell counties, and almost weekly he added more information to the file urging this site to show why it would be an excellent choice. For example, in October he forwarded to appropriate officials a letter from the Lone Star Gas Company saying it would be able to provide all the natural gas such a base near Killeen would need.[33]

To Mayborn's great disappointment, however, Senator Tom Connally in early November of 1941 announced that the new base would be located at Valley Mills. Still refusing to concede defeat, Mayborn led a delegation of county judges from Bell, Lampasas, and Coryell counties, along with citizens from Gatesville and Killeen, to San Antonio for a meeting with General Richard Donovan, commander of the Eighth Service Command and the officer in charge of site recommendation. To General Donovan, Mayborn pointed out the weaknesses of the Valley Mills location. Among the most important considerations was an oil pipeline from West Texas that crossed through the middle of this location. Moving it would cause the vital flow of petroleum to be closed off for weeks or even months. In addition there was a village of Norwegian-speaking people whose stone houses would have to be relocated at great expense. Moreover, there were few access roads in this area, many small farms that would drive up the cost of acquiring a large block of land, and "not a highway to anywhere." Moreover, Mayborn noted that on October 11, just a month earlier, the Eighth Service Command had announced that the area between Killeen and Gatesville would be a good site for a cantonment.

When Mayborn concluded his description of the problems the Army would have with the Valley Mills site and the advantages of the Killeen-Gatesville area, General Donovan said, "Young man, you don't think much of the United States Army, do you?"

Mayborn held up the report on the Valley Mills site and replied, "I don't think much of this report. But if I weren't thinking a lot about the United States, I wouldn't be down here."

Donovan studied him carefully before asking, "Where are you talking about?"

Mayborn pointed to a location on the general's map, and Donovan put his thumb on the spot. This was the southwestern corner of Bell County from Killeen running north and west into Coryell County. The Temple newspaper publisher then traced a line around Donovan's thumb on the map, and the general initialed it, promising that he would order a new inspection of the area.[34]

The Japanese attack on Pearl Harbor on December 7, 1941, and the subsequent declaration of war on Japan and Germany by Congress brought an urgency to the Army's needs and the necessity of quick decisions. It was less than two weeks after Pearl Harbor that Colonel Bruce slipped out of Washington in civilian clothes for a personal inspection of the various sites proposed for a major Army base, one that could house his Tank Destroyer Tactical and Firing Center. Accompanying him were four of his staff members from Fort George Meade: Colonel Richard Tindall, Lieutenant Colonel Charles S. Miller, Lieutenant Colonel H.T. Mayberry, and Lieutenant Colonel George Beatty. Also in the party were Major G.R. Tyler of the construction division, Office of the Chief of Engineers, and L.H. Zach, a civilian engineer in the Chief Engineer's Office.

When the colonel and his staff arrived at Temple on December 19 to make their unannounced and incognito visit to Killeen and Gatesville, they were surprised to be met by Frank Mayborn and members of his Defense Projects Committee. Jim Reinhold, the Santa Fe's agent in Washington, had learned of the trip and had alerted Mayborn about it. As Mayborn later said, Reinhold "was the bird dog of all this. He was invaluable."[35]

On December 20 Mayborn escorted Colonel Bruce and his staff over the terrain north of Killeen and southeast of Gatesville, pointing out the advantages of the site. In Killeen they found only one person downtown that cold Sunday morning. He was sitting in back of Wood's Drug Store reading a magazine. Bruce was strongly impressed by what he saw. Here was a huge block of land, sufficient for tank training and firing exercises, that could be had inexpensively with the removal of only a few hundred people. Two railroads served the area: the Cotton Belt could bring men and supplies to Gatesville on the north side of the proposed camp, while on the south side at Killeen and Copperas Cove the Santa Fe provided easy access to and from all parts of the nation. Bruce also noted that there were few pipelines across this area, which was ideal in terms of climate and topography. Nearby Temple had excellent hospital facilities and sufficient office space for a temporary headquarters along with land for an airport to serve the new base. And there were several cities in the area close enough that soldiers could go to them for recreational purposes. Finally, Mayborn pointed out–and Bruce recognized and was impressed by–"the patriotic attitude of the people" in the area.[36]

Bruce and his staff had only one reservation about this location: the availability of an adequate supply of water. As the colonel and his staff departed, Mayborn promised to demonstrate that sufficient water could be had in the area. Far faster than anyone thought possible, the Temple publisher and his Defense Projects Committee arranged for some deep wells to be drilled on the Lampasas River. The drilling site, where Stillhouse Hollow Dam years later would be located, was chosen by Dr. E.H. Sellards of the University of Texas and Charles F. Reaney of the Wyatt C. Hedrick Company of Fort Worth, which had won the bid to construct the new post. In record time a drilling rig was put to work at the chosen site, but the driller kept reporting difficulties. Mayborn later recalled, "It looked like they were never going to get it dug." At last he became suspicious, and he conducted an investigation which made him suspect that the driller was under the influence of people in Waco, where the firm already was drilling several wells. Perhaps the people in Waco hoped that if sufficient water for the Killeen-Gatesville site could not be guaranteed, the Army would decide to locate the camp at Valley Mills.

To counter this possibility, Mayborn on January 9 announced in the *Temple Daily Telegram* that the Santa Fe Railroad was going to put up $25,000 and the city of Temple another $25,000 and that drilling would commence closer to the proposed base site in the Trinity sands, which were known to produce an excellent flow of water at 1,600 feet. "That night the well came in," Mayborn later said of the effort by the Waco firm drilling on the Lampasas River. Water was flowing in abundance from a depth of 922 feet from a water sand that extended toward the cantonment site. The next day, January 10, 1942, his telegram to Colonel Bruce jubilantly told the result: "Well now flowing one fifty [gallons] per minute (stop) pumping five hundred with inadequate pump (stop) estimated seven hundred through eight inch hole."[37]

Mayborn's years of work on behalf of Temple suddenly began to pay off in dramatic fashion. In December of 1941 there already had been an announcement that Temple would get a federal grant of $335,000 to build a municipal airport. Then on January 6, 1942, the same day the Waco drilling company found water on the Lampasas for the Army base, Congressman Poage announced that the Army would build a general hospital in Temple at a cost of $2.5 million; Temple had won out over Fort Worth, Corsicana, and Waco in the contest for this hospital.[38]

Then on January 10, the Army announced that the new Tank Destroyer Technical and Firing Center would be located at Killeen and would require 109,000 acres, making it the largest military post in the United States Army, and some 1,800 buildings would be erected there, all at a cost of $35 million. Until the land was acquired and temporary buildings were erected, the headquarters for the base would be at Temple. The telegrams from Senator Tom Connally and Congressman Bob Poage announcing the creation of the new fort both stressed that it would be "PERMANENT," each stressing this by sending this word in capital letters.[39]

The location of this Army camp thus had been determined by two men, each an expert at what he did. Frank Mayborn, a publisher, had fought through the echelons of politics, both state and local, to call this site to the attention of the Army, and Colonel Bruce had chosen it as the ideal location for a school to train destroyers of tanks. Therefore what at the time was considered a temporary post would be built in Central Texas.

# Chapter Three

# Acquiring the Land

EARLY in March of 1942, while government agents were still in the process of acquiring title to the land that would become Camp Hood, Walter R. Humphrey, editor of the *Temple Daily Telegram*, set out by automobile to have one last look at this slice of Bell and Coryell counties. "Did you ever stop to think how big 108,000 acres is?" He asked his readers, then answered by saying, "It's big," so big that he could cover only a small part of this "fascinating country" in one afternoon. He found Cowhouse Creek, fed by spring rains, "never more beautiful," a "magic land" surrounded by what easily could be called mountains. Surveying the loveliness of the area, Humphrey concluded he easily could understand why settlers went there in the first place and why their descendants hated to leave.

On that afternoon drive, Humphrey took the old "middle road" from Killeen to Gatesville, a route that ran through the heart of the new camp. His first stop was the little town of Palo Alto, known among long-time residents as Old Killeen. Some claimed that at the time of settlement, there was nothing between there and Sugar Loaf Mountain but "sage grass belly high to a horse." This was an area of "no cedar trees" and therefore was "all prairie."[1]

Circling around Sugar Loaf Mountain, Humphrey came to Sugar Loaf Cemetery and there found numerous headstones alive with the history of the region. Still legible on one was an epitaph so graphic it needed no explanation: "John and Jane Riggs, murdered by Comanche Indians, March 16, 1859." Another stated, "Sacred to the memory of Sarah Scoggin, born 1779, died Jan. 12, 1882. Gone to meet her 18 children and three husbands." Nearby in a grove of twisted and aged live oaks was a church where camp meetings had been held by Methodists for more than half a century. Legible on the rocks atop Sugar

Loaf Mountain were the names carved there by men who in their prime considered it a challenge to climb the peak, and in whose shadow whole generations had spread their picnic blankets.

Two miles beyond Sugar Loaf was a tree where in the 1870s two rustlers had been hanged as a deterrent to others who would steal livestock, while at the crossing of Cowhouse Creek was an old, rickety bridge across whose groaning timbers almost every traveler in the region had made his way. Humphrey found the waters of Cowhouse "clear and cool and the rock bed of the stream clean from washing by the fresh waters." Stately pecan trees, huge and majestic, lined the stream. Two miles north of the creek, along the winding road, was the old Maples Cemetery in a grove of cedar. It was there that the first schoolhouse and church in that area had been constructed by pioneers.

Humphrey stopped his trip north at the Silver City store, then circled to the southwest past ranch houses with new buildings and barns. He noted that the old rock fences in the area, built by Mexican laborers, were falling down and would "scarcely be an impediment for the armored vehicles of war" which would soon be maneuvering over them. "We found Brown's creek clear as crystal, as it rippled over the rocks in an almost idyllic setting," wrote Humphrey. Then it was past the Manning community where again he crossed the Cowhouse, this time over a new bridge. "The road winds on," he wrote, "and the car speeds up, through the Elizah community (where the army had bought some land early in the week) and where a stone store-building will go, too...another church...on out of the Cowhouse valley in toward Killeen." Just past Pilot Knob he came upon surveyors with their instruments and poles and flags, "a contrast in time to the farmers I last saw, working those fields."

Humphrey concluded, "I could have steered my car over many another road that day within the camp area and found just as much beauty. It seems to me the United States army has selected an ideal setting for its grind of training and maneuvering."[2]

On that trip in March of 1942, Humphrey had taken a trip not only through the countryside, but also through history, and his was the last report of the region before it was forever changed. The conversion of this region from farm and ranch to Army post was sudden and dramatic, but not totally unexpected. During the late fall and early winter of 1941 the farmers and ranchers of northwestern Bell County and southeastern Coryell County had listened to news of the war in Europe and of American preparedness with close attention, for they realized that if a base was authorized between Killeen and Gatesville they would have to give up their homes. The *Temple Daily Telegram* of September 26, 1941, had told people in the two counties that Army engineers were studying the area between Gatesville and Killeen as a possible site for a cantonment, but somehow the possibility that this site would be chosen seemed remote. A story in the *Killeen Herald* of December 26, 1941, noted:

> *Dame Rumor has built the army camp here two or three times but up to now there is nothing more substantial on the ground than a few stakes and markers. Everyday we hear this one or that one say they have the inside on this or that, but the fact remains we have no army camp up to press time and that is about all we can say on the matter.*

Rumor became fact when on the morning of January 15, 1942, the *Temple Daily Telegram* headlined the announcement that the Tank Destroyer Tactical and Firing Center would be moving from Fort George Meade to an Army camp at Killeen.

Even this announcement did not end the speculation, however, for nothing seemed settled definitely. Rumor spread that the Army was going to take permanent title to only 4,000 acres through eminent domain. The remainder of the land needed for this base, it was widely believed, would be leased for the duration of the war and then the original owners could have it back.[3]

However, just after the public announcement on January 15, 1942, that the post would become a reality, surveyors from the Real Estate Branch of the Division Engineer, Eighth Army, opened an Army Land Office in Gatesville to acquire a post that at first was expected to encompass 80,000 acres. Soon the Army land agents were swarming across the targeted land area, 16,000 acres of it in Bell County and 64,000 acres in Coryell County, talking with owners. By February the government already had title to 22,000 acres for the facility, and a month later it had another 45,000 acres under option. However, some landowners were resisting all pleas to sell their land for the base. This led to a federal district court in Waco issuing a "take order" that gave the government permission to move onto the land on March 18, even those parcels not under option at the time. This "take order" amounted to a partial condemnation and was a clear signal to all hold-out landowners that they were going to have to settle almost for whatever was offered them. In those cases where a title was cloudy and a true owner or owners could not be positively identified, the "take order" from the federal district court in Waco allowed the property to be acquired by the government with funds set aside for payment at a later date when the true owner or owners became known.

The federal government had the right to take this land through eminent domain, as provided in the fifth amendment to the constitution. However, this federal right could be slow because owners could contest through endless litigation, saying the price offered was too low. For this reason Congress on March 27, 1942 passed the *Second War Powers Act*, giving the secretary of war the power to institute condemnation proceedings to take away any real or personal property for purposes of expeditiously prosecuting the war. Eventually there would be 220 trials over the land taken, but the owners were dispossessed immediately and the Army was operating Camp Hood as the trials were underway.[4]

Moreover, government planners were moving swiftly to prepare the base for its training mission. To transport the thousands of men and tons of equipment needed just to construct more than 1,000 buildings in the cantonment area, several types of roads had to be built. At this time the State of Texas required that counties provide right-of-way for all roads; on February 12 the Bell County commissioners agreed to purchase three miles of right-of-way for an access road from Killeen to Camp Hood and the Coryell County line. Then on February 24 the Coryell County commissioners voted to buy the right-of-way for Highway 190 in their county as well as right-of-way for a new road from Copperas Cove to Gatesville by way of the Pidcoke-Topsy area. The next day, February 25, the State Highway Commission announced that $85,000 would be spent to build state access roads to the new military reservation. In addition, the federal government spent $650,000 to grade and hard-surface roads in the reservation area, and it purchased three miles of Highway 190 from the State of Texas (that part from Killeen to Camp Hood). In fact, Camp Hood could claim ownership of one of the shortest officially designated federal highways in the United States. This was the road, designated War Highway No. 1, which connected the main gate at South Camp with Highway 190. Built in the shape of a Y, it was 819 feet long and was constructed by the Texas Highway Department, which, under noted Director Dewitt C. Greer, cooperated with federal planners in every way in providing access to Camp Hood.[5]

As it dealt with the people of Central Texas, the Army tried to make the new post more palatable to them by the name chosen for it. Historically the Army had made an effort to name its new camps and posts for military figures held in high esteem in the area of each base. In the case of the new camp at Killeen, Colonel Bruce on January 30 recommended and the War Department agreed on February 17, 1942, that the post would be known as Camp Hood in honor of General John Bell Hood, the "Fighting General" who led a famous Texas Brigade in the Confederate Army of Northern Virginia.[6] Hood, born in Kentucky in 1831, was a graduate of the Military Academy at West Point in 1853. He had resigned from the Army in 1861 to accept a commission in the Confederate military forces. Rising to the rank of lieutenant general, he had been a bold fighter whose major strategy was attack and who believed in never showing his enemy his back.

Hood demonstrated this attitude in the first action in which his Texans were engaged. On May 7, 1861, a force of Federals estimated at 3,000 to 5,000 was disembarking from gunboats at Eltham's Landing on the York River. Hood was ordered to "feel the enemy gently and fall back, avoiding an engagement, and draw them away from the protection of their gunboats." However, he found the Federals already away from their boats and attacked, driving them back a mile and a half until they were again under the protection of the boats' guns. In this skirmish his Texans had killed or wounded 300 and captured 126 while losing 37 killed and wounded. General Joseph E. Johnston, who commanded the Confederate forces, told him, "General Hood, you have given an illustration of the Texas idea of feeling the enemy gently and falling back. What would you Texans have done, sir, if I had ordered you to charge and drive back the enemy?"

Hood replied, "I suppose, General, they would have driven them into the water and tried to swim out and capture the gunboats."

Hood and his men fought with valor and steadfastness in many of the major battles in the war, including the defense of Atlanta against General William T. Sherman, and he was wounded several times, losing a leg at the Battle of Chickamauga. He left the service in early 1865 and settled in New Orleans where he died of yellow fever in 1879 at age 48.[7]

The selection of this name did not appease all the farmers and ranchers who were told to vacate the 80,000 acres that at first was to be included in Camp Hood. The first major evacuation was ordered to be completed by midnight, April 20th, and all landowners were told to be off the land by May 1, 1942. In addition, they were advised not to plant any crops that spring. As T.C. Cloud wrote in the *Killeen Herald* of February 27, 1942, those being forced to move were "the kind of plain, common, substantial, honest, patriotic home owners, tenant farmers and other people" who were cooperating with the Army "in order that we may put Hitler, Mussolini and Hirohito and all murderers, barbarians, uncivilized inhumans where they belong...." Colonel Bruce and other Army officers went through the area speaking to gatherings to explain the military need for the area, but there were a few people who seemed unable to comprehend what was happening to them. One eyewitness later wrote:

> *The most touching scene I witnessed was the group of ranchers and farmers under the Ewing tabernacle when [Colonel] Bruce told them that the United States needed their land for a training field. Many of them were gray and stooped; they had been born upon that land; and their forefathers were buried there. They had labored to improve it and expected to pass it on to their sons and daughters. No tears were shed, nor were there many words spoken. Each family group went its own way, but on their faces could be seen the deep hurt.[8]*

Apparently few of them thought their Congressman, W.R. Poage, could do anything to help them, for on February 27 he commented in a letter to Temple publisher Frank Mayborn,

*I have received a few complaints from land owners in the Killeen
area; however, the number has not been great and I think the
main difficulty was more a worry over when they would receive
the money [for their land from the government] than as to the
amount to be received. I am extremely glad that this matter has
not caused much complaint from the owners of the land.*[9]

Gra'Delle Duncan, a local historian who spoke to many of the
members or descendants of the 470 families that had to move off this
land, saw this dislocation as far more difficult that Congressman Poage
believed. In 1984 she wrote that this was a "heart-rending, searing
experience, leaving lifetime marks on all, and actually killing some."
It was her contention that these people were heroes, "unsung, unrec-
ognized and almost unnoticed." One of those who agreed with her
assessment was Preston Edwards, whom she quoted as saying of that
time when government agents came to take the land, "No one wanted
to seem unpatriotic–they just suffered in silence." An article in the
*Killeen Herald* of February 27, 1942, bears out her conclusion, the
editor of the paper noting, "The exodus of our people is a great sacri-
fice for our country but all are taking it with a good will and a fine
spirit. None have complained about moving but some feel that they
should have more compensation for their losses in dollars and cents
but all are willingly turning over their holdings to help our great
country."

Shortly after World War II ended, a study of attitudes among those
in Bell County who had lost land to the Army concluded that most of
them were not bitter.[10] However, those dispossessed in Coryell County
seemed more inclined to echo the opinion of long-time resident, Buzel
"Buck" Blackwell; he commented that losing land, most of which had
been owned by the same families since before the Civil War, was "like
nothing imaginable. The closest thing might be the unexpected death
of someone you loved very much."[11]

During the first weeks of the government's efforts to take the land
needed for Camp Hood, some families, after signing over their property, were allowed to pay for their homes and move them. Most of
those exercising this option bought one or more lots in Killeen along
Eighth Street. However, this was an option not extended past the first

weeks of land acquisition. Thereafter all whose land was taken were required to leave all fences, walls, water tanks, and one dwelling on each piece of property for use by the Army.

General Bruce did grant one exception to the rule of leaving houses in the impacted area when it was called to his attention that Mrs. Irene Elms, age 92 and blind for five years, wanted to move her home from its location about five miles north of Killeen at the village of Palo Alto. She and her husband originally had lived in a log cabin at that site, and their six children had been born there. In 1914 the family had built a new frame home. In 1942 the family petitioned the Army to remove the home, which the elderly Mrs. Elms knew so well she could find her way about without assistance. When General Bruce approved the request, the house was jacked up, and moving trucks took it down a road so narrow that at times the trucks had to halt while trees were cut down or fences moved.

During this time of change, Mrs. Elms displayed true pioneer courage. When told that her home had to be moved to make way for the Army, she replied, "Well, I have lived through the Civil War, the Spanish American War, and the World War, and if it's necessary for this war that I move, I can do it." The home was placed on a new site at 1802 N. 8th Street in Killeen, and there Mrs. Elms lived until her death a year later.

One house not moved–and not bulldozed to make way for new construction or destroyed during maneuvers–was the one built by Hiram B. Reynolds in 1914. Originally constructed as a farm home of 10 rooms, it was on the Reynolds farm of 384 acres which the government purchased. The barn, a two-story seed house, and several smaller outbuildings were torn down, but the home, situated on a hill with a commanding view, was converted for use as a residence for top-ranking officers. The old farm home was wired for electricity, and a modern heating and water system were added. The picket fence which had surrounded the house was torn down and replaced by a split rail fence, and the screened porch at the back was remodeled into part of the kitchen. For years the old Reynolds home, around which a housing addition known as Walker Village would be built, was usually the residence of the commanding general at Hood.

Several schools in the impacted area had to close: Clear Creek, Antelope, Silver City, and Palo Alto. Their buildings were converted to uses not imagined by the builders; for example, one of the two rooms in the old Clear Creek school became the office for a construction company, and the other room was appropriated as an office for government land agents.[12]

Because of the haste with which everything was being done in order to get Camp Hood ready for troops, some residents found troops on their front porch and Army trucks in their flower beds even before the government bought their land. Most had to move off their land before they were paid for it, which worked a great hardship on them in trying to buy new land on which to make a home. Many later claimed that they were not paid promptly when their land was taken, some saying they had to wait for as long as a year and a half for their check from the government. Once land was taken, the residents were given 10 days in which to gather their stock and load their home furnishings and farm equipment. A few saw the homes in which they had lived and the barns they had labored to construct for their livestock being burned or smashed by bulldozers as they rode away.

The suddenness with which ranchers had to move worked a special hardship on them as they tried to find new pasturage for their animals. Leonard Landrum, who lived in the Clear Creek community, later said, "We tried to move our ewes [sheep] to West Texas, but lost a good third of them, and the rest of the stock we sold at a loss." Another well-known citizen of the area was John Pace, who owned the 2,500-acre Pilot Knob Ranch. Born in 1858 at Salado, he refused to sell to the government. His property was condemned, declared unimproved, and taken for $1 an acre, at which time he was given 30 days to vacate his livestock.

In order to help these ranchers, Congressman Poage insisted that grazing rights be made available to those who had owned the land that became Camp Hood. Eventually more than three-quarters of the Camp Hood reservation would be leased to ranchers on a prorated basis (depending on the amount of their land taken). In return the ranchers paid a nominal grazing fee. Livestock grazing on the range actually were exposed to little danger, for soldiers made an effort to remove them from an impact area before firing began. Those that were left behind would begin running to get out of the way of exploding shells when firing began. Of course, a few animals were killed, but the ranchers were so pleased with the grazing rights extended them that there were few complaints—except a few from landowners immediately adjacent to the post who complained that cattle were straying off the Army reservation to eat grass on their land.[13]

Also forced from the reservation were several rural churches, such as those at New Hope, Sugar Loaf, and Antelope. Newspaper accounts of the last services at these little churches reflected the agony of the settlers, for these buildings were far more than just places of worship. They also served as social centers for people living lonely, rural lives. On April 12, the final Sunday of meetings at Sugar Loaf Methodist Church, the Reverend E.R. Barcus, the presiding Elder of the Georgetown district, preached the 11:00 a.m. worship service. That afternoon another service was held with Judge Mallory Blair coming from Austin to be the principal speaker; he was an ex-resident of the area whose mother was buried in the Sugar Loaf Cemetery. Ninety-two-year-old "Aunt Rennie" Elms, the only surviving charter member of the church, was unable to attend, so a "memory book" was prepared for her.[14]

Memories of a different kind came to Second Lieutenant Thomas M. Blackwell, who was stationed at the military base in 1967. His great-great-grandfather, Joseph Blackwell, after fighting for Texas independence at San Jacinto with Sam Houston, had built a ranch in what became the artillery range impact area. Later he was killed during the Civil War in the struggle for Southern independence. Lieutenant Blackwell's great-grandfather, G.W. Blackwell, had run a general store and post office at the Beverly Stage Station; he had fought Indians as a Texas Ranger, and as a Baptist preacher he had battled lawlessness and sin from the pulpit, for which he was ambushed and shot by gang members operating in the area. In 1967 young Lieutenant Blackwell, with permission from range control, found the ruins of his great-grandfather's general store. Later, as he trained at Fort Hood, he told a reporter, "It sure seems strange at times to fire into the area that was once home for your family."[15]

Perhaps even more difficult than the loss of their homes for those forced to leave the military reservation was the relocation of cemeteries on the land taken from them to surrounding towns such as Killeen,

Gatesville, and Copperas Cove. Some of these cemeteries were well known, but most were little more than family plots. And there were burial places used in the distant past that were small and scattered, most with headstones either rotted away, vandalized, or even stolen. The government made a concerted effort to move these bodies with as much dignity as the pressing need for haste allowed, but some 15 known cemeteries would remain within the Camp Hood reservation. For years the story persisted that when bodies were moved from graves with no headstones, the government "named those previous unnamed ones."[16]

In July of 1942, two months before Camp Hood was to be completed, the Army decided to enlarge the reservation to approximately 108,000 acres in order to accommodate an additional 15,000 soldiers, and thus another round of condemnations and acquisitions took place. Yet more people had to be removed and additional "take orders" issued by the federal court. The following January the War Department decided to purchase another 16,000 acres in Bell County, south of the main camp, to be used for training purposes. Moreover, the Army wanted an additional 34,943 acres in Coryell County, south of Gatesville, to house the Tank Destroyer Basic Replacement Training Center and Tank Destroyer Basic Unit Training Center; this addition in Coryell County was referred to as North Camp and was considered a sub-camp for the post. When the 200 additional families were removed, the total acreage of Camp Hood had increased to approximately 160,000 acres, making this post the largest training center in the nation.[17]

Most of those who were moved from the original 80,000 acres were paid about $12 per acre for grazing land that was improved–that is, land which was cleared, fenced, or terraced and on which there were homes, barns, and outbuildings. In later years it would be argued by many that the government appraisers were ignorant of land values in Central Texas and that the correct amount they should have been paid for grazing land was about thirty percent higher; others said these bureaucrats had no sympathy for those being moved and were interested only in taking the land for the least amount possible. Those with good farming land were paid more than those with grazing land so that Congressman Poage later could say the average price paid was $18 per acre because members of Congress were balking at paying an average $30 per acre for this land. Still later in 1942, when the amount of land taken was expanded to 108,000 acres, the average price per acre was yet higher. At a hearing of the House Appropriations Committee in Washington, one member pointed out that the total cost of the 108,000 acres was $3 million, which made the price of the entire reservation average out at almost $30 per acre.

When asked to comment on this, a spokesman for the Army Corps of Engineers agreed that this figure was correct, saying, "This land is fairly well populated, and there are quite a number of operating farms with farm buildings. There is no question that the land itself is worth less than $30 an acre, but the overall cost of relocating the facilities and utilities will result in a considerable increase in the total cost of the land." A member of the House Appropriations Committee then asked why a site with fewer families could not have been selected, to which the spokesman for the Corps of Engineers replied, "Well, 108,000 acres, even in Texas, is quite a chunk of land." The later expansion of the post to approximately 160,000 acres was made at a cost that, like the earlier purchases, averaged some $30 per acre.[18]

The Army's choice of Central Texas for Camp Hood caused far more change than simply the removal of almost 700 families from farms and ranches. It likewise had a permanent effect on the surrounding towns of Temple, Killeen, and Gatesville. Of the three, Killeen was most profoundly changed. What had been a small, rural village of 1,263 people providing goods and services to farmers and ranchers suddenly was transformed into a far different kind of town. Gone were half the people who had come to town to buy, sell, and trade—the farmers and ranchers—when the Army took the land for Camp Hood.

Coming to town, however, were thousands of civilian construction workers employed in putting up buildings at Camp Hood. The population of Killeen jumped to more than 6,000 by July of 1942. Despite heroic efforts by local contractors to build new houses, apartments, cafes, and stores, not enough could be erected because of severe shortages of building materials for civilian uses. Killeen never was designated a Defense Area, which would have given it priority in getting lumber and other building materials to construct new housing. A story has persisted for years that Killeen suffered politically because the mayor at that time, T.H. Minor, also president of the First National Bank, was unhappy because his farm west of town, on which he lived, was taken by the Army to be part of the new camp. His dislike of the military led to a misunderstanding with General A.D. Bruce. Reportedly Bruce came to Minor to suggest ways Killeen might help the Army. "General," the mayor told him, "you run the camp and I'll run the town." Bruce found officials in Temple much more cooperative, and he worked with their chamber of commerce, whose stationery was headed, "Gateway to Camp Hood."[19]

In July of 1942 Killeen city officials estimated that 3,848 people were living in houses, another 1,229 in trailers, and 1,219 in tents. Some of the trailer parks were inside the city limits and could be regulated, but several were outside town and subject to almost no rules. The Hudson, the City, and the Killeen hotels were so filled to capacity that they closed their dining rooms, filling the space with beds—which were quickly rented, while some 15 "cot houses," with capacities ranging from 15 to 50, were either built or improvised.

So acute was the housing shortage that townspeople who previously had never thought of renting spare bedrooms opened their homes to the swarm of civilians and the Army wives coming to town to be with their husbands. Reliable witnesses tell of construction workers and Army families so desperate for quarters that they rented hen houses. C.R. Clements, a cashier at the First National Bank of Killeen, later said, "People slept in their cars, put up their cots along the highway and in pastures. Every home, outhouse and yard in Killeen was occupied." In 1986 Marjorie Baker of Copperas Cove commented that in that town during the early part of the war there was nothing north of the railroad but tents. The men living in them would get up in the morning at sunup, walk to the base where they were employed as construction workers, and then walk back to their tents at sundown. She remembered that both workers and soldiers would stop by the drug store owned and operated by her and her husband and "drink anything cold for sale."[20]

Feeding this horde of people was difficult, and the number of "restaurants" in Killeen jumped from three to more than a hundred in the first few weeks of the boom. Even so, there still were too few to satisfy the demand of both soldiers and workers at the post. D.H. Kramer, a soldier who came to Camp Hood in July of 1942, later recalled, "You couldn't get into a cafe to eat because they were so crowded." Solving problems of water and sewage proved far more difficult, while schools could not be built fast enough to provide classroom space for the children of both civilians and soldiers. All during the war there was a shortage of doctors in Killeen to contend with normal illnesses and a polio scare. The Rural Telephone System's out-of-date equipment never was able to handle the volume of business; those wanting to place long-distance calls usually had to wait for hours to get a connection. The Post Office likewise was inundated, suddenly getting mail for 100,000 and more soldiers and civilians rather than for some 3,000 townspeople and rural residents as before the war. And the First National Bank faced chaos as it tried to provide service to the construction workers who would line up for half a block to cash their paychecks on Friday evenings.[21]

Gatesville, like Killeen, was suddenly overrun with soldiers, construction workers, and their families, and like Killeen fought to provide the housing, services, and goods needed. On February 6 a survey was made of housing in the Gatesville area to find room for incoming appraisers and engineers. When local authorities found they were far short of the amount needed, they asked local homeowners with spare bedrooms to rent them. The Gatesville Chamber of Commerce served as a liaison between the Army and local people in every way, especially in finding housing. In fact, the Chamber had a full-time staff arranging housing, even urging local citizens to rent rooms on weekends to soldiers on weekend passes so they would have somewhere to stay as they went to local movie theaters, ate in the crowded local restaurants, or just played softball at one of the local parks. With apartments and rent houses in great demand and extremely short supply in the Gatesville area, a few landlords raised rents to the point that soldiers began complaining, leading to Gatesville and all of Coryell County having rent controls placed on rent property.[22]

Belton, like Killeen and Gatesville, was strained by the influx of workers and soldiers, but because it was located several miles east of the Army base it did not suffer as much disruption as those two towns. However, it did grow because that was where the employment office was opened by the state to process the 12,000 to 15,000 workers initially hired by the construction industry for Camp Hood. Most moved closer to the post, but many chose to live in Belton, as did some soldiers and their families. Belton's major problem was to provide housing for the workers, soldiers, and their families who chose to live there despite its distance from the post. This influx of population caused rents to rise and the construction of some new housing; also it strained the water and sewage systems, and additional schools had to be built. However, none of the young ladies studying at Mary Hardin-Baylor College ever had to worry about getting a date. Nor did many of their dates have far to travel, for in March of 1942 the college made two of its dormitories, Heard and Ferguson Halls, available to the Army for use as temporary housing for military personnel.[23]

Most of the soldiers assigned to Camp Hood did not pause in Killeen or Belton for recreation, choosing to go to the nearby and much larger city of Temple. However, almost no enlisted men and few officers had private automobiles in which to get from the post to Temple, and those who did faced the problem of gas rationing. There was public transportation for the thousands trying to make the trip, especially on weekends. The two railroads serving Camp Hood–the Santa Fe at the main camp near Killeen and the St. Louis Southwestern (Cotton Belt) at North Camp near Gatesville–primarily brought troop trains in and out of the area, but there were some passenger cars. In fact, every morning a special passenger train ran from Temple to Killeen carrying workers to the cantonment area, and every evening these commuters were returned to their homes and apartments by this special train. On all Santa Fe trains making this thirty-mile trip, every seat was filled both eastbound and westbound, a round-trip ticket from Killeen to Temple costing 70 cents. However, the primary purpose of the two railroads serving Camp Hood was to move freight. At these two camps the traffic was so heavy that there were approximately 16 miles of trackage; at Camp Hood this included warehouse tracks, four tracks with concrete end ramps, and four side ramps, all lighted with floodlights, while the North Camp had three loading tracks with temporary end ramps, all lighted with ordinary street lamps.

Providing transportation for most small groups of people and individuals were the two competing bus lines, which at the height of their operation were running 108 round trips daily. The oldest of the two was the Cramer Bus Line, which operated between Killeen and Temple. Competing with it was the Southwest Transit Company, begun by Churchell W. Duncan of Killeen and Roy Sanderford of Belton, which ran in a more direct line between the two cities. On Saturdays and Sundays both Cramer and Southwest ran as many buses between the base and Temple as possible, every seat filled and the aisles packed with those willing to stand, and always there was a long line waiting at both ends to get aboard. There were loud complaints that these two bus companies were inadequate to move everyone who wanted to go from post to town, but such was the case at almost every Army reservation in the nation, not just at Camp Hood.[24]

The announcement that Camp Hood would be located in northwest Bell and southeast Coryell counties and that the temporary headquarters for the Tank Destroyer Training and Firing Center would be in Temple caused both merchants and citizens in this city of 15,000 to brace themselves for a period of great expansion. And the city did expand–to 30,000 people by February of 1944.[25] Working with General Bruce and his command to make the Army feel welcome in Temple during this period was Frank Mayborn and his *Temple Daily Telegram*. Colonel Stanley J. Grogan, chief of the Press Bureau in the Bureau of Public Relations at the War Department in Washington, wrote General Bruce on April 20, 1942, to note the importance of Mayborn's help, commenting, "With civilians like Mr. Mayborn helping you..., you certainly have fine public relations backing."[26]

In January of 1942 all residents of Temple were asked to report anything that was available for rent because the Chamber of Commerce was swamped with letters from across the nation asking about housing. By February 17 there were some 30 officers and several civilian employees in Temple to staff the temporary headquarters of the Tank Destroyer Training and Firing Center. The need for housing for these people, as well as for the additional Army personnel and their families expected to arrive in the near future, was so acute that on February 22 an officer was appointed to consult with a civilian rent committee, consisting of two local businessmen; this committee had the authority to control all lease arrangements with anyone connected with the Army. In addition, this committee determined what was fair rent for the quarters available in Temple. So well did this arrangement work in Temple that the same procedure also would be followed in Belton, Killeen, Copperas Cove, and Lampasas.[27]

So acute did the housing situation become that on February 21 the Regional Defense Housing Coordinator recommended to Washington that Temple be designated a Defense Area, giving it priority in getting the materials needed to construct houses and apartment units. On April 13 the city was designated a "private housing priority locality," in large measure because of the Army hospital located there. This designation enabled contractors in the city to build housing even during the war. Temple also had difficulties keeping up with the demand for water, sewage facilities, schools, shops, and recreational facilities, but the city fathers had planned so carefully that the impact of the war was not as great there as elsewhere.[28]

Major Gerald R. Tyler was the Army Engineer in charge of the construction of the Camp Hood cantonment. A member of the team of inspection that chose the Killeen-Gatesville site for Camp Hood, he previously had been in charge of the construction of an armored division post at Pine Camp, New York. Arriving in Temple on January 20, 1942, he studied the surveys and began drafting plans. These then were submitted to the War Department for approval. The plan finally accepted called for mobilization type construction (semi-permanent, 15-year life) of facilities to handle 23,475 troops but with utilities and hospital buildings based on an eventual garrison of 35,000 troops. Everything was to be completed by August 15, 1942. Including the amount paid for the land, the estimate was that the total cost of Camp Hood would be $22.8 million.

One of the first problems to be confronted was getting water to the cantonment site. This Major Tyler handled in early February by letting a contract to the H.B. Zachery Company of San Antonio for construction of an 18-mile water line to run from six artesian wells near Belton to a point some three miles northwest of Killeen, and an additional contract was let to Wiegand and Company of San Antonio for drilling yet more wells. Later the main source of water for Camp Hood would be the Lampasas River, at which time the wells near Belton became a standby supply for those years when scant rainfall caused the Lampasas to be unable to provide a sufficient amount.

On March 12 bids were opened for actual construction, and that day

contracts were let. Camp construction was to be handled by Taylor and
Byrnes of Fort Worth along with Tankursley Trapp Associates of Okla-
homa City, while clearing and site grading would be done by the R.M.
Ball Construction Company of Fort Worth. Fuel storage facilities and
gas distributing pipelines were to be constructed by the J.W. France
Company of Corpus Christi, the electrical distribution system by Taylor
Construction Company of Taylor, the water and sewage system by the
H.B. Zachery Company of San Antonio, the sewage disposal plant by
McKenzie Brothers, Williams and Whittle of Dallas, and the power
hook-ups by the Industrial Electric Company of New Orleans. Also let
was a contract to build a camp railroad system so that troops and tanks
and guns could be moved to any part of the post quickly; this went to
Martin and Grace of Dallas.[29]

Helping in the construction of this base were the young men in the
Civilian Conservation Corps (CCC) stationed in Bell and Coryell
counties. A New Deal program begun during the heart of the Great
Depression, the CCC employed young single men who were paid $21
a month and who lived in military style in rural areas. The young men
in the CCC camps in Bell and Coryell counties had been used to do soil
conservation work, build fences, and prevent erosion. One Bell County
project of long-term significance had been to build a dirt road between
Belton and Killeen using only picks and shovels. At the request of
Colonel A.D. Bruce, the CCC camps in Bell and Coryell counties were
not disbanded early in 1942, as had been scheduled, but rather on
February 25 were assigned to work at Camp Hood. Nor were their
camp buildings near Temple and Gatesville to be moved; rather these
were to be left intact either for military or civilian housing.[30]

The employment office in Belton took applications for those who
wanted to get jobs with the contractors, and it was swamped with
applicants from Dallas, Fort Worth, Austin, San Antonio, and cities
out of state. The lines were long indeed at this office, for the country
was trying to pull itself out of the Great Depression, and patriotic
women were leaving their homes to take employment at jobs previously held by men.

Across the hills and valleys and bottom land of the newly acquired
government post, thousands of workers soon swarmed. Because of the
haste with which they had to work, there was almost total disregard for

the structures already on the land, which caused extremely hard feelings among the people either just moved or still in the process of vacating the land. On the first 108,000 acres taken were dozens of windmills, hundreds of gates, miles of barbed wire, untold thousands of good fence posts, excellent lumber on sheds, barns, and houses, and galvanized iron and tin from roofs. In the haste of building the new post the construction companies knocked down fences and buildings and burned the wood. People who were being forced to move from their farms and ranches watched in agony as what they and their ancestors had built was destroyed, and they were incensed that what they had left behind was being destroyed by bulldozers and flames. Equally enraged at the destruction of scarce building materials were the people in nearby Killeen, Gatesville, and Copperas Cove who could not construct the housing so desperately needed because civilians could not get building materials during the war.

Congressman Poage received many complaints about this. Later he would say that he fully understood and sympathized with these constituents, but he said he also had an understanding of the Army's viewpoint. In that time of national emergency, the Army could ill-afford to have hundreds of civilians swarming across the area.[31] The old made way for the new in wasteful fashion, but the demands of wartime left no alternative.

Not wasted, however, was the steel in several structures inside the Army reservation. This was salvaged as scrap and sent to be melted and used in tanks or planes or ships. One of the first such structures to be torn down was at Mason's Crossing, located in the middle of the impact area. This was a three-span, 230-foot steel bridge across Cowhouse Creek. It was demolished by the Pioneer Section of the Tank Destroyer School. Explosive charges were placed on the main span so it would be shorn at each end and drop upright into the creek. This worked perfectly, and the steel then was salvaged.[32]

Actual construction began on April 7, at which time there were some 5,000 carpenters and more than 12,000 skilled and unskilled laborers at Camp Hood erecting frame barracks, office buildings, sheds, and the dozens of other structures needed at a major military installation. However, the needs of war were so pressing that General Bruce could not wait for the post buildings to be erected. On March 31, 1942, the 893d Tank Destroyer Battalion arrived to erect a field camp, mainly with materials salvaged from abandoned CCC camps in the Eighth Army area. Two weeks later, on April 14, the 753d Tank Battalion arrived, and training began even as civilians were still living on many parts of what would become the Army reservation.[33]

Work by civilian contractors proceeded at a high rate of speed despite shortages of manpower and materials and rainfall that was greater than average. Moreover, there were constant changes in the plans. In July, two months prior to the date scheduled for completion, orders came to build for an additional 15,000 troops, and the same contractors were awarded the new construction contracts. However, despite all difficulties, the work was always on or ahead of schedule. In mid-September, when the base officially was opened as an Army camp, much remained to be done, but the station hospital was the only major facility not completed. Some wards became available for use on September 24, but not until February of 1943 was the 1487-bed hospital totally completed and operational.[34]

Hardly had all this been completed when in January of 1943 the War Department announced plans to purchase an additional 80,000 acres. A small part of this land was to be in Bell County south of the main cantonment, the remainder in Coryell County. Eventually the War Department scaled back its purchase to just 50,000 acres, 16,000 south of Killeen and 34,943 in Coryell County. The land near Gatesville was to be used as a cantonment for the Tank Destroyer Basic Replacement Training Center and the Tank Destroyer Basic Unit Training Center; the land taken would be used as training areas by these two units. The cantonment area selected was seven miles south of Gatesville and 20 miles north of the main camp. All the buildings, except a mobilization type 1139-bed hospital, for the 40,000 troops expected at this sub-camp were to be of the theater of operations type (temporary, five-year life span).

A. Farnell Blair, a contractor from Decatur, Georgia, was given the contract to construct the buildings at this sub-camp, which became known as North Camp. Construction began on January 4, 1943, and was to be completed by June 30 that year. This contractor was blessed with a mild winter and good weather during the spring, and he faced few shortages of manpower or materials. Thus the work went forward so rapidly that on May 23, 1943, the personnel of the station complement were able to move in. Six days later the sub-camp officially opened. At this time Camp Hood, in all its various areas, had quarters to accommodate 80,000 soldiers.

Two roads were built to connect North Camp with Camp Hood, one around the west firing ranges and entering the west end of North Camp, the other following the east firing ranges and entering the east part of North Camp. Because time was such an overriding consideration, these two roads were poorly built and were kept usable only by constant repair. The water supply for North Camp came from 12 wells drilled in the Leon River Valley on the Camp Hood reservation.

In addition to military construction at both Camp Hood and North Camp, the Army found it necessary to erect civilian war housing quarters in both areas. R.D. Jones Construction Company built the apartments at Camp Hood. Named Hood Village, it consisted of 765 dwelling units plus 389 dwelling trailers and 88 laundry and utility trailers. The work at North Camp was done by A. Farnwell Blair. It was known as North Village and consisted of 465 dwelling units with no trailers. First to be occupied were the trailer units at Hood Village, beginning in April of 1943. The dwelling units in both villages were completed–and fully occupied–in August that year.

Two other groups of buildings were erected at Camp Hood during World War II. These were for German prisoners of war. Theater of operations (temporary, five-year life span) quarters were erected for approximately 1,000 prisoners at Camp Hood, and similar buildings were erected at North Camp for another 3,000 POWs; B.B. Smith of Dallas built those at Camp Hood, while A. Farnwell Blair of Decatur, Georgia, erected those at North Camp. The 4,000 POWs were the responsibility of the Service Command, which guarded them, oversaw the work they performed on nearby farms and ranches, as well as on the post itself, while their supplies were provided by the post exchange system. During the time German POWs were held at Camp Hood, there were few attempts at escape. In July of 1943 a 22-year-old German prisoner fled from a work detail at North Camp Hood, but he was recaptured that same day not many miles away. Later two young prisoners fled the detention facility at North Camp Hood and began making their way to the southwest. When they were captured at West

Fort Hood, they said they thought they were almost at the Mexican border. In 1944 about 3,000 POWs were transferred to other camps in Texas, leaving only about 1,000 at Hood until the end of the war. During the last week in June of 1944 the vacated POW quarters at North Camp became the Southern Branch of the United States Disciplinary Barracks to hold men sentenced to Army prison.[35]

All construction was completed at both the main cantonment and at North Camp by September 1, 1943. When completed, the base consisted of 160,000 acres, making it one of the largest military installations in the world and certainly the best maneuvering area in the United States. In addition to its 35 firing ranges, it had 5,630 buildings. Included in this number were 18 chapels, 1 field house, 26 recreation buildings, 35 post exchanges, 1,384 barracks, 367 mess halls, 373 bachelor officers quarters, 4 clubs for officers, 4 clubs for enlisted men, 2 laundries, 2 hospitals with a total of 132 buildings, 12 theaters, 1 bus station, 1 post office, 516 warehouses, 432 shops, and 2,014 miscellaneous buildings.

There also was a landing field near the South Camp. The first airstrip at the post, built in 1942, had only a dirt surface running northwest-southeast and was used by 10 light aircraft belonging to the artillery unit assigned to help in training Tank Destroyers. The next year a more permanent airstrip was constructed; this consisted of a hard-surface runway 150 feet wide by 3,600 feet long with two taxiways; in addition, there were several bulldozed landing areas in the reservation area suitable for use by liaison planes.

Recreational facilities at Camp Hood included 3 swimming pools, a nine-hole golf course, several tennis courts, a football field, three bowling alleys, and several basketball courts and baseball and softball diamonds. The total cost of everything—land and buildings—was approximately $35 million (additional construction during the period from 1942 to September of 1945 would bring the total government expenditure for land, improvements, and construction to $75,961,000).[36]

All this work at the first 108,000 acres of Camp Hood was completed in just eight months (between January and September of 1942) and in little more than a year and a half when North Camp was completed in September of 1943, bringing the size of the post to 160,000 acres. Totally transformed was an area where previously cattle, sheep, and goats had grazed and where farmers had tried to eke a subsistence living out of the stubborn soil in the form of cotton, corn, and hay. There had been scenes of personal tragedy as third- and fourth-generation Texans were uprooted from their land. Some had died of shock, others of heartbreak, and a few by suicide. There was anger at the heavy hand and insensitivity of bureaucrats, at the low prices paid for their land, at delays of up to three years in paying for the land, and at the destruction of homes and outbuildings and fences when materials were scarce for building elsewhere. Yet most of these Central Texans endured these hardships with the same fortitude as had their ancestors when faced with Indian raids, outlaws, rustlers, drought, tornadoes, and grasshopper plagues.

Not only did these people endure, but in a spirit of total patriotism they tried to welcome the servicemen–enlistees, National Guardsmen, Army Reserves, and draftees–suddenly thrust into their midst. However, one of the first efforts by people in Killeen to extend the hand of friendship to the soldiers almost ended in disaster. While the post was under construction, people in Killeen, many of them belonging to conservative religious denominations that frowned on dancing, decided to stretch their convictions and hold a street dance for the troops already bivouacked in the field nearby. This was because almost all the soldiers seemed to think of Killeen as someplace to get through, not a place to stop. A considerable amount of work went into preparations for this dance, which local leaders hoped would make the soldiers know they were welcome in Killeen. Housewives baked cakes and cookies, the street was cleaned, decorations were put up, and the young ladies of the town and surrounding communities excitedly readied themselves for an evening of fun and festivity.

When the date for the dance arrived, townspeople were discouraged to see soldiers leaving the post and speeding through Killeen, as usual bound for the city lights of Temple or Waco. At last someone remembered that no one had taken responsibility for delivering an invitation to the soldiers. A group of civic leaders immediately went to the bivouac area and explained the situation to the commanding officer. He released all the men still in camp he could spare, and the street dance of welcome was a success.[37]

A similar welcome, this one with invitation delivered early, was

held in Gatesville, leading Major F.G. Felber, commander of the First
Tank Battalion, to write:

> *Since organization of this battalion, your invitation of last
> Saturday night was the first of its kind that has ever been received
> from the civilian community. Members of my command were
> delighted not only with the quality and quantity of your fine
> barbecue and the fine entertainment and dance that followed,
> but with the exceptionally fine spirit of friendliness and good
> neighbor attitude that everyone of your community extended to
> every individual in the command. For that, many thanks, and my
> deepest admiration to an American Community as unselfish,
> congenial, and hospitable as yours.*

Colonel Hugh T. Mayberry, commandant of the Tank Destroyer School,
wrote to express his feelings about the way people in Gatesville had
opened their homes to provide quarters for soldiers before quarters
were built at North Camp. He concluded, "This is the first time in the
United States History of the American Army that officers from Maine
to Oregon, Florida to California were housed by a civilian population,
and it was a huge success."[38]

Although General Bruce and his entire command had moved from
the Camp Hood staging area at Temple to the main cantonment near
Killeen effective at 8:30 a.m. on August 21, 1942,[39] it was not until a
month later, September 18, that ceremonies were held to mark the
official opening of Camp Hood. An estimated 25,000 people, soldiers
and civilians from the surrounding area, gathered to watch as a huge
flag, 20 by 38 feet, was raised, and Under Secretary of War R.P. Patterson took the salute as troops marched in review. Special guests that
day included Major General Richard Donovan, commanding general
of the Eighth Service Command; Major General Harold Bull, commanding general of the School and Replacement Center, Birming-
ham, Alabama; and Major General Harry Twaddle, Camp Swift, Texas.
Also an honored guest was Colonel (Ret.) John Bell Hood, son of the
Confederate general for whom the post was named.[40]

During the ceremonies that day, Lieutenant Colonel G.R. Tyler, the
area engineer for the Corps of Engineers, officially turned Camp Hood

over to General A.D. Bruce as commander of the Tank Destroyer Center and to Colonel Charles M. Thirlkeld as post commanding officer. Passing in review in that opening day ceremony were the first two units that had arrived at Hood, the 893d Tank Destroyer Battalion from Fort George Meade, Maryland, and the 753d Medium Tank Battalion from Camp Polk, Louisiana. These two units had formed the nucleus of the permanent school cadre–the men used to train Tank Destroyers.

During the opening day ceremonies, there was a demonstration of firepower by the weapons mounted on the half tracks of the Tank Destroyer Battalions, while a commentary on the use of Tank Destroyers was given over the loud speaker. Then at 1:45 that afternoon on Range Road north of the center of camp came the official opening of Camp Hood. Broadcasting this event was Frank Mayborn's radio station KTEM of Temple.

The principal speaker of the day, Under Secretary of War R.P. Patterson, told those assembled that the only way for the United States to win the war in which it was engaged was expressed in the slogan of the Tank Destroyers: Seek, Strike, and Destroy. "You have," he said, "one of the largest training centers in the country, or in the world for that matter, occupying ground that gives you the opportunity to try out almost every tactical problem."[41] Such indeed was this new post–as General Bruce and his Tank Destroyer command already had been demonstrating by their use of its facilities long before the buildings on it were completed.

*Chapter Four*

# Camp Hood:
## *The Tank Destroyer School*

BY orders dated November 4, 1941, Lieutenant Colonel Andrew D. Bruce was named commanding officer of the Tank Destroyer Tactical and Firing Center, a new chapter in Army history. His task and that of his command was defined twenty-three days later. The Tank Destroyer Center was to open temporary headquarters on December 1, 1941, at Fort George Meade, Maryland. The command was to consist of a Headquarters, a Tank Destroyer Board, a Tactical and Firing Center, and a Tank Destroyer School. The commanding officer of the Tactical and Firing Center also would serve as commandant of the Tank Destroyer School. The mission of this command was to formulate tactics and methods of training for Tank Destroyer forces, to develop Tank Destroyer weapons, and to organize and operate the Tank Destroyer Tactical and Firing Center, the Tank Destroyer Board, and the Tank Destroyer School. In short, Bruce had to find a way not only to stop tanks but also to develop antitank tactics that would free other parts of the Army for offensive operations.[1]

At the same time he was studying reports about potential base sites and visiting Central Texas to make his choice, Colonel Bruce also was organizing his command at Fort Meade. He arrived at this post on December 1 with his secretary and the few officers who already had joined his command. The War Department had given him a staff of 18 Regular Army officers of field grade and 14 reserve officers holding the rank of captain to lieutenant colonel. By the end of December Bruce had made great progress. He had selected the area between Killeen and Gatesville, Texas, as the location where his command would undertake its training, and he had an organizational framework developed.

Bruce quickly had a Tank Destroyer Board operating. Its chief functions were to develop new weapons and equipment, to improve existing weapons, to formulate tank destroyer tactical doctrine, and to prepare tables of organization. Another pressing problem in organizing a Tank Destroyer Tactical and Firing Center was training for the officers and men who would operate it. Therefore on January 19, 1942, Bruce recommended that 24 officers and 232 enlisted men be sent to service schools for the specialized training they would need to become instructors at the Center. Tables of organization were prepared for all units needed at the Tank Destroyer Center and the Tank Destroyer School, and these were submitted to the War Department along with a budget to finish out the fiscal year ending June 30, 1942. Additional estimates had to be prepared for the ammunition, gasoline, and other supplies that would be needed to operate the Center and School.[2]

Yet another part of Bruce's command was seeking the perfect antitank weapon. As recommended in the summer of 1941, the M-3 Tank Destroyer—a 75mm gun mounted on a halftrack—was being produced. The other antitank weapon then being produced was the M-6, a 37mm gun mounted on a $^3/_4$ ton truck; Colonel Bruce saw this as a temporary training expedient while a better light armored car antitank weapon was being devised.[3]

Each of the tasks assigned to Colonel Bruce's command was complex, and each had to be moved forward with dizzying speed. Simultaneously, the command was in transit. Temporarily its headquarters were at Fort Meade, Maryland, but by the fall of 1942 it would be at Camp Hood, Texas. So pressing was the mission of the Tank Destroyer Board, the Tank Destroyer Tactical and Firing Center, and the Tank Destroyer School that even during the period of transition from one location to another there could be no slowing of the pace of work.

Bruce's forward echelon arrived in Temple on January 16, 1942, under the command of Major Thomas G. Shaffer, and by early February seven officers of the Tank Destroyer Board were in this Central Texas city. Bruce arrived on January 24 and moved into the office space his command had rented in the First National Bank building. On February 13, 1942, the Army recognized the tremendous responsibilities given Bruce, and he was promoted to brigadier general. The next day the activities of the Tank Destroyer Center closed at Fort Meade, and at the exact same date and hour the Center Headquarters were officially opened in Temple.[4]

This was a time of considerable confusion for both soldiers and civilians in Temple, Belton, Killeen, Gatesville, and other communities in the area. Roads were being drawn on maps and then turned into reality by gangs of construction workers. Land procurement officers were swarming across the future site of Camp Hood asking, pleading, and demanding that land owners move. Army engineers were drawing plans for the base buildings and letting contracts. And off the Army reservation, other officers were in every town and village inspecting public eating places to insure sanitary conditions, while additional efforts were being made to keep houses of prostitution from opening in the region. Another area of major concern was sufficient housing at reasonable rental rates for the families of soldiers coming to Camp Hood.

Some of the soldiers who arrived during the first three months of 1942 later would recall this time of confusion. J.A. Warren, Jr., visited the area 25 years later and recalled his first hours in Temple:

> *I arrived in Killeen in mid-February, 1942, with orders from the War Department in Washington assigning me to the "Tank Destroyer Tactical and Firing Center." It was Sunday morning and the very small town was quiet. Only a few people were about. I drove around town for about 30 minutes, looking for some evidence of a military establishment befitting the impressive title in my orders. None was evident, so I parked and walked. I met an elderly gentleman and asked him, "Where are the soldiers?"*
>
> *He said, "What soldiers?"*
>
> *"Any soldiers," I replied.*
>
> *"Mister," he told me, "you are the first soldier I ever saw in this town."*
>
> *I thought he was joking, so I wandered farther and asked several more people. I even showed them my orders. All professed ignorance of any military establishment. I went back to Temple and registered at the Kyle Hotel with the view of calling Washington the following day. That afternoon, I saw another officer in Temple and he had orders similar to mine. By Monday*

*there were more arrivals. Someone learned that an office had*
*been rented in Temple and that we–members of the faculty of the*
*Tank Destroyer School–would start work. I, a "horse caval-*
*ryman", became a tactical instructor in "Reconnaissance and*
*Security."*[5]

With the activation of the command at Temple on February 14,
General Bruce had his staff hold conferences with officers of the
Eighth Corps Area Headquarters at Fort Sam Houston in San Antonio
to work out details of supply as well as coordinate with Army Engineers in planning the cantonment, the firing ranges, the airfield, and
other facilities at the new camp. A Camp Hood Quartermaster was
created on March 3, 1942, and the 124 enlisted men in it were put on
detached service at Camp Bowie, Texas, to train and organize personnel and to forward supplies to appropriate areas at Camp Hood. A
detachment of the Camp Hood Quartermaster unit arrived in Temple
on April 7 under the command of Major A. Murphey to establish a
warehouse in that city and to operate railheads at Gatesville and
Copperas Cove; it would be to these places that troops and supplies
bound for Camp Hood would arrive.

From March to September of 1942, supplies came by rail to Killeen
on the Gulf, Colorado and Santa Fe and to Gatesville on the St. Louis
Southwestern. Troops detrained at Copperas Cove from the Santa Fe
and at the depot in Gatesville from the St. Louis Southwestern. Out-
going units usually entrained at Gatesville because facilities at that
town included thousands of feet of loading track and a number of
heavy duty loading ramps.

Later, when the camp was fully operational, all freight was received
directly at the Camp Hood cantonment near Killeen, but units with
equipment had to be unloaded at Copperas Cove. Not until April of
1943 were loading facilities completed at the Camp Hood cantonment
that would enable units with equipment to be entrained there.

From the spring of 1942 until December that year, the Quartermaster unit would receive 4,769 carloads of freight destined for Camp
Hood, and 343 carloads would depart from there; most of these cars
were filled with units being sent to ports of embarkation. In addition,

hundreds of trucks were unloaded at the post. None of these figures include the shipments destined for civilian contractors.[6]

While Quartermaster units were doing their work, the faculty for the Tank Destroyer School busied themselves writing text materials and drafting training procedures to be used when trainees arrived. To do this they had to familiarize themselves with the terrain of Camp Hood, then coordinate their needs with the engineers preparing the firing ranges. J.A. Warren, Jr., was one of those who went out for a lesson in Central Texas geography:

> *Toward the first of March, 1942, we obtained two jeeps and saw the land for the first time. We drove from Temple along a narrow paved road to Belton and thence to Killeen. From Killeen we took off across country exploring Cowhouse Creek, the high points and areas suitable for demonstrations of school techniques. It took at least a day to make the round trip. The main road from Hood to Temple had not then been built....*
>
> *The countryside was beautiful. The area we used had been cattle and sheep country. Some parts had supported goats and looked like a park, with trees uniformly cropped at the height of a goat reared up on its hind legs.*
>
> *But there were other "animals," too. Chiggers were voracious. I still have scars on my legs to remind me of my service at Hood. Also, rattlers!... [One] lad was washing his truck in Cowhouse Creek and backed up too close to the bank. A rattler was disturbed and bit the soldier in what the ladies would call the hip.*
>
> *When summer arrived, the heat made for considerable hardship, day and night.... In 1942, we would have paid a great premium for an electric fan.[7]*

The first troop unit actually on the ground at Camp Hood was the 893d Tank Destroyer Battalion, which arrived at the Gatesville railroad depot on March 31. Victor Stanley, a member of this unit, later would recall that he and others in the unit had been told they were moving to Camp Hood, "but we couldn't find it on a map." The reason was the post was not yet on any map. When they arrived at Gatesville, they "asked a man along the road where Camp Hood was, and he pointed to a pasture down the road." The 1,000 men and officers of the 893d, commanded by Major Samuel E. Mays, moved into tents in the field. As other tactical troops arrived, they also were quartered in tents in the field.

Supplies for the men of these first units to arrive were issued directly from boxcars and trucks, while water purification units were put to work and water was taken directly from any running stream that could be found nearby. There was no post exchange, no theater, no service club, just an occasional movie shown under a canopy of stars at some improvised setting. The young men in these units were painfully aware that the nation indeed was at war.[8]

Increasing their pain were the animals and insects that already inhabited the land on which their tents were placed. So long as there has been a United States Army, there have been stories about the snakes and biting insects at every post to which soldiers have been sent. During World War II there were endless tales, each told authoritatively about every post in the country, about troops crawling infiltration courses and coming face to face with rattlesnakes, as also there were innumerable "true stories" of soldiers crawling into sleeping bags or awakening in them to find rattlers sharing their beds.

At Camp Hood some of these stories could have been based on truth, for a list of things that crept and crawled there read like a list of the top ten venomous things in North America–the diamond-backed rattler, the copperhead, the coral snake, the cottonmouth moccasin, the black widow spider, the tarantula, and the scorpion. There even was one variety of caterpillar known to cause severe skin disorders and nausea, and ticks carrying Rocky Mountain spotted fever were numerous. In addition, even the vegetation was dangerous; poison oak and poison ivy were common hazards.

Because of these snakes, insects, and plants, the troops were carefully indoctrinated about how to avoid being bitten or infected and about what to do in case of an injury. Snakes rarely were found in what became the cantonment area at North and South Camp, but on the ranges the troops had to be aware of the danger. The young inductees and volunteers were told that rattlesnakes, because of their number, the amount of their venom, and their willingness to strike with unpredictable suddenness, did not always rattle before they struck, contrary to legends about them, but on occasion they would give an introductory buzz. And their razor-sharp fangs could go all the way through tough GI boots.

The cottonmouth also was of mean temper, was quick to strike, and was dangerous because of his habit of lying along the banks of creeks in concealment. With proper precautions, both the rattlesnake and cottonmouth usually could be avoided. And their bites were not necessarily fatal if the proper treatment was administered quickly, as the soldiers were taught.

The brightly banded coral snake, by way of contrast, had more deadly venom than the rattlesnake or the cottonmouth but an extremely small mouth and no fangs. It had to chew on loose skin, as between fingers, in order to inflict any damage. However, his poison worked on the nervous system, and his bites usually resulted in quick death. Fortunately these small snakes were shy, usually not coming around people and rarely were seen in daytime.

There were three harmful insects on the post: the black widow spider, the tarantula, and the scorpion. Both types of spiders could inflict painful bites, while the scorpion stung its victims. All three could cause great pain and suffering, but the black widow, the soldiers were informed, was capable of paralyzing those it bit.

To counter the threat of snakebite, post commanders at Camp Hood eventually would employ professional snake hunters. These men, usually local citizens familiar with all the dangers involved, would take to the field in early spring while the cold-blooded snakes were still holed up in their dens hibernating. The hunters would spray gas into the dens, and when the reptiles groggily came out the hunters would shoot them with rat shot. Thousands of rattlesnakes were killed each spring, but always a sufficient number survived to constitute a threat and to perpetuate the species.[9]

On April 13, 1942, two weeks after the arrival of the first tactical troops, a station complement was activated at Camp Hood and relieved the tactical troops of administrative, supply, and service duties. Soon the station complement consisted of Post Headquarters, Quartermaster, Ordnance, Finance, and Post Engineers; the men for these units were part of the 1848th Corps Area Service Unit. Transportation was furnished by units transferred to the vicinity of Camp Hood from other posts, such as one unit that came from Fort Sill, Oklahoma in early April of 1942. D.H. Kramer, a member of that unit, would recall that his group was headquartered in Gatesville "in the old mill yard, billeted in tents."

Another unit moving to Camp Hood was a Military Police company. These MPs had myriad duties, including guarding gates and supplies, performing police duties in nearby towns, and apprehending those who were absent without leave (AWOL). And the MPs at Camp Hood had one extraordinary duty: riding horses to patrol the 35 firing ranges adjacent to the East and West Range roads and other outlying areas. These military policemen had to be part cowboy, herding cattle and horses that had wandered into the cantonment area from outside the military reservation. Helping the MPs in their duties on the ranges were members of the K-9 Corps, sentry dogs that were especially useful in guarding water wells.[10]

Because Camp Hood was growing so rapidly, the station complement quickly had to be increased—and many of the personnel sent to it were untrained. To keep things running smoothly, additional veteran Eighth Corps Area officers and enlisted men were sent to Camp Hood, and hundreds of civil service workers were assigned to the post. So large did the post quickly become that on July 21, 1942, at his request, General Bruce was relieved as camp commander in order to devote all his efforts to the work of preparing men and weapons to combat enemy tanks. Named commanding officer of Camp Hood Cantonment was Colonel Charles M. Thirlkeld.[11]

In the weeks that followed the arrival of the first training units, the build-up of troop strength at Camp Hood was steady, but all of these soldiers had to be bivouacked in the field while the buildings were being constructed by civilian contractors. One of the men coming to Camp Hood as part of the Unit Training Center in June of 1942 was Lieutenant Harry H. Hiestand. However, the Tank Destroyer Battalion was so short on officers that for several weeks he was assigned to that unit. When he was relieved from this duty by the arrival of additional officers, Lieutenant Hiestand rejoined the Unit Training Center whose task it was to develop new concepts of attack, defense, and ambush of enemy tanks; once developed, these then were tested under battlefield conditions.

Hiestand and other officers developed the first tank hunter course, which consisted of a number of antitank problems. One of these involved "Dismounted Tank Hunting Units," consisting of tank destroyer personnel whose equipment had been destroyed or become inoperative, along with security elements; these men would become a ground assault force against enemy tanks. During two days of intensive training, later expanded to a week, in this part of their work at Camp Hood, the Tank Destroyers were taught night firing under simulated combat conditions. As they moved forward, the tank hunters had to spot simulated tank targets. Moving through a dark tunnel, the men learned to shoot quickly at a flash of light or a sudden noise. When their ammunition was expended, the lights would be turned on and the exercise scored. However, some of the early training was conducted under conditions that would have been laughable had not the situation been so earnest. For example, Adolph Gresak, one of those early trainees, later would recall that his battalion had to train with BB guns mounted atop the 75mm guns on their M-10 tanks in order to save ammunition.

This training was conducted on the Tank Hunting Course, later renamed "Battle Conditioning." This facility was based on courses used to train British commandos. It had a simulated battlefield which also included a village known as Nazi Town, fashioned entirely from scrap lumber and used for instruction. Here the men learned to shoot immediately at targets in windows and doorways, to take cover behind the first available object, to avoid the surprise traps built into the village, and to cross intersections as safely as possible. They were taught to fire at a crouch with the butt of a rifle in the stomach, thereby knocking out close targets without aiming. It was in this course that, beginning in July of 1942, live ammunition was fired over advancing troops for the first time in the history of the United States Army.[12]

All these methods of training were specified in FM 18-5, the field manual developed by General Bruce's command between January and March of 1942. Entitled *Tank Destroyer Field Manual, Organization and Tactics of Tank Destroyer Units*, this said the "major objective of training must be the development of aggressive individuals and units whose skills with weapons have instilled in them confidence in their ability to destroy the enemy both at long range and in close combat." This meant the teaching of every possible means of destroying tanks–from the massive firepower on self-propelled weapons to the actions of individuals in close combat. Despite the emphasis on destroying tanks without regard to personal safety, the training at Hood instilled a high morale in the men who passed through it.

These men were taught the long range destruction of enemy armor by Tank Destroyer units whose weapons combined a strong armor-piercing firepower, light armor for speed and maneuverability, generous amounts of communications equipment so they could move into position quickly, and a strong defensive capacity against attacks by enemy aviation. Simultaneously the men in "Dismounted Tank Hunting Units" would ambush tanks on the move and raid enemy tank parks with small arms, grenades, mines, and improvised weapons. Among these was the Molotov cocktail, a bottle of gasoline with a rag fuse, but the special pride of the Tank Destroyers was the "sticky grenade." This was a GI sock filled with dynamite and then dipped in a bucket of tar with a 30-second fuse attached; it was to be lit and thrown against the side of a tank where it would stick and then blow a hole through the armor. The Dismounted Tank Destroyers were then to throw a Molotov cocktail through the hole.

Thus the heart of Camp Hood, both before and after its official activation on September 18, 1942, was the Unit Training Center, renamed the Advanced Unit Training Center on August 17, 1942. It was this unit that organized and trained new battalions of Tank Destroyers. Later there was an Individual Training Center and a Replacement Training Center along with a Tank Destroyer School giving specialized technical training to officers and enlisted men. By the end of 1942 these units had trained and shipped out six Tank Destroyer battalions and had begun the instruction of seven more battalions.[13]

The shoulder sleeve insignia for Tank Destroyers, designed to set them apart and give them pride, was a black panther crushing a tank between his jaws and encircled by the words, "Seek, Strike, and Destroy." The insignia was designed by Lieutenant Harry Larter, who was inspired by the World War I Tank Corps mascot, "Black Tom." On at least one occasion, however, this shoulder sleeve insignia led to a case of mistaken identity. In 1943 Private LaVerne Kinsman was home on furlough in Detroit and sitting in a restaurant. A civilian patron also in the restaurant stared at Private Kinsman's Tank Destroyer shoulder insignia for a while, then came over to ask, "Are you a member of the Detroit Tigers?"[14]

General Bruce and his staff quickly realized that one of the greatest needs of the Tank Destroyer battalions being created was officers trained for this specialty, which previously had been unknown in the United States Army. Therefore on June 26, 1942, the War Department issued a memorandum authorizing the establishment of a Tank Destroyer Officer Candidate School at Camp Hood. This command was activated on July 16 and made a part of the Tank Destroyer School; that day the Tank Destroyer School activated an Officer Candidate School Regiment which would train its students in weapons, tactics, communications, automotive details, military procedures, and academics. The first class of 150 began training at Gatesville on July 20. These officer candidates were billeted in Gatesville public buildings and private homes because permanent base quarters were not available for them. In fact, so pressing was the need for junior Tank Destroyer officers that these candidates held their gunnery classes on the front lawn of the Gatesville high school.

The men of this first OCS class along with those who entered in the classes immediately behind them participated in the first formal retreat and review ever held at Camp Hood. This was on the evening of August 25, 1942, when more than 800 officer candidates passed in review on a parade ground north of the Tank Destroyer school on the eastern end of the cantonment area. By the end of 1942 the OCS school had graduated 496 officers. In fact, by the time the 23rd class entered on December 28, 1942, the Officer Candidate School had reached its peak enrollment of 2,005 students.[15]

One of those going through the basic training course operated at Camp Hood during the period shortly after it became an official Army camp was Frank W. Mayborn, publisher of the *Temple Daily Telegram* and owner of radio station KTEM, which served the Temple-Killeen area. In September of 1942, General Bruce and Mayborn were talking one day about the relationship between the soldiers at Camp Hood and the civilians in the surrounding area. Bruce said, "I need someone out here like you to run my public relations office," adding that nothing in Army life had trained the members of his staff in this area.

Mayborn considered the offer but knew he could not be given a direct commission and then posted to this position. "The time is over for getting a political commission," he told Bruce. However, the more he thought about the idea, the more convinced he became that he should "just enlist" and take his chances on getting a commission and being posted as base public relations officer at Camp Hood.[16] This was a serious undertaking for a man approaching his 39th birthday.

After passing the Army physical, Mayborn was sworn in as a private at San Antonio on October 7, 1942. He then had four weeks of basic training at Camp Hood that involved heavy physical activity, such as marches of 15 miles with pack, rifle, and field equipment which severely tested the strength of 18- and 20-year-olds. Mayborn successfully completed basic training and then was assigned to Class 15 of the Tank Destroyer Officer Candidate School which began on November 2, 1942, and concluded on January 28, 1943, after 13 hard weeks.[17] Forty years later Quintus C. Atkinson, then a retired Army colonel, would write Mrs. Sue Mayborn, "Your husband has every right to be very proud of going through the Tank Destroyer OCS at the 'old' age of 39. There were many younger men who could not meet the very demanding physical requirements placed on them by a very tough course." Mayborn served for several months as Public Relations Officer at Camp Hood, then transferred to Washington, D.C., eventually serving with high distinction in the Public Relations Office of SHAEF in Europe.[18]

Also undergoing officer training at Camp Hood was Charles Thomas, one of the first blacks to complete this course. He and other black officers then were assigned to all-black Tank Destroyer battalions also being trained at Camp Hood. Thomas graduated in the 21st Tank Destroyer Officer Candidate School class in March of 1943 and by early 1945 was serving in Europe as a captain in the 614th Tank Battalion. Near the Alsatian town of Climbach, Captain Thomas was leading a group of infantrymen, tanks, and Tank Destroyers sent to take the village. His jeep was at the top of a hill when the enemy opened fire. Although injured, he grabbed a 50 caliber machine gun and raked the woods while his wounded men crawled out of the line of fire. Before he allowed himself to be evacuated, he moved his men into favorable positions. For his action he became the first living black soldier to win the Distinguished Service Cross.[19]

Because of the rapid increase in the size and scope of the command at Camp Hood, A.D. Bruce was promoted to major general on September 23, 1942 (with September 9 as date of rank). And still his command continued to grow. The Tank Destroyer Replacement Training Center, established earlier that year, had enabled the command to give uniform training to replacements, but this made it evident that there was a need for the standardized basic training of all men coming into Tank Destroyer units and programs. Therefore a Tank Destroyer Basic Unit Training Center was created. However, owing to a shortage of facilities at Camp Hood, this unit, when it was activated on November 28, 1942, was temporarily located at Camp Bowie, Texas.[20]

It was the creation of this Basic Unit Training Center and the Tank Destroyer Replacement Training Center which caused the Army to decide to purchase additional land and create facilities at North Camp Hood beginning early in 1943, enlarging the post to some 160,000 acres. When this land was acquired and suitable buildings erected on it, the two new units were housed there. For example, the Basic Training Program, as the effort was renamed, moved to North Camp Hood from Camp Bowie when quarters for it were completed in late 1943. Activated on November 23, it was under the command of Colonel Maurice C. Bigelow.[21]

The official ceremony marking the opening of North Camp Hood came on May 29, 1943, and appropriately the principal speaker was Lieutenant General Lesley J. McNair, the Commanding General, Army Ground Forces—and in many ways the father of the Tank Destroyer concept. "I know of no war training agency which was conceived, planned, built and put into full operation with greater speed, skill and soundness than Camp Hood," General McNair told the audience that day.[22]

Among those in attendance at this ceremony were members of the Women's Army Auxiliary Corps—WAACs. The 159th WAAC unit, consisting of 331 enlisted women and three officers, had arrived at Camp Hood in April of 1943 and was attached to Post Headquarters Company. The women were housed in two detachments, one of which was a medic's station. They were assigned duties as librarians, stenographers, clerks, telephone operators, theater and service club hostesses, receptionists, and chauffeurs, thereby releasing the men who had been performing those tasks for combat assignments. A second unit, the 164th WAAC Post Headquarters Company, later was assigned to Camp Hood, and two days after it arrived its commanding officer reported that her 160 enlisted women and three officers had replaced 110 enlisted men in the Replacement Training Center and 31 enlisted men in the Basic Unit Training Center.[23] It was extremely appropriate that WAACs be assigned to Camp Hood, for commanding this branch of the Army during World War II was Colonel Oveta Culp Hobby, a native of Killeen. In 1943 she visited the post in connection with her duties as WAAC commander.

The Tank Destroyer School likewise was growing as dramatically as Camp Hood itself, reaching its maximum enrollment of 4,810 students on December 31, 1942. This included 12 officer candidate classes, nine courses for officers, and 24 courses for enlisted men. A publications department of the Tank Destroyer School began operations on December 28, 1942, to get the manuals and text materials needed into the hands of instructors and trainees. And always there seemed to be expansion at the Advanced Unit Training Center to ready still more battalions of Tank Destroyers for deployment to combat zones around the world.[24] The success of these units reflected the wisdom of creating a Tank Destroyer Center. In the Center's Information Bulletin No. 7 of May 19, 1943, General Bruce wrote, "It will be noted that our tactics continue to be epitomized in our shoulder sleeve insignia and in our motto. Panther-like, we seek *information* of enemy tanks and of suitable firing positions; panther-like, we strike and destroy by *gunfire* from favorable positions."[25]

In addition, there were decisions made during this period about the weapons and equipment to be used by Tank Destroyer forces. Constantly General Bruce worked with Ordnance and other creative agencies of the War Department to design and build a better Tank Destroyer weapon. Through 1942 the standard equipment for Tank Destroyer battalions was the M-3, a halftrack carrying a 75mm field piece mounted on its bed. The other weapon of expediency was the M-6, a ³/₄ ton truck with a 37mm gun mounted in the rear. Except for the gun shield, the M-6 had no armor. Bruce's recommendation was a "fast moving vehicle mounting a weapon with a powerful punch which could be easily and quickly fired" and which had "armored protection against small arms fire." Bruce's goal was a self-propelled weapon that had speed, maneuverability, and flotation superior to those of hostile tanks. [26]

Created after extensive experimentation was the M-10, also known as the T-70, the first real antitank destroyer, which has been called "one of the most important weapons of the war" by military experts. This consisted of a chassis from the M-4 Sherman Tank with a three-inch antiaircraft gun on a fully rotating open-topped turret. Originally this three-inch gun was designed to be mounted on the M-6, a super tank weighing approximately 65 tons and powered by a 1,000-horsepower engine. However, the M-6 was deemed too heavy for Tank Destroyer needs, and the three-inch gun, with its special recoil mechanism, was mounted in a special turret on the M-4 and proved an excellent weapon. The gun had a range of 16,000 yards and, with armor-piercing ammunition, could penetrate four inches of the best German armor plate at 1,000 yards. The M-10, weighing approximately 30 tons, had a crew of five, a top speed of 30 miles per hour, and a range of 200 miles, and it carried a three-inch gun.

The M-10 was first exhibited and tested at the Aberdeen Proving Grounds on May 2, 1942. General Bruce did not approve of the M-10, feeling its production would slow development of a much superior antitank weapon. This was the M-18, which eventually came into use early in 1945. In May of 1942 General Bruce was overruled, and the M-10 became the standard vehicle of Tank Destroyer units until early 1945. Another weapon added to the armament of Tank Destroyer units was the M-1 Rocket Launcher, known universally as the "bazooka." The Tank Destroyer Board also oversaw the testing of dozens of other items of potential use by the men of Tank Destroyer battalions–even the helmet liners they used. [27]

On May 25, 1943, Major General Bruce was relieved of command of the Tank Destroyer Center at Camp Hood and transferred to command the 77th Infantry Division. By this time most of the tasks assigned General Bruce in November of 1941 had been accomplished. The Tank Destroyer Center, including excellent firing ranges and maneuver areas as well as housing facilities for 80,000 troops, had been built, while yet more tens of thousands of men were bivouacked in the field; an administrative structure had been planned and then carried into reality; sound tactical and training doctrines had been formulated; and suitable weapons had been developed to replace the expedients placed in service before the war started. All this had been accomplished with a speed unknown in American military annals; just 18 months had passed since the order had been issued to create the Tank Destroyer Tactical and Firing Center and train Tank Destroyer battalions.

By this time Tank Destroyers had virtually become a separate arm of the Army, equal to infantry, armor, artillery, and engineers. By early 1943 there were 106 active battalions of Tank Destroyers, each consisting of just under 800 men. This was only 13 fewer battalions than armor itself.[28]

Replacing Bruce at Camp Hood was Major General Orlando C. Ward. A veteran of the North African Campaign where he had commanded the First Armored Division, General Ward was well acquainted with what Tank Destroyers could do in battle, and thus he was an ideal choice to command the Center because of his realistic knowledge of battlefield conditions and his belief in the Tank Destroyer concept. Because his predecessor, General Bruce, had created an excellent administrative framework for the Center, General Ward could concentrate his efforts and time on improving the combat training given at Camp Hood.[29]

General Ward would command the Tank Destroyer Center for just six months, but he would leave his strong imprint on it, bringing to the training given in Central Texas the lessons the Army had learned in North Africa. His special concern was improved gunnery training; it was his desire to correlate all practice firing with what actually took place in combat. Therefore he requested that all officers associated with the instructional staff have combat experience. The battle conditioning course became more realistic by the addition of instruction in night infiltration and the use of live fragmentation grenades. There were courses in fighting in wooded terrain, and there was increased emphasis on "terrain appreciation" for officers and enlisted men; this was accomplished by placing signs near all the ranges at Camp Hood indicating good and bad combat positions under that particular terrain. Moreover, there was increased emphasis on training for such secondary missions as indirect fire and beach defense.

One change General Ward made was the result of a tragic accident. About three weeks after he assumed command at Camp Hood, a company of soldiers was marching on a tank trail when a column of tanks came rolling down it. These tank trails ran parallel to each main road on the post and had been constructed to prevent the treads of the heavy vehicles from doing damage to hard-surfaced roads. In this case the tank drivers did not see the company of soldiers because a dust storm obscured their vision as well as that of the soldiers. Before anyone realized what was happening, twenty-five soldiers had been run over and killed by the tanks.

General Ward called North Camp's post public relations officer, Lieutenant Frank Mayborn, to ask how the incident should be handled. Mayborn's advice was blunt: "You have to tell the truth" to the press, he advised. "You get on the phone and talk to the parents of every one of the dead soldiers, telling them that their son was lost in action in training and that you are writing a letter that will be mailed with their belongings and things. You work out funeral arrangements, and you get the whole post busy accommodating their families." Because of this tragedy, General Ward issued orders that troops never were to march on tank trails.[30]

As late as the summer of 1943 the Army had not overcome many of the problems associated with the rapid build-up of the nation's military forces. Years later Gilbert Jethro would recall being transferred from Camp Bowie at Brownwood, Texas, to Fort Hood; many of the men told to report to the base at Killeen had to walk the 100 miles separating the two posts because there were no trucks available to take them. "The worst thing about the training [at Fort Hood]," Jethro later would say, "was the heat, ticks, and rattlesnakes. Live ammunition was flying over our heads when we were crawling on the obstacle course, so if you crawled up on a rattlesnake you couldn't jump up because you would get shot."[31]

General Ward, like General Bruce, considered the integration of Tank Destroyers with other forces on fields of combat to be of paramount importance. He wanted those trained at Camp Hood to be able to coordinate their efforts with the infantry, armor, artillery, and the Air Corps. Thus in July of 1943 the Training Brigade–soldiers assigned to Hood to assist in training Tank Destroyers–was increased by the addition of the 1st Battalion of the 51st Armored Infantry, 4th Armored Division, and on November 4, 1943, the 264th Field Artillery Battalion arrived. In addition, General Ward on September 22, 1943, recommended that eight liaison airplanes, with needed personnel from the Army Air Corps, be assigned to Hood to work in training Tank Destroyers.

All Tank Destroyer classes were made aware of the need to guard against loose talk that might help the enemy. It was difficult to believe that enemy agents might be operating in Killeen, Gatesville, or Temple, but the base newspaper, the *Hood Panther*, began an anti-loose talk campaign that urged the need for secrecy. Reinforcing this effort were the signs posted above all barracks mirrors that stated, "If you talk too much, this man may die." There were many other restrictions at the time for reasons of security. For example, during the war soldiers were not allowed to have cameras on the post without a permit from their company commander. If they had a camera, they were forbidden to take pictures of military personnel and equipment in training or on maneuvers, just as they could not photograph any ordnance.[32]

And during General Ward's tenure at Camp Hood, the basic manual for Tank Destroyers, FM 18-5, was updated to bring it in line with the lessons of North Africa and other combat zones as well as with the latest in equipment and tactics. One major change was that the Tank Destroyers were given additional training in indirect firing as well as their normal efforts at destroying enemy tanks. Early in the life of Camp Hood, when the manuals were written for training Tank Destroyers, the emphasis had been placed on training the men in methods of indirect fire–support work for infantrymen. However, during the war effort, Tank Destroyers increasingly were called upon to destroy enemy fortified positions, such as pillboxes, and thus the replacements at Camp Hood were trained to do this job.[33]

On October 23, 1943, General Ward was transferred. Replacing him as Commanding General of the Tank Destroyer Center was Major General John H. Hester, a veteran of two combined operations in the Southwest Pacific. During Ward's six months at Camp Hood, it had reached its maximum size–some 130,000 soldiers and officers, permanent staff and trainees; of this number approximately 80,000 were at South and North Camp, while another 50,000 were bivouacked in the field. Troop strength would fluctuate slightly, but would remain at a high level for the next several months after General Hester assumed command. This made it the largest and one of the best-equipped camps in the United States. During General Hester's tenure at Hood, he continued the training policies of his predecessors while stressing perfection in gunnery and teamwork. Also, he added emphasis on initiative and leadership, pointing out the absolute necessity of knowledgeable combat leaders.[34]

However, the Tank Destroyer Center had accomplished its goals of training men to destroy tanks so well that curtailment of its activities became necessary late in 1943. On October 25 General Lesley McNair wrote Hester that the Tank Destroyer Center, along with almost all branches of the Army's Training Command, save the Air Corps, would begin a gradual reduction. Then in November General McNair announced that Army Ground Forces had reached sufficient strength to attain the strategic objectives of the war. In short, all that would be needed to achieve the final victory would be the training of replacements for those killed or wounded. By early 1944 Camp Hood therefore began a rapid shrinkage in manpower numbers as Tank Destroyer battalions completed their training and were shipped to ports of embarkation. The number of men assigned to the Tank Destroyer Center was reduced even more drastically early in 1944 as the Tank Destroyer Unit Training Center was deactivated on February 18. By this time the training of Tank Destroyers largely was confined to North Camp Hood near Gatesville.[35]

Although fewer men were training at Camp Hood, there was no change in the rigorous daily work schedule. During the winter of 1943-1944, reveille was at 6:15, breakfast at 7:00, and the men at their tasks by 8:00. Lunch was at noon, drills then continued, and dinner was at 6:00 p.m. with taps each evening at 11:00. Offices were open seven days a week, although regulations did stipulate that all personnel were to get one day a week off. Moreover, in order to be able to respond to any emergency, the regulations stipulated that no one could live further from the post than where they could report for duty within one hour of a telephone call. When spring arrived that year and the days lengthened, reveille was moved back to 5:45 in the morning. And under some conditions, the workday could be lengthened; on August

1, 1944, for example, a general order was issued placing the men in the maintenance shop and the laundry, as well as post engineers, on a nine hour work day that began at 7:00 a.m. and concluded at 5:00 p.m. at South Camp and ran from 7:30 a.m. to 5:30 p.m. at North Camp.[36]

There also were major efforts at post-wide savings during these years. For example, in February of 1944 a general order was issued about "Handling of Salvage, Garbage and Trash." This noted that "Garbage from kitchens furnishes food for cattle and hogs when properly segregated. It is also an important source of revenue for the Government." Mess personnel were instructed to separate kitchen garbage into specific categories: that which was fit for animal consumption, grease, and trash. They were to salvage tin cans and scrap metals, and they were to save rubber scrap of any kind, crates, glassware—even that which was broken—as well as burlap and cotton bags and onion and sugar sacks. There even was a separate order to save scrap lumber.[37]

Another general order bluntly stated that all paper of any type was to be saved. In this was a notation that "PAPER IS SO VITAL A WAR MATERIAL that in Great Britain destruction of any form of paper has for years been a penal offense."[38] And another general order concerned long distance telephone calls. This directed that a record of all such calls be kept showing the subject matter discussed as well as the time and date. This order concluded that if the base commanding officer deemed any call unwarranted, it would be charged personally to the officer making the call.[39]

By the time General Hester was reassigned on June 26, 1944, there had been one other major change—a new Tank Destroyer weapon was in production. The armament on the basic weapon used by Tank Destroyer forces, the M-10 (T-70), had been a three-inch antiaircraft gun. Because German tanks had been given additional armament, the three-inch gun was not as useful as it earlier had been. This led to the development of the M-18, which seemed almost a race car with its top speed of 55 miles per hour. It carried a 76mm gun in a special turret which had a full 360-degree traverse. The gun fired tungsten carbide ammunition and had a muzzle velocity of 3,400 feet per second, making it the death of German tanks. Its ammunition could penetrate 7.3 inches of armor at 1,000 yards. With its crew of five, it had a cruising range of 150 miles.[40]

Yet as the war progressed, German tanks continued to increase in size and armor–the Tiger with its superb 88mm gun and the Panther with its high-velocity 75mm piece. It was suicide for either the M-10 or the M-18 to engage one of these in head-to-head combat. The answer coming from weapons' developers in the United States was to mount a 90mm gun in a modified turret on the M-10 chassis. On December 29, 1943, Army Ground Forces ordered the Tank Destroyer Board to test and report on this new effort at a better tank destroying weapon. After extensive tests the Board on February 18, 1944, concluded that this weapon, the M-36 (or T-71), was satisfactory for use as a Tank Destroyer. The 90mm gun could throw a shell 19,000 yards and at 1,000 yards would penetrate 4.5 feet of reinforced concrete. The first M-36s arrived in Europe in September of 1944 and soon showed that they could match German tanks in firepower.[41]

Taking command of the Tank Destroyer Center when Major General Hester was reassigned on June 26, 1944, was Brigadier General Ernest J. Dawley, a veteran of the Mediterranean campaign. His lesser rank than the man he replaced reflected the reduced size of the Center. By May of 1944 it had dropped from 85,000 troops (at the end of December, 1943) to only 22,032, of whom 10,999 were permanently assigned there to train the Tank Destroyers needed as replacements for those killed or wounded. The total strength of Camp Hood at that time was 49,591.[42]

Commanding Camp Hood during this period of great growth was Colonel Charles M. Thirlkeld. Assuming his post on July 21, 1942, he had taken a skeleton staff and had built a complete and efficient post command headquarters unit that oversaw the expansion of Camp Hood to the largest military installation in the United States Army. Colonel Thirlkeld could look back with great satisfaction on what he had achieved when he was transferred on January 23, 1944. Replacing him as camp commander at that time was Colonel L.A. Kurtz, while Brigadier General W.R. Nichols was designated Commanding General of Camp Hood as of March 5, 1944. Three and a half months later, on June 30, 1944, General Nichols was forced to retire from the Army for reasons of health, and the following day he was replaced by Colonel Benjamin F. Delamater.[43]

The reason Camp Hood had as many troops as it did in May of

1944–almost 50,000–was a new assignment given the post. No longer was it to be solely a post for training tank destroyers. In early February of 1944 the first Field Artillery battalions arrived, and in the months that followed the training of artillerymen became a major activity at North Camp.

Even more important to the future of the post was the activation there on March 10, 1944, of the Infantry Replacement Training Center at the main cantonment near Killeen. Its task was to receive inductees and train them in infantry tactics as replacements for battle casualties. Under the command of Brigadier General Thomas F. Bresnahan,[44] the Infantry Replacement Training Center in just three short months became the largest activity at Camp Hood, reaching a peak of 31,545 troops on September 21, 1944. Because of these changes, Camp Hood's population did not drop as drastically as might have been the case when the Tank Destroyer Center's work was curtailed. Between May 1 and December 31, 1944, the average strength of the camp was approximately 55,000 with the largest number, 62,557, coming on August 3.[45]

Boosting the number of military personnel at Camp Hood during this period was a less desirable unit but one necessary in the Army during World War II. This was the Southern Branch, United States Disciplinary Barracks, which was activated at North Camp Hood on May 10, 1944. Although housed in an inactivated prisoner-of-war compound that had been reworked, this facility was listed as a Class I Installation of the 8th Service Command and was commanded by Colonel Wilson T. Bals. It soon had approximately 800 officers and men stationed there to guard approximately 2500 prisoners.[46]

Because of the training of infantry replacements at Camp Hood, the Army began using this base for one type of special training that would save thousands of lives and help win the war in the Pacific. As the Army moved from Australia northward across the South Pacific, fanatical Japanese soldiers fought desperately from mountain dugouts and caves on the islands being invaded and caused so many casualties that the War Department created Project Sphinx. This was a task force to research Pacific island battle problems and devise better tactics for this type of combat.

The officers of Project Sphinx chose the Elm Mountain area of Camp Hood, specifically Manning Mountain and Clabber Point, as the site of this research because the terrain there closely resembled some of what would be found on Okinawa and in Japan itself. Hundreds of civilians along with large numbers of German prisoners of war, from the POW compound at North Camp Hood, worked at Manning Mountain and Clabber Point to construct some 3,000 caves, spiderholes, and dugout positions, as well as numerous pillboxes. Most of the caves could not be seen except from the air. Army Air Corps pilots from bases across Texas were sent over the area to spot the caves. Once they were located, the area around them would be defoliated by napalm jellied gas dropped from planes or by tank-towed "snakes" which pulled down the vegetation.

Once the land was cleared of vegetation, the next step was to seal off the caves. This tactic, when used in combat, would avoid the hazardous job of trying to force Japanese soldiers out of their underground hide-outs. Sealing the caves was done by low-flying airplanes armed with rockets and by large-caliber artillery rounds fired into cave entrances. Once the caves were sealed, 18-man assault teams moved to the caves where they dropped satchels of dynamite charges into them. Thus the strategy for attacking typical Japanese fortifications involved close work between Infantry, Artillery, Engineers, the Air Corps, and Tank Destroyers.

Project Sphinx saved the lives of many of the soldiers trained at Manning Mountain and Clabber Point. After the war there were miles of burned grass and scores of craters that once had been man-made caves on this section of Camp Hood, an odd monument to the success of Project Sphinx.[47]

On November 2, 1944, the population at Hood was 57,540 soldiers and 3964 civilians, a number that dropped to 47,156 soldiers and 3927 civilians by January 4, 1945, and then to 40,961 soldiers and 3676 civilians by May 2, 1945. Clearly the planners in Washington could see the end of the war. However, the Infantry Replacement Training Center at South Camp Hood continued to operate on a moderate scale all during this time as did the Basic Training Program at North Camp Hood. Each week through 1944 and into the spring of 1945 hundreds of raw inductees arrived at the Basic Training Program,[48] and each week hundreds of well-trained fighting men departed for service overseas from either the Infantry Replacement Training Center or from the Tank Destroyer schools. This continuous effort required great coordination of administration, supply, and service units.

A glance at reports made during late 1944-early 1945 reveals that the urgency felt in 1942 during the opening days of the war was a thing of the past. In the interim between November 1, 1944, and May 8, 1945, the commanding general reported that his major problems were a shortage of both skilled and unskilled civilian workers and an increase in the laundry load at Camp Hood caused by the closing of laundries in nearby military installations which then began sending this work to Hood. The previous spring the post commanding officer had allowed commercial dry cleaners from off-post to come onto the reservation to offer their services; however, the prices they could charge were closely regulated: 25 cents to clean and press trousers, 20 cents for shirts, and 25 cents for alterations to the length or waist of trousers. Even this proved inadequate, and in late 1944 a large dry cleaning plant, the largest in the state of Texas, was opened at Camp Hood with the capacity to give three-day cleaning service to 20,000 people.[49]

As busy as the laundry facilities at Camp Hood during the first months of 1945 was the combined Maintenance Shop, one of the largest in the Army. It had been designated by the Eighth Service Command as the place where thousands of vehicles, guns, and other types of Army equipment would be reworked for all installations in the Service Command. By rail this equipment came, and by rail it departed, creating much paperwork for post headquarters and much labor by the Quartermaster facility operating the railroad loading docks. Meanwhile, Eighth Service Command activated a Quartermaster Reclamation Center at North Camp on March 19, 1945. To it came clothing and equipment from the Eighth Service area for cleaning, repair, and disposal as directed. So great was the volume of this business that for several months the Quartermaster Reclamation Center operated on a 24-hour-a-day basis.[50]

Meanwhile at South Camp, the Tank Destroyer Replacement Center continued to train replacements. General Dawley, like those who preceded him in command, stressed realistic battle conditions along with great speed in gunnery. In late 1944 there was considerable talk about combining Armor and Tank Destroyer schools at the Army base at Fort Knox, Kentucky, an idea with which General Dawley vigorously disagreed, saying that if the Center was to be moved it should be combined with the Field Artillery at Fort Sill, Oklahoma. On November 1 Army Ground Forces decided that officer candidate schools for Cavalry (Mechanized), Tank Destroyers, and Armor should be combined at Fort Knox. The Tank Destroyer allotment for officer candidates that week was only 11.[51]

Much of General Dawley's tenure as commander of the Tank Destroyer Center was spent working with his staff to draft recommendations about the postwar status of Tank Destroyers. Dawley eventually made a strong plea that a Tank Destroyer battalion be included as part of every Infantry division because Tank Destroyers were essential to Infantry in combat. And he argued that the Center should be continued, for Tank Destroyers were specialists whose training was basically different from all other parts of the Army.

The final World War II commander of the Tank Destroyer Center was Brigadier General A.O. Gorder, who replaced Ernest J. Dawley on March 18, 1945. General Gorder continued to stress teamwork, accuracy, precision, and good training. By the time General Gorder assumed command, however, it was obvious that the war in Europe would last only a few more weeks. Therefore the training at Camp Hood began to focus on how Tank Destroyers could work with Infantry to knock out pillboxes and attack Japanese troops in caves. As part of this effort, the Tank Destroyer Center worked closely with the Infantry on Project Sphinx. In fact, it was Lieutenant Colonel V.W. Pyland, a veteran Tank Destroyer officer from the European Theater who supervised construction of the caves at Manning Mountain and Clabber Point, and Tank Destroyers were closely involved in devising the best strategy for attacking these fortifications. Fortunately Japan surrendered before these tactics had to be tested in actual combat.[52]

Beginning in March of 1945 there were numerous rumors circulating that Hitler's forces had collapsed and that unconditional surrender was at hand. Finally on May 8 came an official announcement from President Harry S. Truman that the long-awaited event finally had occurred. This news was broadcast over post and chapel loudspeakers. All regimental newspapers carried extra editions telling of the surrender of Hitler's forces as did the post newspaper. Military Police were sent into all surrounding towns where people had spilled into the streets to shout and dance in spontaneous celebration of the news. The MPs loaded the troops on pass onto buses so they could be brought back to participate in the ceremonies of thanksgiving ordered at the post.[53] Similar observances were held at Hood on August 11 when the Japanese surrendered.

The Army post created in 1942 as a Tank Destroyer Center certainly had performed the task set for it in late 1941. By the end of World War II, the Center had given instruction to 5,187 officers and 17,062 enlisted men; 5,299 second lieutenants had been graduated from the Tank Destroyer Officer Candidate School; the Replacement Training Center had processed 42,000 enlisted men; tank destroyer weapons, especially the M-18, had been developed along with numerous training manuals; and tremendous advances had been made in the methods of direct and indirect fire from Tank Destroyer weapons.

Moreover, during the first three years of Camp Hood's existence, 56,313 infantry replacements had been trained at North Camp Hood and sent to become an integral part of the Allied forces fighting in World War II. Another study revealed that slightly more than three percent of all United States military personnel serving in combat had been trained at Camp Hood, and that 12 of the 100 Tank Destroyer battalions sent from Camp Hood into combat situations had been awarded unit citations.[54]

As World War II ended, Lieutenant Colonel John Gest issued statistics that showed how complicated had been the role played by the service unit at Camp Hood during the first three years of its existence:

> *If all the frankfurters which I have bought and inspected for consumption here at Hood were rolled into one frankfurter, the don-gone thing would stretch from Austin to Texarkana, and if all the cans of evaporated milk which we have consumed here were laid end to end, they would stretch 350 miles.*

The various mess halls on the post also had used 63,814,040 eggs and 3,228,404 gallons of milk.[55]

Between the end of the war in Europe in May and the Japanese surrender in August, the population of Camp Hood fluctuated between 40,000 and 48,000 troops. Once the Japanese surrendered, however, there was a dramatic decrease, the strength falling by thousands each month. A separation center began operating at Hood on September 17 to process and discharge some 200 troops a day until it closed on December 13, 1945. On the last day of that year North Camp had 1,307 prisoners and 1,266 troops, while the main camp had 9,584 troops for a total of slightly more than 13,000. North Camp, its 2,660 buildings outnumbering the number of troops there, seemed a ghost city, and most of the 2,970 buildings at the main camp were empty.[56]

After the Japanese surrender, the pace of work and training slowed dramatically at Camp Hood. Beginning on September 1, 1945, both civilian and military personnel went on a 40-hour training and work week, by far the fewest number of hours soldiers and civilians had worked in years. Wednesday and Saturday afternoons were not work times for soldiers, and Wednesday morning was for participation in a sports program. At the same time the Infantry Replacement Training Center eliminated battle courses using overhead artillery fire as well as infiltration and close combat courses, and then on October 2, 1945, it closed, its function no longer needed in an Army rapidly demobilizing.[57]

In the first nine days of January, 1946, the post population shrank from 13,206 to 10,847. However, the Army had no intention of closing this giant post and returning the land to its original owners. A study done the previous September noted that Camp Hood's 158,579 government-owned acres were ideal for Army purposes. It was not located in a highly populated area, but Temple, Waco, and Austin were sufficiently close for recreational purposes. The climate was so temperate that little time had been lost due to adverse weather conditions. At South Camp Hood, according to this study, there were housing facilities for 28,909 troops based on 80 square feet per man. The water system was adequate, the sewage system was satisfactory and of a permanent nature, and transportation facilities were excellent. North Camp Hood had a capacity of 18,750 based on 80 square feet per man, but largely the buildings here were unsatisfactory. The report concluded:

From an engineering standpoint *South Camp Hood is considered quite satisfactory for postwar retention. North Camp Hood* *is not recommended for retention, for the reason that, the facilities at this camp will not be required for the proposed postwar strength of the Post. In addition to improvements to the sewage disposal plant..., the cost of providing permanent housing for the officer complement, for the first three grades of NCO's and for remodeling the existing mobilization type barracks for the postwar use of 22,290 enlisted personnel at South Camp Hood would be in the neighborhood of $32,000,000.*[58]

Funds of this magnitude were not available in 1946 as an economy-minded Congress cut appropriations to the Armed Forces. Therefore the work recommended would have to wait. In line with these recommendations, North Camp Hood virtually was closed, and most of its buildings were sold. A few structures–warehouses, post exchanges, chapels, headquarters, and workshops were retained, and concrete slabs for tents were poured. Together these would accommodate the National Guardsmen and Army Reserve units that came to Hood each summer to train. From across Texas, Oklahoma, and Arkansas they would arrive to use North Camp's tank and small arms ranges. In fact, as these men came, some 10,000 at a time, they would put up so many tents that North Camp often was called "tent city." Each spring the permanent personnel of Camp Hood would move into the North Camp area and prepare it for the annual influx of Guardsmen and Reservists that late spring and summer brought, then return in the fall to put the area back in mothballs.[59]

Not immune to this slowdown in Army activity at Camp Hood was the Disciplinary Barracks, which housed Army prisoners. At the time of its annual report on July 1, 1945, the installation had approximately 2500 prisoners. A year later there were about the same number there because the Disciplinary Barracks at Camp Bowie had been closed and its prisoners moved to North Camp Hood. An annual report submitted on August 15, 1946, covering the previous fiscal year noted that these prisoners were receiving training in job skills that would serve them once they were released, skills that included vocational training, motor maintenance, carpenter shop, farm work, printing, the repair of shoes, bicycles, typewriters, and radios, barbering, and plumbing. In the previous year a vigorous program of clemency had been instituted that had resulted in 1902 men being paroled between November of 1945 and June of 1946, and even more would receive an early release in the months ahead as the Army tried to rid itself of these men.[60]

The one major exception to this rule of retrenchment was the construction of an Army Air Corps base on the west side of Camp Hood. During this period there was considerable discussion in military circles that in future wars entire armies would be moved by air. By the fall of 1946 there were rumors circulating among Army people and civilians in Central Texas about construction of an air base at Camp Hood. These rumors grew to the point that many people thought that a runway four miles long would be built and that underground hangars would be dug into hillsides. On November 8, 1946, Major General F.L. Parks, chief of public relations for the Army, announced that $1.5 million would be spent to build a runway of 7,000 to 8,000 feet at Camp Hood to give training at the post in air transportation to all units. When the airfield was completed, more than $5 million had been spent on it. In addition to a runway 8,000 feet long, an additional 1,000 feet had been cleared at each end of the runway. This provided an airstrip that could handle the weight and runway length needed by the largest airplanes, not only those then in service but also those projected by military aircraft designers to come on line in the foreseeable future.

This 1,800-acre facility was turned over to the Air Force when the Armed Forces were reorganized in 1947 and was named Robert Gray Air Force Base in honor of a local hero. Captain Robert M. Gray, who had ridden his pony "Whiskey Pete" through the streets of Killeen in the 1930s, had been one of the bold young Air Corps men who flew with General James Doolittle to bomb Tokyo in 1942. On October 18 that year, shortly after the raid on Tokyo, Gray was killed in action in China.[61]

The downward slide in Camp Hood's population ended in mid-January of 1946 with the arrival of the 2nd and 20th Armored Divisions, bringing the number of troops on the post to 14,000. The 20th was deactivated on April 2 that year, many of its personnel being discharged, the remainder transferred to the 2nd Armored or to other posts.[62] This began a long association between Camp Hood and the 2nd Armored.

The 2nd Armored Division had been organized on July 15, 1940, at Fort Benning, Georgia, and prepared for combat overseas during maneuvers in Louisiana, Tennessee, and the Carolinas. Its first commander was Brigadier (later Major) General Charles L. Scott; he was succeeded by the colorful General George S. Patton, Jr. In fact, while it was in training under Patton, the 2nd was the most maneuvered division in the Army, earning for itself the nickname "Hell on Wheels." The division was a combination of tanks, mechanized infantry, and self-propelled artillery, of engineers and armored cavalry, and was supported in combat by the Air Corps, a mobile logistics system, and a flexible communications network. In November of 1942 the 2nd Armored had been involved in the Allied invasion of North Africa. Eight months later it was part of the assault in Sicily where it met and defeated the elite Herman Goering Panzer Division.

Withdrawing to England, the 2nd trained on the Salisbury Plains, then went ashore at Normandy at Omaha Beach on June 7, 1944, engaging the enemy at Carentan and pushing him back. At St. Lo it shattered strong German defenses, then turned east to help close the Falaise Gap and trap thousands of German soldiers. In September of 1944 the 2nd was the first Allied unit to enter Belgium after a 60-mile drive from the Somme River in just 36 hours. During the Battle of the Bulge in December of 1944, the 2nd raced 75 miles overnight, and the next day met and destroyed its opposite number, the 2nd Panzer Division. Then it was on toward Germany, the "Iron Deuce" racing through crumbling Nazi defenses. Division engineers set a new record by spanning the 1,152 foot Rhine River in just seven hours while under intense fire.

Because of its outstanding record, the 2nd was chosen to be the first American unit to move into Berlin, arriving there on July 4, 1945. During the 1,700 mile trail it took from Normandy to Berlin, the Hell on Wheels Division earned 10 Distinguished Unit Citations–and its men 6,000 Purple Hearts. The 2nd furnished the honor guard for President Harry Truman at the Potsdam Conference. It was a division indeed proud of its history that came to Camp Hood early in 1946.[63]

However, even this heritage would be tested in the lean years that followed the end of World War II, for the 2nd would experience the same shortages of men and supplies as other Army units. And the deactivation at Camp Hood continued as it did at almost every other American military installation. All remaining prisoners of war were shipped to ports of embarkation for return to their homeland in the spring of 1946, and on May 10, 1946, the Service Command Unit at the POW camp was deactivated. The last day of that same month the WAAC detachment was closed down. Commanding Camp Hood during this period was Colonel Benjamin F. Delamater, Jr., who had assumed his post on June 30, 1944. When he transferred on May 13, 1946, his replacement was Colonel O.P. Houston, who served until June 9 that year.[64]

Then came a major Army reorganization, one for which planning began in the final months of World War II as top officials in Washington projected what the peacetime military needs of the country would be. When put into effect in June of 1946, the old Service Commands were abolished and the United States divided into six zones of interior armies and a Military District of Washington, D.C. Each of the six Army zones would be under the command of Army Ground Forces (AGF) with regard to training and troop issues but directly responsible to the War Department for supply and administrative functions.

Under this new arrangement, Camp Hood became part of the Fourth Army, which was headquartered in San Antonio and which oversaw the five-state area of Texas, Arkansas, Louisiana, New Mexico, and Oklahoma. The major military installations in this new command were Fort Hood, Fort Sam Houston, Fort Bliss and Fort Wolters in Texas; Fort Chaffee, Arkansas; Fort Sill, Oklahoma; and Fort Polk, Louisiana. The major commands consisted of the III, VIII, and XIX Corps. Fourth Army contained armor at Camp Hood, artillery at Fort Sill, air defense and missiles at Fort Bliss, and aviation through helicopter training at Fort Wolters; for this reason the Fourth Army sometimes was called the "Quadruple A."[65]

Under orders issued by Fourth Army, the commanding general of the tactical troops at Camp Hood became the commanding general of the post. This meant that Major General John W. Leonard, who commanded the 2nd Armored Division, also was commanding general of Camp Hood. Colonel Houston then was designated deputy post commander.

General Leonard's tenure was brief. On July 4 he transferred, and

Brigadier General J.H. Collier then assumed command of the division and the post. On July 22, less than three weeks later, Brigadier General John M. Devine replaced General Collier as division and post commanding general. He, in turn, was replaced on October 10, 1946, by Major General L.S. Hobbs. From the time General Hobbs took command until the end of December that year, the population of Camp Hood shrank from 14,000 to just 4,629.

Simultaneously it was necessary to cut the number of civilian employees at Camp Hood. The reduction was dramatic–from 3,014 civil service workers in August of 1945 to just 810 by the end of 1947. During 1947 South Camp Hood was thinly populated, the men of the 2nd Armored performing routine duties and using only a small portion of the facilities of the post. Some former barracks were converted into apartments for military personnel and dependents.

It was Major General J.G. Christiansen who commanded the major training exercise that year. On September 27, he replaced General Hobbs as division and post commander, and it was he who participated in an amphibious maneuver staged in October and November. In "Operation Seminole," as this exercise was known, the division boarded ships in the vicinity of San Jacinto, Texas, made a landing at Panama City, Florida, and established a beachhead at this point. The troops returned to Camp Hood on November 17.

By the end of 1947 almost 2,000 buildings, mainly those at North Camp, had been declared surplus and sold. Of the remaining 3,647 structures on the post, only a small number were in use. However, all buildings not declared surplus were kept in a good state of repair in case they might be needed. The population of the camp on the last day of 1947 was 3,394.[66]

At this time the post seemed little more than a ghost of its former self when 130,000 men were working and training there. Clearly some new role would have to be fashioned for it, else it would be closed.

*Chapter Five*

# A Permanent Two-Division Post

In the postwar Army of 1945-1948, Camp Hood and its contingent of troops fared about the same as most other American military posts. An economy-minded Congress and president were bent on demobilization–reducing the size of the Armed Forces–as rapidly as possible. Starvation budgets and Spartan conditions became the new reality for Army personnel, not only in Central Texas but also around the world. Thus in the months following the end of World War II, most of the buildings still standing at Camp Hood slowly deteriorated as they stood in long silent rows, weeds growing between them. The merciless Texas sun caused the yellow paint which covered them all to crack and begin peeling to expose the wood underneath to the elements. Only those structures in use by the 2nd Armored and permanent base personnel were in good repair.

During this period the housing provided for enlisted men's families, called Hood Village, was a public disgrace. These structures, in reality little more than tar paper shacks, had been built during World War II by the Federal Public Housing Authority for civilian workers at the post. After the war they had been turned over to Army control and renovated–making them actually better than some of what was being offered to soldiers as rental property in surrounding towns. Hood Village had 571 apartments ranging from two to four bedrooms, and in the area were a Post Exchange, a food store, a barber shop and a recreational building known as a "Youth Center." Married officers' quarters and bachelor officers' quarters were only slightly better.

In what might have seemed an exercise in wishful thinking, the commanding general at Camp Hood in 1946 created a Post Planning Board, consisting of representatives from training, logistics, personnel, engineers, and communications. The task of the Post Planning

Board was to plan for a permanent facility that would allow the phasing in of permanent structures alongside the temporary buildings, which gradually would be retired from use.

A major restriction placed on the Post Planning Board was that no permanent housing could be built if a temporary structure had to be demolished to make way for it. Therefore the members of this board almost unanimously agreed that the first structures it would recommend for construction were those in the category of welfare and morale facilities, then woefully inadequate if Hood was to be a major peacetime installation. The Post Planning Board made this decision because its members knew that a large amount of nonappropriated money had accumulated in Washington from welfare funds generated at post clubs and theaters throughout the world at bases that had been closed. The Post Planning Board decided, in line with Army Engineers' recommendations, that all construction at Camp Hood, even that relating to welfare as well as to military needs, would be buildings of cream stucco and clay tile.

Camp Hood officials were successful in getting 2 million dollars allocated to the Central Texas facility because of its distance from large cities that could provide recreational facilities. Moreover, they could argue that Camp Hood was in a part of the country where segregation was still a reality, and thus integrated recreational facilities were greatly needed for minorities on the post itself. The $2 million in unappropriated funds that were allocated for Camp Hood were used to construct an air-conditioned Main Post Theater that seated 1,006; a 4,560-seat reinforced concrete Post Stadium that included a football field; the first nine holes of a permanent 18-hole golf course; three swimming pools; five baseball diamonds, including the main post diamond with bleachers for 3,000 spectators; and 17 tennis and volleyball courts.

Officials at Camp Hood subsequently secured additional unappropriated funds, and these were used to construct the Main Post Exchange and Cafeteria, the noncommissioned officers open mess and swimming pool, an enlisted men's service club, and an officers' open mess with pool facilities.[1]

However, the Planning Board was less successful in its efforts to provide better housing for base personnel. A review of its efforts in 1954 led to major criticisms:

*There are times when it appears that the Planning Board has blacked out and lost all contact with the world of reality, for it is not too uncommon for a fiscal year's program to include major buildings being authorized for construction and the supporting utilities and access roads to be deferred for not only one, but for several years. Perhaps the most difficult to explain is why the Colonels' family quarters have fireplaces when the General Officers' do not...and both constructed under the same authorization in the same fiscal year and under the same contract.*

In fiscal year 1948 Congress authorized the construction of 272 family housing units at Camp Hood, 184 for enlisted men and 88 for officers. However, a rider on this appropriations act limited each housing unit to 1,080 square feet and specified that all quarters were to be of eight-family row-type construction. This square footage met the requirements only for enlisted personnel, falling far short of that authorized for all grades of officers. Therefore all these units were designated for noncommissioned officers, but housing for officers was in such short supply that as late as 1956 officers, ranging in grade from lieutenant to colonel, were occupying 88 of the units. Moreover, general officers were found to be paying their full housing allowance of $171 for quarters very similar to those occupied by enlisted personnel, who were paying only $96.90 a month.[2]

However, the Planning Board did accomplish the broad mission given it to draft a "Future Development Plan" for the post. In fact, this plan was the first to receive approval from the Department of the Army in the entire Fourth Army area. This plan called for housing and training grounds for force troops with an Armored Division and a Corps Headquarters as the major elements. In drafting this document, the Planning Board, in the interest of economy, adhered to the World War II layout at Hood to the greatest extent practicable. By using existing utilities, roads, and drainage and by retaining troop housing and motor park areas, the Planning Board saved an estimated $8.3 million, while it saved another $1 million by using streets, rail facilities, and utilities in the warehouse area.

What the Planning Board did was analogous to a city drawing a zoning map as it looked to the future. The members of the Planning

Board knew that areas of the post would be needed for work, other areas for recreation, and yet other areas for housing a population equal to that of a small city. The plan involved 2,650 buildings totaling 9.5 million square feet, 448 miles of roads, 104 miles of electric distribution lines, 408 miles of natural gas distribution pipelines, 137 miles of water mains, and 111 miles of sewer lines.

The troop housing belt, planned for armored units, provided for both battalion and regimental echelon facilities, each accommodating approximately 3,300 men. Until the mid-1950s the standard barrack housed 225 men, and 24 of this type would be erected at Hood; after 1955 the standard barrack housed 326 men. Unfortunately Congress would not provide the funds to air condition these barracks–although another military facility 150 miles to the north was found to meet the criteria for air conditioning. As one inspector commented, "It's just a matter of perspective!"

Each of the barrack areas was served by streets, and each had easy access to supporting motor pools located in adjacent areas to the rear of the barrack blocks. Also, each block was fronted by a clear area for athletics, recreation, and parade fields. Interspersed throughout the barrack area, which extended some six miles through the central section of the post, were enlisted men's service clubs, theaters, and guest houses for visitors.

Near the Corps and Post Headquarters area, 18 acres were set aside for the main shopping center that would be central to both troop and family housing areas. In this area were the 1,000-seat Post Theater, the Main Post Exchange, Post Cafeteria, Commissary, Post Office, a public telephone and telegraph facilities building, and bank and concessionaire shops.

The area designated for family housing, both enlisted and officer, was on high ground to take advantage of prevailing wind patterns. By the mid-1950s, in addition to the 272 units of eight-family row-type quarters, an additional 435 units had been authorized and consisted of 113 separate and 322 duplex units. Almost all of these were wood-framed with brick trim and had low-pitched roofs with wide overhang that was suitable to the climate. To reduce maintenance costs, all exterior wood was cedar or redwood with stained finish.

Home to many Army families was the Wherry Housing Project,

which contained 568 units. Opened in 1952, these were in an area of dependent housing known as Walker Village. These units were constructed at a cost of $8,100 each and were for enlisted personnel. Providing medical attention for all Army personnel at Camp Hood and their dependents was a 300-bed hospital dating from World War II; it consisted of some 111 wooden buildings. When specialists were needed, patients were transported to Brooke Army Medical Center in San Antonio at Fourth Army Headquarters.[3]

The streets in the Wherry Housing Project were named for twelve Central Texas war heroes. Bowen Circle was named for Sergeant John G. Bowen of Killeen, who died in a plane crash in 1943. Carrol Drive was named for Master Sergeant M.D. Carroll of Killeen, who was killed in action in Italy in 1943. Clement Circle was named for Private Cecil R. Clement, who was killed in the Philippines in December of 1941. Cole Avenue was named for Private Walter R. Cole of Belton, who was killed in Italy in 1943. Seaman First Class Earl L. Derrick of Gatesville died when the *USS Cooper* sank near the Philippines in 1944; Derrick Circle was named for him. Krause Avenue was named for Sergeant Jim A. Krause of Belton, who died on D-Day at Normandy. Lieutenant Grover C. Martin, Jr., was killed on a flight over Munich in 1944; Martin Drive was named for him. Scott Avenue was named for Private William Scott of McGregor, who died in the Meuse-Argonne section just before World War II ended. Oswalt Drive was named for Private First Class G.C. Oswalt, Jr., of Temple, who died in the Korean War. Graves Avenue was named for Private Riley W. Graves of Temple, who was killed in Korea in 1950. And Waskow Drive was named for Captain Henry T. Waskow of Temple, who won the Legion of Merit and who was the subject of a column by the famed correspondent Ernie Pyle. The main street in the Pershing Park area, Hoover Hill Road, honored A.J. Hoover, a pioneer resident of Killeen. Other streets named for 1st and 2nd Armored Division soldiers who died in action in World War II included Wales, Yeakel, Dillingham, Kilder, Rowe, Northrup, Cutler, Boyd, Hughes, Moore, Carter, Large, and Bixby.[4]

Because so many enlisted men and officers brought their families to Camp Hood in the years just after World War II ended, the new peacetime Army had to provide schooling for the children. In the spring of 1946, Major General John M. Devine, the post commander, ordered that a Camp Hood school system be established. By August, Major Barney Barrows, serving as school officer, had overseen the conversion of Building 909 to classrooms, and in September approximately 250 children from Hood Village began attending the eight grades taught. Supervising the effort was the Killeen school system with R.E.L. Jones serving as principal.

During the 1947-1948 school year a building expansion program was undertaken under the supervision of Lieutenant Colonel B.E. Meadows, and several needed facilities were completed: classrooms, auditorium, cafeteria, home economics department, and a woodworking shop. This enabled the Camp Hood school system to expand to nine grades, and enrollment swelled to 475 as a kindergarten was added along with an athletic program and a school band. In addition, a school for the children of black soldiers at Camp Hood had to be started, for this was the era before the Supreme Court ordered school desegregation and facilities still were separate, even in the Army.

During the summer of 1948 came yet more expansion as three classrooms in Building 910 were set aside for the Camp Hood school system and another three in Building 924. Buildings 1137, 1138, and 1139 were converted into two gymnasiums and a dressing room, and in September that year yet another grade was added, giving the Camp Hood system 10 grades, 24 teachers, and approximately 575 students.

In the spring of 1949 a full four-year high school was added to the Camp Hood system, and eight new classrooms were allotted it, four in Building 925 and four in Building 911 and 912. Added enrollment brought the school to 734 with 33 teachers. In 1950 Barney Barrows, who had been Camp School Officer in 1946, became president of the school board; serving on the board with him were John Bruner and Ray Moore.

On September 1, 1952, the Fort Hood Independent School District and the Killeen Independent School System formally consolidated, but it was not until 1953 that students from Fort Hood actually began attending Killeen schools. That fall Killeen's school enrollment jumped from 1,260 before consolidation to 2,140 afterward. However, most Army dependents saw little difference after consolidation, for they continued to go to class in the same buildings as before. Then in 1953 the United States Commissioner of Education provided funds to construct a modern 29-classroom elementary school building at Fort Hood. This was located between the officers and enlisted family housing area and, when completed, was operated by the Killeen Independent School District. In addition, a new high school to serve both Army post and city, was erected on the edge of the military reservation adjacent to the Wherry Housing area, built in part with a grant of $410,000 in federal funds; the remainder came from a local bond issue. The Killeen Independent School District became one of the first in Texas to desegregate following the Supreme Court ruling of 1954. Prior to this, young blacks had attended a segregated elementary school in Killeen, and older students were bused to an all-black high school in Belton.[5]

The financial fortune of residents of Killeen rose and fell with appropriations for Camp Hood during the late 1940s. As the tempo of life at the post slowed immediately after World War II ended, so also did the pace of affairs in Killeen's business district. Some of the slack was taken up when the city issued $75,000 in revenue bonds for street improvements, and funds were voted to build a water treatment and distribution system. However, from 1945 to 1948 the economic climate in Killeen was depressed as fewer and yet fewer soldiers and their families came to town to spend their money. Always during this period there were rumors about the Army base–that it would be closed, that it would be enlarged. In 1947-1948 the rumors about growth increased dramatically when Robert Gray Air Force Base was being built.[6]

Actually most of these rumors centered around a second military installation on the west side of Camp Hood. This was Killeen Base, which was a Defense Atomic Support Agency facility used to store components of the nation's nuclear defense system–exactly what that might be was classified top secret. This was a post of some 982 acres carved out of what had been the Fort Hood Reservation. When it was being built in the fall of 1947, miners were flown in by Air Force planes from Kentucky and kept in total ignorance about where in the United States they were working. It was their job to dig tunnels 20 feet wide and 30 feet tall into the hilly countryside of the Camp Hood reservation in both Coryell and Bell counties, but there has never been any official confirmation of what use these tunnels had during this period, leading at the time to the circulation of many rumors about it in the nearby civilian area. The most persistent was that atomic bombs were being stockpiled there. These rumors even grew to the point of the absurd, one holding that what actually was being built on the west side of Camp Hood was a submarine refueling base that was linked by an underground waterway to the Gulf of Mexico.

Originally this facility was named the Armed Forces Special Weapons Project Activity, but was designated Killeen Base on October 1, 1948, and passed to Air Force jurisdiction. In February of 1952 command of this post would change from the Air Force to the Army when it would come under the jurisdiction of the Defense Atomic Support Agency at Sandia Base, Albuquerque. Even when the post was under Air Force jurisdiction, there were no landing facilities there; rather planes landed at the adjacent Robert Gray Air Force Base or at the 4,712-foot-long air strip at Fort Hood. And it was guarded by Army ground units. Richard Cavazos, later to be commanding general at the post, was at Fort Hood in 1953 as a first lieutenant commanding a company of armored infantry. He later would recall being assigned guard duty at this atomic facility for a week at a time about every six weeks. "We would spend a whole week circling it," he said. "We never knew what was inside it, but we guarded it with weapons cocked and loaded."[7]

The gradual decline in numbers at Camp Hood, which began even before World War II ended, continued until the spring of 1948 when a gradual reversal began. From a low of 3,400 men, there came a slow climb to approximately 4,800 officers and men by the end of June that year. Then the effect of the Selective Service Act of 1948 became evident. The act of 1940 had been extended in 1945, but enthusiasm for military training was so low that in 1947 the draft was allowed to lapse. Then in June of 1948 came a new Selective Service Act which was to remain in effect for two years and provided that young men were to be trained during a year of active service, followed by a long period in the reserves.[8]

At Camp Hood, following passage of this act, Post Engineers rehabilitated and renovated buildings dating from World War II in preparation for the influx of trainees expected. The 2nd Armored Division was designated a training unit for eighteen-year-olds who enlisted for one year, and Combat Command "A" was organized into a Replace-

ment Training Center; eventually seven training battalions were used
to train the eighteen-year-old enlistees. By October 6 the Replacement
Training Center had grown to 2,857 men, but this gradually decreased
because the Army's starvation budget would not allow it to accept
more enlistees. On December 4, 1948, the last training battalion was
discontinued.

During this same period Camp Hood was a training camp for Reserve
Officer Training Corps (R.O.T.C.) and National Guard units. That
summer of 1948, 427 students from 15 colleges passed through North
Camp Hood as they trained for the infantry, cavalry, or military police.
National Guard units coming to the post, undergoing what was termed
"Civilian Component Training," included the 45th Infantry Division
from Oklahoma, the 36th Infantry Division and the 49th Armored
Division of Texas, and the 112th Armored Cavalry Regiment of Texas.
Army Reserve units training at North Camp Hood included the 75th
and 90th Infantry Divisions.

The increase in Army strength at Camp Hood was matched by increased civilian employment, the number rising from just more than
800 in January of 1948 to some 1,400 by the end of the year. About 200
of the increase was in the Post Laundry, and many more were involved
in the renovation of buildings.[9] However, no significant changes took
place in 1949 as the Army–and Camp Hood–continued to receive
inadequate funding from Congress.

Behind the scenes, however, there was an intense lobbying effort
taking place to make Camp Hood a permanent Army installation. For
a time after hostilities ceased in the summer of 1945, the people of
Central Texas, like most Americans, believed there would follow a
period of world peace and that a large military establishment would
not be needed. They applauded as President Truman and Congress
announced that the Army would be cut to 1,950,000 and then by July
1, 1947, to 1,070,000, figures that included both Army and Air Corps.

Then came the National Security Act of 1947 which separated the
Air Force from the Army and created the Department of Defense. This
further reduced the size and scope of the Army–in the face of a growing awareness of the territorial ambitions of the Soviet Union. However, both military and civilian strategists concluded that the deterrent
to war would be atomic bombs and airplanes, not ground soldiers, so

the Army continued to receive scant funding during this period. Army officers could do nothing but obey their superiors and watch in frustration as the number of soldiers in uniform decreased.

There were civilians aware of the needs of the country who felt free to walk where Army officers dared not visibly tread–the corridors of political power. Moreover, every cut in Army strength brought an intensified struggle among civilian leaders across the country to see that bases in their own particular area not be reduced or closed. "Cut somewhere else, not here," was the universal cry. Closing a military base meant the loss of jobs and federal dollars, which severely impacted many areas of the country. And usually the first to be closed were the "temporary" bases built during World War II.

The leader of a group of Central Texans anxious to see that Camp Hood not be closed but rather grow in size and strength was Frank W. Mayborn, the Temple publisher and broadcaster who in 1940-1942 had led the fight to get an Army post located at Killeen. Almost immediately following his separation from the Army in 1945, Mayborn began a concerted effort to get Camp Hood declared a permanent post. On August 16 he convened a group of city and county officials from Bell, Coryell, and Lampasas counties in Temple, and the next day on their behalf he wrote Senator Tom Connally of Texas:

> *Now that the war has ended and the disposition of Army facilities is being considered by the War Department, we feel that the time has come to take active steps to see that this installation is made permanent for the reasons which are stated in the attached resolution.*[10]

Then–and in the months and years ahead–the argument for Fort Hood was that it was the ideal place to train armored soldiers, as several high-ranking officers had pointed out.

Mayborn's efforts kept Camp Hood open, but in the immediate postwar years there was no announcement that the base would become a permanent post. On September 20, 1945, Jim Reinhold of the Santa Fe, still in Washington and guarding the interests of both Central Texas and the railroad, wrote a confidential letter to Mayborn about how the Army felt about Camp Hood: "The latest rating on the confidential list as of this date shows Camp Hood with a 1A priority and refers to both the south and north camps. This, of course, is the highest priority and indicates the present thinking on the part of the Army to keep Hood as a permanent post. Nevertheless I think you should continue through the Senator [Tom Connally] to watch the matter closely as these lists are subject to revision from time to time."[11]

In November of 1945 came word that the 2nd Armored Division would make Camp Hood its permanent home when it returned from overseas, which was reassuring to Central Texans and showed the truth of what Reinhold had written about the Army's intentions for Camp Hood.[12] However, Mayborn had been involved in political lobbying efforts long enough to know that constant vigilance was required. Therefore in late January of 1946 he was in Washington as part of a three-man committee representing the interests of Central Texas; on the committee with him were Charles Eubanks of Waco and Judge Floyd Ziegler of Gatesville. General Jacob Devers, chief of Army Ground Forces, assured them that Camp Hood's usefulness to the Army extended into the distant future. In his story about this meeting, written for the *Temple Daily Telegram*, Mayborn stressed that "the policy of the army will be to handle the economic angles in such a way as to benefit all towns and cities in the area."[13]

Mayborn's major worry in this lobbying effort was that people in some area towns might get disgruntled and break the unified front needed to convince officials in Washington to make the post permanent. Especially was Mayborn worried that some in Waco would not fully cooperate, and thus in February of 1946 he began a series of "unity meetings" designed to convince everyone to work together.

Mayborn's worries were justified–but not so much about Waco as Gatesville. Some leaders in that town were seeking to get South Camp Hood closed while making North camp a permanent facility. On September 20, 1945, Frank C. Higginbotham, manager of the Gatesville Chamber of Commerce, forwarded a lengthy report to the Army and to members of Congress urging this, writing that this would be "of vital importance to the taxpayers of the nation, to the military personnel to be trained at the camp [Hood], and to the area contributing the training grounds." This report, sent under the signature of Gatesville Chamber of Commerce President John Gilmer, argued that North Camp Hood was more accessible to populated areas of Texas and to recreation centers of the state, that North Camp Hood had a better supply of water available and a better sewage system, that North Camp Hood was "a more healthful location," and that there was greater economic stability in the Gatesville area.

Interestingly, the Gatesville group in February of 1942 suggested that the post, should it be made a permanent facility, be renamed Fort McNair in honor of General Lesley McNair, who had received little public recognition for his contributions as commander of Army Ground Forces during World War II; also, according to the people of Gatesville, such a designation would be fitting, for General McNair had been the principal speaker at the formal dedication of North Camp's facilities in 1943. Accompanying this petition was a "brochure outlining the advantages and the disadvantages to the proposal of making a permanent military establishment of North Camp Hood or South Camp Hood"; this was submitted by the Industrial Department of the St. Louis Southwestern Railway Lines (the Cotton Belt); this concluded that "North Camp Hood [the area served by the Cotton Belt] presents the more favorable location for a permanent military establishment."

Four months later people in Gatesville and Coryell County submitted yet another petition to its congressman and senators. This one urged, as had the one before it, that North Camp Hood be made the permanent Army base in the region. However, if South Camp Hood was to be the major cantonment area for the post, the petitioners asked that the Army take 130,000 acres for such permanent military reservation from "the Chalky hills and lands, over in Bell County, that is located between Belton and Killeen and North of the Santa Fe Railroad." Then the Army could declare surplus some 130,000 acres already taken and used as part of Camp Hood during World War II, allowing it "to be disposed off [sic] back to the citizens of Coryell County for rehabilitation as farms and ranches."[14]

The Gatesville idea to rename the post after General Lesley J. McNair found considerable support in the Army–and briefly brought the hope of its designation as a permanent installation. On June 1, 1947, the War Department Memorialization Board announced that at its next meeting it would consider a suggestion from the Army Ground Forces Command at Fort Monroe, Virginia, that Camp Hood be redesignated Fort McNair. The next day Major General L.S. Hobbs, commander of the 2nd Armored Division at Camp Hood, wrote the commanding general of Army Ground Forces that "This headquarters deems it most fitting and proper that such an honor be rendered." However, General Hobbs pointed out that Paragraph 2c of Army Regulations No. 210-10, issued by the War Department on May 6, 1947, stipulated that any post made permanent will be designated a fort. Thus naming the post Fort McNair would change Hood's status from temporary to permanent.[15]

General J.M. Wainwright, commanding the 4th Army at Fort Sam Houston, which was the next level of command above the 2nd Armored Division, endorsed the idea of renaming Camp Hood in honor of General McNair, but he pointed out that it should be called "Fort Lesley J. McNair" because "there have been several distinguished officers named McNair." However, General Wainwright added his own idea about an appropriate permanent name for Camp Hood, writing, "In view of the fact that Camp Hood has for many years been the seat of Armored activity, and in all probability will so continue..., consideration [should be] given to the name Fort George S. Patton."[16]

Officials at Army Ground Forces headquarters at Fort Monroe, Virginia, concurred in recommending a change of name from Camp Hood to Fort Lesley J. McNair, but the War Department Mobilization Board disagreed. In February of 1948 came the announcement that the Army War College had been renamed Fort Lesley J. McNair.[17]

Frank Mayborn tried to get all of Gatesville's leaders to work in concert with representatives from Copperas Cove, Killeen, Belton, and Temple–and continued his quiet, steady efforts despite Gatesville's independent attitude. In 1947 he organized a Temple Army Advisory Committee at the request of Fourth Army Headquarters in San Antonio. Many of the members of this committee, which Mayborn chaired, had been on his War Projects Committee in 1940-1942, and it worked in close cooperation with its Congressional delegation, particularly with Congressman Bob Poage and Senator Tom Connally, to secure permanent status for Camp Hood. And after he was elected to the United States Senate in the fall of 1948, Lyndon Johnson, with whom Mayborn also had a particularly close relationship, became another major supporter of the effort.[18]

Mayborn likewise kept a close eye on federal appropriations for dependent housing at Camp Hood, for he believed that if sufficient money was invested at the post the Defense Department would not close it. Through 1948 and 1949 he and members of his Military Affairs committee monitored this spending and kept each other informed as information became available. It was a distinct pleasure for them to see that in the fiscal year 1948-1949 the Army planned to build 272 housing units and that under the Wherry Act there would be more than 500 housing units built in 1949-1950 with another 150 housing units to be constructed at Robert Gray Air Force Base.

Another Mayborn effort was to get funding to build permanent training facilities for the Texas National Guard at North Camp Hood near Gatesville. The structures left from World War II on the north side of the post were deteriorating badly by the late 1940s, and Mayborn knew that unless new buildings were erected the Texas National Guard might be sent elsewhere each summer. After a long effort, the goal was achieved when in October of 1950 Major General Raymond H. Fleming of the Texas National Guard Bureau announced that $294,000 had been allocated for construction of mess halls, kitchens, and latrines and the repair of other facilities.[19]

One of the major obstacles to getting Hood declared a permanent post was the periodic droughts which threatened the camp's water supply. There were years in Central Texas when the spring and fall rains did not come, causing creeks and reservoirs to dry up, and concerned officials would declare an emergency that restricted water use. Frank Mayborn had long been aware of this problem, which he began addressing in 1934 with a campaign to get a dam built on the Leon River near Belton. All his work had come to naught before World War II, but finally on December 15, 1945, Mayborn and those working with him–Representative Bob Poage, Guy Draper, Dr. A.C. Scott, Byron Skelton, and Roy Sanderford–got the U.S. Army Corps of Engineers to produce a report favoring the project to build a dam on the Leon.

Getting a recommendation favoring the dam was easier than getting the money to build it, for at the end of World War II there was a great backlog of civil engineering projects awaiting federal funding. Finally in 1947 Congress appropriated $100,000 for planning for a dam on the Leon River, but then in 1948 the House refused to vote any construction funds for it. Mayborn and his committee continued to fight, however, and at their urging Senator Tom Connally got $1 million for the project inserted when the money bill came to the Senate that year. This was cut to $500,000 in the House-Senate conference committee, but this was a beginning. Formal ground-breaking ceremonies were held on December 10, 1948, and work on the dam began immediately thereafter.[20] This meant that Camp Hood, if made a permanent post, would have a guaranteed supply of water.

The lobbying effort by Mayborn and his committee of Central Texans, the political action of Congressman Poage and Senator Johnson, and several behind-the-scenes efforts paid off in the spring of 1950. On April 13 Sarah McClendon, Washington correspondent for the *Temple Daily Telegram*, telegraphed the long-awaited news:

> *The Army General Staff has given its approval to making Camp Hood a permanent military installation and to changing its name to Fort Hood.... The formal order is expected to be issued by the Adjutant General's office within two or three weeks.*
>
> *Approval by the General Staff is believed to be tantamount to final definite approval of permanent status and change of name for Hood.*
>
> *This achievement is the result of the efforts of Rep. W.R. Poage, 11th district, and a group of Temple citizens, who also are largely due the credit for getting the camp near Temple and for keeping it there....*
>
> *For some time now it has been understood in military circles that the government had such a large investment in Camp Hood that it did not wish to move the installation. Location of the military center itself is strategically important, far inland as it is, in addition to providing excellent training and firing ground.*[21]

The next day the Army Department confirmed the story, and on May 8 came General Orders officially changing the name of the post to reflect its permanent status: "Effective as of 15 April, 1950, Camp Hood, Texas, a class I installation under the jurisdiction of the commanding general, Fourth Army, was redesignated Fort Hood, Texas." The order was signed by J. Lawton Collins, Chief of Staff, United States Army.[22] What had started as a mushroom camp of temporary buildings, created to train Tank Destroyers during World War II, had become the Army's major post for armor. This designation speeded the construction of permanent buildings on the post, both military and civilian. Frank Mayborn's long-held vision had become a reality.

The designation of Fort Hood as a permanent post also made possible long-range planning in nearby towns such as Killeen. As the *Temple Daily Telegram* reported on April 15:

> *Businessmen [in Killeen] were already talking projects, such as a new hotel, which have long been planned but were being held off pending the status of Hood.... Killeen today was assured of the biggest boom ever as merchants breathed a sigh of relief and concluded that their investments were safe.... A population of 20,000–more than double the present estimated population of 7,900–was forecast by Postmaster Earl Massey.[23]*

The timing of this change in the status of Fort Hood was fortuitous, for on June 24, 1950, the Communist forces invaded South Korea and began a three-year conflict sometimes mistakenly called a "police action" by President Truman. In reality this was a war, a dirty war in which American and United Nations forces were forced to fight not for victory but rather to achieve political goals. At first the Joint Chiefs of Staff and the Department of Defense thought this would be a conflict in which American participation would be limited to air, sea, and logistical support, with ground combat the responsibility of the South Koreans. However, the Army of the Republic of Korea had no tanks or heavy weapons, while the Russians were supplying the North Koreans with both. Both General Douglas MacArthur and the Department of Defense soon realized that American ground troops would have to be committed to battle–and in such numbers that a partial mobilization became necessary in the United States.[24]

At Fort Hood the 2nd Armored, known as the "Hell on Wheels" Division, began training in earnest when word came of the outbreak of conflict in far-off Asia. The 2nd also was given the responsibility for training some 20,000 reservists, most of whom had no military service since World War II and whose military skills thus were in great need of being updated. Several units from the 2nd Armored went to

Korea and saw combat there: the 6th Tank Battalion, two companies each from 66, 67 Armored Regiment, two companies from the 82nd Recon Battalion, and the 92nd Armored Field Artillery Battalion. Also going to Korea were thousands of replacements trained by the 2nd, while additional tens of thousands of National Guard troops came to North Fort Hood each summer during these war years to prepare themselves for duty if needed. Moreover, the 2nd was heavily involved in training the draftees inducted into the Army when the draft was reinstated during the Korean War.[25]

Early in 1951 came a major change at Fort Hood as high-ranking officers in Washington finally realized that ground forces would continue to be needed as the United States faced Russia and its allies in the so-called Cold War. On March 7, 1951, came orders for the 1st Armored Division to be reactivated at Fort Hood, Texas.

The 1st had a proud history, tracing its origins to the basement of a schoolhouse in Alexandria, Louisiana, in 1940. Among others present at this gathering of officers concerned about the nation's preparedness in the face of aggression in Europe were Lieutenant General Adna R. Chaffee, Major General Frank M. Andrews, Major General Bruce Magruder, and Colonel George S. Patton, Jr. The result was orders dated July 15, 1940, creating Armor as a separate branch of the Army and ordering the formation of the 1st Armored Division at Fort Knox, Kentucky, under command of General Magruder. The 1st quickly pioneered the development of tank gunnery and the use of forward observer fire direction. As it trained at Fort Knox, the 1st also had responsibility for guarding the gold at the Federal Gold Depository there.

During World War II, the 1st Armored had embarked on the *Queen Mary*, trained in Northern Ireland, then confronted General Erwin Rommel's Afrika Korps in North Africa, after which it landed at Anzio during the invasion of Italy, becoming the first Allied unit to reach Rome. The 1st was officially inactivated on April 26, 1946, several of its units becoming part of the United States Constabulary (occupation force) in Germany.[26]

Assigned to command the newly activated 1st Armored Division at Fort Hood was Major General Bruce C. Clarke. He was no stranger to the 1st, for in 1940 as a young captain he had commanded the 16th

Engineer Battalion of the 1st. Born in New York in 1901, he had enlisted in 1918 as a private. In 1921 he received an appointment to the United States Military Academy, from which he graduated in 1925. Following years as an engineering officer, he assumed command of Combat Command A (1st Brigade) of the 4th Armored and, in June of 1945, became commanding general of the 4th Armored Division. In 1949 he was assigned to Munich, Germany, as commander of the 2nd United States Constabulary Brigade. It was from this post that he was ordered to Fort Hood to assume command of the 1st Armored, also known as the "Old Ironsides" Division. He officially began his duties with the 1st AD on March 10, 1951. On May 24 General Clarke, in addition to his duties with the 1st, would become post commander of Fort Hood.[27]

The initial troops for the newly activated 1st Armored, the training cadre, came from the 2nd AD and were augmented by reservists and some officers. Shortly after he took command of the 1st, General Clarke addressed the first group to begin training:

> *We must spare no effort to make the 1st Armored Division, from the start, an outstanding combat force. We have one great advantage over our predecessors of ten years ago when this Division was first activated. We have the advantage of their experience and those of the members of other units who fought in World War Two, and who are fighting in Korea....*
>
> *You have been sent to Fort Hood to become a part of this great Division. During your training you will be taught only the things necessary to enable you to take your place as a member of this Armored fighting team. Learn fast and well. We cannot tell you when you will need to use in battle what you are being taught.*[28]

The ability of the 1st AD's cadre to train recruits was quickly tested, for draftees began arriving at Fort Hood at the rate of some 400 a day, young men fresh from the farm and city awkward and ill-at-ease at the start of their Army service. Six weeks of basic training–in dust and sand, in hot summer or windy winter, in isolation from friends and family–made them begin to look and sound like soldiers, but for some of them much more was needed. General Clarke and his staff found that half these young inductees had never graduated from high school, while some five percent of them were functional illiterates–and half of that five percent were foreign-born and spoke little or no English. The 1st AD had to start and maintain a grammar school for this five percent, eventually teaching the ability to read and write English to 1000 men.[29]

With the reactivation of the 1st, Fort Hood was only temporarily a two-division post. On May 10, 1951, came orders for the 2nd Armored to move to Germany where it was feared the Russians might try some adventure while American attention was focused on Korea. The "Iron Deuce," as the 2nd sometimes was known, departed during the summer of 1951 and for the next six years would serve as the "Mailed Fist of NATO." Constantly the division would be in training for any emergency, simultaneously working to win friends in what had been the major enemy of the United States during World War II.[30]

At Fort Hood the 1st AD increased the pace of its training after the 2nd moved to Europe. Once the draftees and recruits completed basic, they were given advanced training. Once that was completed, there were two still more advanced courses taught at Fort Hood, innovations of General Clarke himself. These were the Tank-Infantry Combat Training Course and the Individual Tank Training Course. In the 5800 yards of the Individual Tank Training Course, the trainees were confronted by eight different types of targets so that they might learn a "quick and accurate reaction to every type of problem." In both courses the purpose was to simulate actual combat as closely as possible, including firing problems using moving targets, enemy counterfire, and cooperation between tank and infantry units.

In addition, a Non-Commissioned Officers' Academy was initiated in June of 1951. This was modeled on a similar academy started by General Clarke at his command in Munich, Germany. This academy stressed leadership not only in combat positions, but also it had subsidiary schools that specialized in clerical, stenographic, radio, and mechanical fields. This academy greatly increased leadership in ways important both to the graduates and to their units.

Through the summer and fall of 1951 the hills around Fort Hood echoed with the thunder of cannon fire as the men of the 1st trained on the post's numerous firing ranges, and everywhere it seemed there were NCOs barking commands to troops marching in close order formation. By February of 1952 General Clarke could report that the 1st Armored–Old Ironsides–once again was a combat-ready division. By the spring of 1952 the 1st Armored was sending men to overseas units on a replacement basis, and 75 "Old Ironsiders" went to Korea to serve with I Corps in front-line combat units.[31]

Just after the men of Old Ironsides completed their training in early 1952 and were declared combat ready, they were joined at Fort Hood by tens of thousands of soldiers from other units coming to participate in the largest Army maneuvers in the United States since the exercise held in Louisiana in 1941. Dubbed "Exercise Longhorn," this was a field-training exercise in which an aggressor force supposedly attacked from the south, landing at Corpus Christi, Texas. The battle area was a huge area of Central Texas in Lampasas, Bell, Coryell, Hamilton, Mills, and San Saba counties, all in the vicinity of Fort Hood. The 1st Armored played a major role as one of the defending units of the United States.

Planning for this operation began in the summer of 1951. The purpose was to train Army and Air Force units in planning and conducting large scale offensive and defensive operations, defense on a wide front, and tactical employment of defense against chemical and atomic weapons, all the while trying "to inject realism wherever we could in the play." This battle commenced on March 25 and lasted to April 10, 1952, the men of the 1st Armored and other units at Fort Hood acquitting themselves well in the battle. Just after this exercise concluded, the commanding general of the 1st Armored wrote, "It is believed that Exercise Long Horn provided an excellent climax to an excellent program of training which has left the men going on overseas levies prepared to receive any assignment in their fields and carry more than their load."

Another by-product of Exercise Longhorn was the construction of a third air field at Fort Hood. Named Longhorn Army Air Field, it was located at North Camp Hood and had a runway 3500 feet long.[32] In addition, Operation Longhorn marked a renewed effort at cost consciousness and supply economy at Fort Hood. Cost placards were placed in all unit areas on vehicles and in displays of charts with stress on savings in every way possible, and formal instruction in supply economy became part of each week's training schedule. When fiscal year 1952 ended on June 30, the estimated savings were impressive; as one report noted, "The idea that 'If I have too much, somebody else is doing without,' prevailed throughout the command."[33]

However, Exercise Longhorn proved to have a long-lasting negative impact on the Army's public relations program in Central Texas. Many of the field officers participating in this exercise had received their training during World War II and were not sensitive to the feelings of civilians in the area in which they were training. Fences often were cut without asking permission from local landowners, and tracked vehicles operated across pastures and fields without thought about the consequences. When farmers and ranchers sought compensation for the damages done to their land and property, some claims officers, intent on short-term economies, browbeat them into taking less than what appraisers had recommended. Moreover, those farmers and ranchers who refused a quick payment at low rates had to wait months for a settlement. The result of Exercise Longhorn was lingering bitterness among some civilians at the Army, anger that would resurface the next time the Army wanted to hold major maneuvers in the region.[34]

Another result of Exercise Longhorn was projections by Army Engineers of land needs for test firing the bigger and heavier weapons being developed. Thus in the spring of 1952 Army officials began declaring that Fort Hood should be significantly enlarged. Containing some 160,000 acres by September of 1943, Fort Hood had been reduced by 1,800 acres when Gray Air Force Base was taken from it, and another 1,700 acres had been given to the War Assets Board for disposition in 1948. However, in 1951, some 1,400 acres had been added to the southern end of the post, leaving approximately 158,000 acres in 1952 when word began circulating about the need for an increase in size. At first officials at Fort Hood tried to reassure local residents, releasing a story in November of 1952 "that no further expansion of the present reservation boundaries was planned before May 1953." Local farmers and ranchers on the land that might possibly be annexed were urged "to proceed with normal operations until a final decision is reached."[35]

Late in 1952, when Congressman Bob Poage announced that the Army indeed wanted to enlarge its post in Central Texas, he noted that the greatly increased range of new military guns made Fort Hood obsolete for proper training unless additional land was taken. Some of the Army plans drafted at this time called for adding as much as 200,000 acres to the 158,000 acres already part of this sprawling Army base. At last it appeared that the amount of land the Army would ask Congressional permission to purchase would be about 85,000 acres. This included some 3,000-plus acres to straighten the base boundary on the west. The remainder would be on the east side of the reservation.

As rumors flew about the Army's intentions, civilians in the area grew alarmed, fearing there would be a repeat of the chaos of early 1942 and 1943. Rural landowners in Bell and Coryell counties organized and began bombarding Congressman Poage with their thoughts. James H. Russell, in one of these letters, expressed the general opinion in the area: "If such expansion is to be made..., it should be done with the least possible disturbance and inconvenience to people of the affected area." What especially alarmed some residents was the Army's open interest in taking some land bordering on what would be Lake Belton when the dam then under construction was completed. As James Russell stated:

> *Sportsmen and many others who have looked forward to using the lake for recreational purposes have suffered sore disappointment that so much of the proposed lake front will be taken into the reservation and thus preclude the possibility of its use for recreational purposes. All of Central Texas has looked forward to developing this area as a sportsman's paradise and using the lake and lakeshore for recreational purposes....*

Attached to Russell's letter were the signatures of some 600 local people who agreed with his sentiments.[36]

Congressman Poage replied that he continually had urged Army officials to take as little land and to dispossess as few families as possible. However, he pointed out that if the Army did not get additional land, the usefulness of Fort Hood for training purposes would be reduced, causing the troops there to be sent elsewhere for training "or be denied the complete training to which I think, and I am sure you will agree, all of our boys are entitled before being sent into combat." As to the Army taking part of the Belton Reservoir, Poage responded that amphibious training seemed a necessary part of the Army's future. He concluded:

> *I full well understand the hardships and heartaches which this removal means for each and every family involved. I know that many of these hardships cannot be compensated for in money; but I have sought, and I hope with some little degree of success, to secure more favorable economic treatment in the way of compensation for those who are to be called on to sell their homes. If the Senate retains the provision which we in the House of Representatives placed in the Authorization Bill, it will be possible to assist families who are to be compelled to move, by paying them something additional over and above the value of their land to cover moving expenses.*[37]

Both Poage and the Army hoped to avoid the difficulties associated with moving civilians that had occurred in 1942-1943.

In hearings before a Congressional committee about this projected purchase, Fort Hood Commanding General L.L. Doan testified that when Fort Hood had been built the basic weapon was a 75mm cannon. By the early 1950s, however, 90mm cannon were in use, and the Army was receiving 120mm weapons at Hood which could not be fired because these demanded a range longer than what then was available. Some members of the Congressional committee were unhappy because they felt the estimated average cost of $85 an acre for this land was much too high.

Approval of the expansion of Fort Hood finally passed Congress in July of 1953, by which time the amount of land to be taken had been cut to slightly less than 50,000 acres. Most of this would be along the eastern border of the reservation, extending the boundary to a point above the junction of Cowhouse Creek and the Leon River. Disappearing as separate communities would be Sparta and Brookhaven. Also included was a portion of Belton Reservoir, which had not yet been completed. The total amount paid for the 49,600 acres taken was approximately $2.9 million (slightly less than $60 an acre). With the addition of this land, Fort Hood grew to 207,551 acres.[38]

This time when the Army took land, it had the full cooperation of local citizens who, in the words of historian Gra'Delle Duncan, had decided, "What's good for the post is good for Killeen." Indeed it was, for during the Korean War the town boomed with activity. There was another great housing shortage, and everywhere the noise of construction could be heard. Then late 1952, with the Korean War stalemated and President-elect Dwight Eisenhower promising to end the conflict, the pace of military activity at Fort Hood slowed dramatically. Troop strength at the post again declined, standing at just 17,858 by the end of August 1952.[39]

By early 1953 Killeen seemed almost a ghost town. Everywhere there were vacant housing projects and empty apartments. Compounding the economic misery was a drought that saw water use curtailed until 1954 when Belton Dam was completed. The attitude of young businessmen in town was summed up by Ray Lott, who was quoted as saying, "One thing I can say for the recent business decline–it caused businessmen to take their minds off making money, since money isn't coming in, and concentrate on making the city grow and develop." Killeen had voted in a home-rule charter in 1949, and by the early 1950s its first city manager, Raymond Baca, had instituted stringent building codes for streets and residential construction.[40]

Because of the economic downturn in Killeen's fortunes, some local businessmen began complaining that officers at Fort Hood were against free enterprise because of the number of "concessions" (businesses located on-post under contract with the Army). General Clarke and his staff held a large meeting with area businessmen to explain the operation of the Post Exchanges, clubs, and food stores on the base. General Clarke pointed out to these businessmen that the military personnel on the post could not always travel several miles in order to get items necessary for their daily needs, and he pointed out how the profits from the concessions were used to provide entertainment and recreation facilities for servicemen. As for housing, Clarke noted that Army regulations provided that military personnel had to occupy government quarters when these were available. He also explained that housing projects, such as Walker Village, were common on most military posts as authorized under the National Housing Act of 1949. Finally, he asked area businessmen to work together with Army officials in order to serve the needs of both townspeople and military personnel. Thereby, he said, they could make Killeen the type of community that can be of the most service to everyone.[41]

To call attention to themselves and their city, the residents of Killeen in April of 1953 raised $11,000 and used it to throw a party of such monumental proportions that it drew national attention and brought approximately 10,000 out-of-town visitors. A highlight of this monumental party was a drawing in which six families were given six weeks of free living–apartment, groceries, and utilities–all of which was donated by 78 merchants.[42]

Officials at Fort Hood were as concerned about public relations and national publicity as were the businessmen in Killeen. When something positive happened at the post, public relations officers tried to get the widest possible coverage. An excellent opportunity came at Thanksgiving in 1952 when the mother of a young soldier in the 1st Armored Division wrote the commanding general to express her regret that she did not have the money to come from her home in New Mexico to spend the holiday with her son. She asked that the Army take good care of her boy.

When word of this request spread, the men in her son's training company "chipped in" to buy the mother a ticket from and to her home in New Mexico to Fort Hood. The story about this visit noted how the woman was welcomed by officers of her son's company and how the visiting mother was "feted" during her stay. This story was carried nationwide on the wire services and contributed to better civilian feelings toward the Army.[43]

The year 1953 was a busy one at Fort Hood in addition to its expansion in size, but the number of troops there did not significantly increase. Training was intensified as the 1st Armored readied itself for combat if the need arose, this done under the watchful eye of four commanding generals. In April General Bruce Clarke departed to take command of the U.S. I Corps in Korea. He was succeeded in command at Fort Hood by Brigadier General Leander L. Doan, who was promoted to major general almost immediately afterward. When General Doan departed for Europe on July 15, Brigadier General Edward G. Farrand assumed command of the division and post. Then on October 18 Major General William S. Biddle was given a welcoming ceremony as the new post and division commander.

It was on April 16, 1953, that the first permanent barracks on the post were dedicated, and later that year the Chief of Military History gave his approval for the official nickname of the 1st Armored to be the "Old Ironsides" Division.Another highlight of the year was the arrival of the M-48 tank, the Army's newest and most powerful weapon for armored divisions. And a record 1,150 babies were born at the Fort Hood station hospital that year, new fathers paying $1.75 a day for food and medication while their wives stayed there.[44]

During this period the 1st AD consisted of two combat commands, A and B, and one reserve command plus division artillery and division trains. There were regular levies of men to be sent to Korea through 1952 and into 1953 with regular training continuing in order to fill the gaps left by those departing for the war zone. For example, in April of 1953 the 1st reported it had 1082 officers and 5245 men plus 8064 trainees. Every commanding general in this period reported that the reenlistment rate was low because of the "isolated location of the post" away from major cities, the few promotions that came through, and the frequent overseas levies. The only favorable factor in the rate of noncommissioned officer reenlistment was the availability of base housing for their families. Nevertheless, all the generals reported that "the morale of the command remained high."[45]

A major problem for the Army in 1953, as it also was for residents of Killeen, was a shortage of water. Almost every year since the post had been built in 1942, there would be a dry period from late spring to early fall, months when Central Texas usually received little rain. During these hot, dry months, the water flow in the Lampasas River would slow to a trickle, but the deep wells on which the Army relied usually could provide enough water for all post needs. However, in August of 1953 came weeks of temperatures above 100 degrees and low water in the river, prompting base commander Brigadier General Edward G. Farrand to issue an order calling for water rationing. Water could be used solely for drinking and sanitary purposes, and then only on a limited basis. For example, showers could be taken only during a two-hour period each day. Washing cars, watering lawns or athletic fields, and any type of prolonged running of water from hoses were prohibited, and military police units were ordered to enforce this restriction. Officials in surrounding communities enacted similar

ordinances, and stiff fines were levied on civilians in Killeen and
Copperas Cove guilty of violating them. During the last week in August,
the heavens opened and brought the Lampasas River back to normal,
ending this crisis.

Then in July of 1954, after Belton Dam had been dedicated in late
May that year, high temperatures and dry conditions caused the
Lampasas and other area streams once again to wither away to almost
no flow. Seven emergency wells were drilled in the Keys Valley area
and drew 4 million gallons a day, but this was insufficient to meet the
needs of the fort, causing an emergency plan to be put into operation.
The 61st Engineering Battalion imported 170,000 feet of six-inch pipe
from Illinois and Tennessee and laid an eight-and-one-half-mile line
from Belton Reservoir to the filtration plant near Stillhouse Hollow on
the Lampasas River as well as almost 30 miles of additional lines,
making available an additional 2 million gallons of water a day.[46]
Eventually a new system would be built at Fort Hood to take advantage of the water trapped in Belton Reservoir, and the almost-annual
shortages of water at last would be a thing of the past.

Almost immediately after the new year of 1954 dawned, rumors
began circulating at Fort Hood and in surrounding towns that the
Army wanted to activate another armored division and station it at the
post. The first hint of this came from Sarah McClendon, Washington
correspondent for the *Temple Daily Telegram*. Such an activation would
give the Army a total of three armored divisions, two of them at Hood
and the other, the 2nd, in Germany. As McClendon noted, "The division, if activated would have approximately 17,000 men. That number
of men, many with families, would again create a housing demand in
the Central Texas area around Fort Hood and set the economy of the
area to booming again." Next came a story in the February issue of
*Army Times* reporting that the 4th Armored would be reactivated and
posted at Fort Hood before June 30 that year. The only question remaining was Congressional funding for the new division.[47]

More solid than the rumors about reactivation of the 4th Armored
was the Congressional appropriation for the construction of permanent buildings at Fort Hood. Early in 1954 work was underway on four
battalion headquarters buildings, additions to eight permanent barracks, and a water intake facility at Belton Reservoir. In February

came an announcement from the District Army Engineer that an additional $4.5 million in contracts would be let to do work on the water supply system from Belton Reservoir, for new sewage disposal facilities, and for buildings for ordnance repair.[48]

And the constant training of the 1st Armored continued to keep it at a peak of combat readiness. Between May 3 and 19, 1954, additional troops came to Hood so that Exercise Spearhead could be conducted. The total strength in this exercise, including simulated enemy troops, was 22,000 men, and it was directed by Lieutenant General I.D. White, commanding general of the 4th Army and the last combat commander (as a major general) of the 2nd Armored Division in World War II. Observing the exercise was Lieutenant General John E. Dahlquist, Chief of Army Field Forces, while close air support, aerial reconnaissance, and aerial resupply was provided by the Tactical Air Command headquartered at Langley Air Force Base, Virginia. The changing nature of warfare was manifest in what was done during Exercise Spearhead: simulated employment of atomic and chemical weapons, and defense against atomic, chemical, biological, and radiological weapons. Secondary training was conducted in defense against air attack, land mine warfare, night operations, logistical support and supply during darkness, anti-guerrilla and anti-sabotage procedures, and the tactics and techniques of electronic countermeasures. Involved in this exercise was the M-48 medium gun tank and the new M-49 carrier for armored infantry.[49]

Before this exercise could get underway, word came from Washington that the 4th Armored indeed would be reactivated and stationed at Fort Hood and that the III Corps headquarters would be moved to the post from California to provide overall command to the two divisions plus any other units that might be assigned to it. III Corps headquarters would begin operating at the post on June 1, and men for the new division were to arrive at the rate of 4,000 a month until the division had its full complement of men. Congressman Bob Poage, in announcing this expansion for Fort Hood, noted that in 1953 when the post had been expanded in size there had been property owners saying it was not necessary for the government to take so much land. However, he noted that Fort Hood never would have been picked as the location for the new division had this expansion not taken place. "This proves that the 'prophets of doom' were wrong," Poage concluded.[50]

"Deeds Alone" was the motto of the 4th Armored, something it had proven in World War II. Organized at Pine Camp, New York, on April 15, 1941, it had landed at Normandy on D-Day at Utah and Omaha beaches. This was followed by 295 continuous days of combat, including 17 furious days of fighting while it moved to rescue the beleaguered defenders at Bastogne during the Battle of the Bulge. Afterward the 4th was the easternmost unit on the Western Front, sweeping past Erfurt, Weimar, and Jena and was racing toward Prague when the war ended. During the period of demobilization following World War II, the 4th was deactivated.[51]

III Corps had an even longer history, some military historians noting that during the Civil War both Union and Confederate armies had units bearing this designation. However, the III Corps which came to Fort Hood in the summer of 1954 dated from its organization at Langres, France, on May 16, 1918.[52] During World War I, III Corps won battle streamers for action at Aisne Marne, Champagne, Oise-Aisne, Lorraine, and the Meuse-Argonne, then was deactivated on July 1, 1919, in Germany.

When the United States began expanding its military forces in preparation for what would become the next world war, III Corps was reactivated on December 18, 1940, at the Presidio in California. Then in 1942 the unit moved to Fort McPherson, Georgia, but soon it was back at the Presidio. From 1942 to 1944, III Corps trained 33 divisions for combat and engaged in four major maneuvers. Then on August 23, 1944, the unit left California for Camp Miles Standish near Boston to sail for Europe. At Cherbourg, France, III Corps was assigned to the 9th Army with the code name "Century," which it retained during the remainder of the war. It was III Corps which organized the famed "Red Ball Express," 45 trucking companies that kept gasoline and ammunition moving to the front to armored and antitank units.

On October 10, 1944, III Corps was assigned to General George S. Patton's III Army and went into battle at the front. It was during the Battle of the Bulge that the unit became known as the "Phantom Corps" because it kept hitting the Germans where they least expected an attack. During the first ten days of this engagement, III Corps liberated more than 100 towns and helped relieve the Bastogne defenders. When the German initiative collapsed, III Corps raced toward the Rhine, capturing the Remagen Bridge and plunging into Germany east of the Rhine. At war's end an examination of battle records showed that III Corps had captured 226,108 prisoners.[53]

Like so much of the United States military establishment, III Corps was deactivated in the rush to demobilize at the end of World War II. This occurred at Camp Polk, Louisiana, on October 10, 1946. However, the Korean War brought new life when III Corps was called back to active duty on March 15, 1951. At Camp Roberts, California, it underwent intensive training and participated in two maneuvers on the West Coast.[54]

In mid-April of 1954 Major General Hobart R. Gay, commanding general of III Corps, arrived to assume his duties at Fort Hood and to become base commander. A veteran of World War II and the Korean Conflict, General Gay commented, "I look forward to the opportunity presented by having a two-division corps here at Hood."[55]

So did the people of Killeen, Gatesville, Harker Heights, Copperas Cove, and Lampasas. As Gra'Delle Duncan pointed out about this era, "Although it was too late for some of the building contractors and realtors who had gone broke, the houses they had built again sold and rented." All could join in singing a song popular during the Great Depression, "Happy Days Are Here Again." Fort Hood had become a two-division post and a corps headquarters, implying a permanent presence in Central Texas.[56]

# Chapter Six

# Fort Hood:
## Biggest Armor Post in the Free World

IN late October of 1954 Major General Herbert B. Powell, Deputy Assistant Chief of Staff for Personnel at the Pentagon stated, "Fort Hood is one thing the United States has that no one else has," noting the post's size and terrain which allowed the best training in the world for combat soldiers. He said that during the Korean War, the troops prepared for battle at Fort Hood were the best-trained and most combat-ready of any soldiers taking the field. The value of this two-division post was well known in military circles, and it ranked high on the list of installations receiving scarce dollars for construction.

In the weeks following the announcement that Fort Hood would be a two-division post had come approval of more than $10 million for construction.[1] These funds were spent according to the Master Plan drawn up after World War II and updated periodically. By 1954 that included plans for the housing and training of ground force troops with two armored divisions and a corps headquarters as the major elements. This plan called for adherence, to as great an extent as possible, to the layout of the post as it was built during World War II. This meant using existing roads, utilities, and drainage and erosion control features and the destruction of no old buildings while new ones that replaced them were being erected. In this way there would be an orderly transition from temporary to permanent buildings.

The heart of the master plan was the allocation of specific areas of the post to the various functions and activities carried on at the installation. There were areas for troop housing, family housing, drilling, training, administration, service, recreation, hospital, and firing ranges. Always the intent was to keep each area operational and functional while retaining sufficient room for expansion and the construction of permanent facilities, then removing the temporary structures. There also was a network of main and arterial roads connecting each of the areas, thereby allowing easy circulation and a free flow to nearby population centers. And all these elements had to be fitted into the geography and topography of the area.

However, those who developed Fort Hood's master plan knew that higher Army officials always could dictate a sudden change in mission for the post as national defense interests dictated. Therefore the planners had to draft contingency plans for alternate land uses as they tried to foresee all possibilities.[2] Thus the master plan had to be updated regularly as construction went forward. And always the greatest priority had to be given to troop facilities essential to the mission of the post at the moment. At no time could temporary structures be demolished if that would reduce the effectiveness of the post in the event of a sudden total mobilization of the country.

By 1967 there had been so much construction at Hood that the replacement value of the post that year was estimated at some $461 million, a figure that included the $13 million in construction taking place in 1967 alone. This gave the government good value in return for the $180 million actually spent on the post since 1942–$120 million of that for permanent construction since the end of World War II. By that year the post had grown slightly to encompass 218,405 acres–341 square miles. The impact area for the 100 firing ranges was 58,000 acres, sufficiently large to allow the firing of the 8-inch Howitzer, the Honest John rocket, and the 105mm tank gun. At Fort Hood were 3,451 buildings and 237 facilities totaling 13.5 million square feet of enclosed space. Connecting these were 504 miles of streets and tank roads, 151 miles of gas mains, 322 miles of electric lines, 233 miles of water mains, and 157 miles of sewage collection lines. Living on the post were 43,474 officers and enlisted personnel along with 8,097 dependents and another 22,806 dependents living within one hour's driving time. In addition, there were 3,652 civilians employed at Fort Hood with a civilian payroll of $15,913,041, while the military payroll added another $98,977,284 to the area economy–a total of well over $100 million each year.[3]

By 1967 a problem during Fort Hood's early years had long-since been solved: an adequate water supply. The completion of Belton Dam and Reservoir provided more than sufficient water for the needs of the post, but a filtration plant had to be constructed at the lake to make the water from it safe for human consumption. In 1966 came improvements to this plant and its distribution lines at a cost of $3.45 million. However, by the mid-1960s the sewage treatment plant which the Army had built and then allowed the city of Killeen to use under contract had become inadequate to the needs of both. Therefore the two negotiated and then built a $2.6 million facility. Opened in 1969, this proved suitable for the needs of 40,000 people at Fort Hood and 50,000 in Killeen.

By this time there had been a major change at the fort. In the years after 1947, when Robert Gray Air Force Base was completed at a cost of $5 million, it had provided training in close air support and air supply for troops in the field. However, the number of Air Force personnel slowly dropped as other bases were used for those purposes. Finally in 1963 the Air Force withdrew its remaining units from the base. By this time the two services had formed the Tactical Air Control Party, and a unit from this was attached to each division at Hood. These units were a liaison at a working level between air and ground forces in joint operations. Whether in combat or in tactical exercises, the personnel of these units established and maintained communications between the Army and Air Force; they received, coordinated, and transmitted requests for air support; and they acted as an on-the-spot air control agency for ground forces. Using jeeps equipped with high-powered radios, these Air Force liaison troops wore the patch of the 1st or 4th Armored on their blue uniforms as they guided aircraft to drop or fire zones.[4]

When the Air Force departed from Central Texas in 1963, Army personnel moved in to what became known as Gray Army Airfield. From its runway would fly the planes and helicopters manned by Army personnel used in air reconnaissance, troop movement, logistics, and supply. In addition, the Directorate for Aircraft Maintenance for the Red River Army Depot would be moved in 1966 from Eagle Mountain, near Fort Worth, to Gray Army Airfield. This provided maintenance for all aircraft in the Fourth and Fifth Army areas. There also were improvements at the Fort Hood Army Airfield with its 4,700-foot-long airstrip; two new hangars were built there, complete with maintenance shops, along with a seven-story flight control tower and new operations building.[5]

It was not this construction which led to friction between the people living in the vicinity of Fort Hood and the Army officials on the post. Rather it was the changing nature of warfare that led high-ranking officers to reassess the way the Army should train its men. By 1954 it had become obvious that dramatic changes were necessary. The development of tactical-size atomic bombs, atomic artillery, and guided missiles required that troops be more widely dispersed, but in order to be shifted about quickly they had to be more mobile. This meant that armor, which had been subordinated to sea and air power in the immediate aftermath of World War II, was coming back into favor.

To test the emerging new theories of warfare, Secretary of the Army Robert T. Stevens announced late in 1954 that atomic-age maneuvers would be held the following year in Central Texas and that ranchers and farmers in the vicinity of Fort Hood would be asked to allow the Army to use some 2 to 3 million acres of land for maneuvers without any rental fees being paid.

A firestorm of protest followed the announcement of the intended "Blue Bolt 1" exercises, the Army reaping the bitterness generated by Exercise Longhorn in 1952. Ranchers and farmers pointed out to their congressmen and senators that these maneuvers would interfere with farming operations and with hunting season, from which they derived substantial rental income from hunters; moreover, they said that property values were declining in what they called "the maneuver area" because of the Army's continual use of it for maneuvers. In addition, they said they had been paid too little for damages inflicted on their land, their fences, their livestock, and their bridges during the previous major maneuver, Operation Longhorn, and the Army had been slow paying even the meager amounts allowed.

Congressmen and civilian advisory groups around Fort Hood proposed that the Army pay a nominal rental, 20 to 25 cents an acre, for the use of the land it needed for the coming maneuver as well as the total cost of any damages. The Army rejected this, counterproposing that it have adjusters go with the troops to write down an immediate estimate of any damages and then pay the landowners. However, farmers and ranchers in the area replied that in the past the payment of such damages had been slow to nonexistent; some claimed they still had not been paid for damages to their land during Exercise Longhorn, held in 1952. The Army thereupon began a school for carpenters at Fort Hood to teach soldiers how to put back the fences that were torn down and to make minor repairs to property. Landowners responded through their Congressional delegation with an offer to rent land to the Army for $1 an acre for five years with small additional payments per acre if the Army actually entered into maneuvers on it.

It was at this point that Secretary of the Army Stevens made what was widely perceived as a threat to Central Texans. Stevens said he would reopen Camp Polk, Louisiana, and make it a permanent post if landowners in Louisiana would make their land available for "continuing maneuvers" at no cost to the Army. When Secretary Stevens commented that Governor Robert Kennon of Louisiana had promised full cooperation with the Army, Senator Lyndon Johnson snorted, "How much land does he own?"[6] Actual Louisiana farmers proved as opposed to the Army's plans as did Texans, and no long-term arrangement could be made there to lease the 7 million acres of land Secretary Stevens indicated he wanted from them.

Nevertheless, Secretary Stevens on June 13, 1955, ordered that Camp Polk be reopened, made permanent as Fort Polk, and that maneuvers in the summer of 1956 be held there despite a greater cost than holding them in Central Texas. Then in July came word that Camp Polk would be reopened as a permanent base, and a "highly placed Army source" told *Temple Daily Telegram* Washington correspondent Sarah McClendon there was "a very definite possibility" that the armored division taken from Hood to Polk for maneuvers would be kept permanently at the Louisiana post.[7]

Frank Mayborn immediately went to Washington to lobby with top Army officers, most of whom he knew personally either from his days in the Army or else through contact with them when they served at Fort Hood. One of these men, with whom he met on November 8, 1955, was Major General Williston R. Palmer, who had commanded at Fort Hood in November and December of 1950; in 1955 Palmer was Vice Chief of Staff of the Army. In addition, Mayborn sent long letters to Speaker of the House Sam Rayburn, Senate Majority Leader Lyndon Johnson, Congressman Bob Poage, and other members of the Texas delegation as well as asking Jim Reinhold of the Santa Fe Railroad to use his influence on behalf of Central Texas.[8]

Operation Sage Brush, as this maneuver was called, began in September of 1955 at Fort Polk with 110,000 soldiers and 30,000 Air Force personnel involved along with 1,200 military aircraft. And for a time it seemed definite that III Corps and the 1st Armored, which journeyed to Louisiana for this exercise, indeed would be stationed permanently at Camp Polk. However, early in November Mayborn's lobbying effort and that of the Central Texas Military Affairs Committee, chaired by banker Roy Smith of Killeen, began to pay a partial dividend. The order moving III Corps headquarters to Fort Polk was rescinded, but orders were issued in Washington saying the 1st Armored was to be kept there when Operation Sage Brush ended. This change was to be made despite inadequate base housing for the dependents of troops and a great shortage of suitable rental property in towns in the vicinity of Fort Polk.

For Fort Hood the situation after the 1st Armored was transferred to Louisiana was not as bleak as local prophets of doom had predicted. With this division gone, the troop population of the post stabilized at some 25,000 including the men of III Corps and the 4th Armored Division.

The move of the 1st Armored to Fort Polk never was a happy one, and the members of the division were greatly pleased in December of 1957 when the Army announced that Fort Polk would be closed. On December 23, 1957, the 1st Armored was deactivated except for Combat Command A (the 1st Brigade). As part of the Strategic Army Corps, it was committed to round-the-clock combat readiness and, in the year and a half that followed it participated in several maneuvers, such as Exercise Strong Army in the spring of 1958 and Exercise Rocky Shoals in October and November of 1958.[9]

During the period of controversy over the leasing of land in Central Texas and the move of the 1st Armored to Fort Polk, there were several III Corps commanders at Fort Hood. Major General Hobart R. Gay, who came to Hood with the move of III Corps from California to Central Texas, commanded only from April to October of 1954 when he was succeeded by Major General Thomas L. Harrold. His tenure was longer, lasting until June of 1956 when Major General William N. Gillmore came to the post. Gillmore departed in August of 1957 when

Major General William S. Biddle returned to Central Texas, this time as commander of III Corps. Previously he had served at Hood in 1943 as commander of the 113th Mechanized Cavalry and in 1953 as commander of the 1st Armored Division. "It is as if I were coming home," General Biddle commented in 1957, "and that is always a good feeling."[10]

It was during General Gillmore's tenure at Fort Hood that a significant new unit came into existence at the post. This was what first was known as the Atomic Support Command, but later was given the designation 2nd United States Army Missile Command (Medium). The nucleus of this unit was seven officers transferred to it from the 4th Armored Division in early 1957, after which the command grew rapidly as personnel came to it from every section of the country. These included technicians, school-trained specialists, and staff officers with unique backgrounds. As one Army spokesman said of these men, "Well, it ought to be obvious that this type of work isn't for beginners or unskilled people." Soon the 2USAMC was second in size only to the 4th Armored at Fort Hood, for it required far more than missile experts to accomplish its goals. An infantry battalion was attached to it to provide security for its rocket emplacements in tactical situations. It had an engineer battalion and a signal company to provide their specialized support along with a Sky Cavalry unit, with both fixed-wing and helicopter aircraft, to provide air support.[11]

At first few people knew what the 2USAMC was to do, and the Army kept a tight lid of secrecy around it. The Defense Department would say only, "The command is primarily to furnish firepower necessary to reinforce the defense capacities of the ground forces."[12] It soon became apparent that this unit's firepower was the Honest John missile, which was capable of delivering a tactical atomic warhead. The Honest John was a 6,000-pound, 25-foot-long rocket propelled by 2,050 pounds of solid fuel; it developed almost 90,000 pounds of thrust that allowed it to travel at more than twice the speed of sound. In short the 2USAMC had its roots and traditions in the artillery section of the Army, and its mission, like that of artillery, was to neutralize or destroy targets that were dangerous to other branches of the Army. The 2USAMC at Fort Hood was the only medium-range rocket command in the Army.[13]

By late July of 1957, 2USAMC was sufficiently trained to give a demonstration of the Honest John to 1,300 R.O.T.C. cadets at Fort Hood for summer training and to newsmen and invited guests. For this demonstration the rocket was armed only with a simulated warhead of concrete. In the pre-firing briefing, Army spokesmen emphasized that the Honest John had a range of some 30,000 yards and that once-fired there was no way of changing its set path; in short, it was set, aimed, and fired much as conventional artillery, and no in-flight course corrections could be made. Those who witnessed the firing were visibly impressed with the power, speed, and accuracy of the missile.[14]

It was during the height of the controversy over the Army's desire to gain the right to maneuver on 3 million acres of Central Texas land that an announcement was made concerning Operation Gyroscope. Fort Hood, the Army said, would be a permanent "home base" for four tactical divisions, two of them serving there and two overseas at all times with periodic rotation. Six other bases in the United States—Fort Riley, Kansas, Fort Lewis, Washington, Fort Ord, California, Fort Campbell, Kentucky, Fort Benning, Georgia, and Fort Bragg, North Carolina—would be two division posts, one division serving at each fort and one overseas. According to an editorial in the *Temple Daily Telegram* following this announcement, local citizens understood this meant "that Hood will become the army's Number One installation in the U.S. in size, facilities, permanent population, etc."[15]

In 1957 came the first switch of a division at Fort Hood with its counterpart division overseas. Dubbed Operation Gyroscope, this was a gigantic effort involving the 4th and 2nd Armored Divisions. By the spring of 1957 the imminent change was obvious to anyone driving around Fort Hood. Word signs in German were everywhere on the post: in barracks, reception rooms, and mess halls, while road signs, as usual in Europe, kept words to a minimum while using pictures to tell the story. The troops and their dependents were given instruction in just about every aspect of what to expect during their tour in Germany, from customs and traditions to etiquette in purchasing *lederhosen*. Just before the move was to get underway, a dependent processing center was set up at Fort Hood to issue passports and give the necessary shots and inoculations. Much the same thing was taking place in Germany, but in reverse, for members of the 2nd Armored Di-

vision and their dependents. During the months prior to this movement, there occurred an Army rarity. Trainees in the 4th Armored wore
the 4th AD patch on their helmets but the patch of the 3rd (Spearhead)
Armored Division, to which they would be assigned in Europe, on
their uniforms.

In August of 1957, an advance group of ninety men from the 4th
Armored arrived at Rhein Main Air Force Base near Wiesbaden, and
a week later a similar group from the 2nd Armored left for the banks
of Cowhouse Creek. The first large element of the 4th to leave for
Europe was Combat Command B (the 2nd Brigade) under the command of Colonel Jackson S. Larence. The men of this unit departed
Hood on October 12 by rail for their port of embarkation, all their seats
prearranged. Only military equipment and clothing could be taken
with them; their personal effects had already been packaged and sent.

The slogan over the gate where men of the 2nd Armored boarded
ships in Germany to take them home read, "Through This Gangway
Pass The Best Damn Soldiers In The World." Others of their number
would fly home. For them, as one journalist wrote, it was "Goodbye
sauerbraten, hello barbecue." The first of the 14,000 "Hell on Wheelers" arrived from Germany to take up their duties at Fort Hood in
December of 1957. Even before all units of the 2nd Armored had
returned, new soldiers were arriving at Fort Hood to begin training
with the Iron Deuce; these troops came over a three-month period and
were assigned to Combat Command B and the 78th Artillery. The 2nd,
even before all its men were at Fort Hood, continued the training of
some 10,000 soldiers for duty with the 3rd AD; the trainees were given
basic combat instruction in more than 100 military specialties. Training young men for duty with armor was a specialty of the 2nd; between
1957, when it returned from Europe, and August of 1961 it would train
89,000 soldiers.

On March 17, 1958, Operation Gyroscope officially ended with the
last man from Combat Command C of the 2nd AD reporting to Fort
Hood. This marked the first time since May of 1951 that all elements
of the 2nd had been stationed in the United States. This had been one
of the most massive command switches in military history and was
deemed a remarkable success.[16]

One of the happy events following the return of the 2nd was ground-breaking in late 1958 for Capeheart Housing Addition, some 500 units for military personnel and their dependents. Turning the first shovel of dirt was Major General Earle G. Wheeler, 2nd AD commander. General Wheeler would command the 2nd AD from October 1958 to March 1960, and he would assume command of III Corps and Fort Hood in March 1959. A graduate of the Military Academy in 1932, he had been in the European Theater of Operations during World War II and had served in several capacities in Washington and elsewhere until promoted to the rank of major general in 1955. In April of 1960 he would be promoted to lieutenant general (and eventually become chairman of the Joint Chiefs of Staff).[17]

In March of 1959 came news that Combat Command A (CCA), the only unit of the 1st Armored Division on active duty, would return to Hood from Fort Polk Louisiana, which was being closed. The other units of the 1st Armored had been deactivated effective in December of 1957. Simultaneously the 2nd United States Army Missile Command (2USAMC), activated at Fort Hood in March of 1957, was to be moved to Camp Carson, Colorado. Both moves were characterized by officials in Washington as moving units to permanent bases. In these two changes, Fort Hood gained some 500 additional personnel. Congressman Bob Poage commented, "This again shows that the Army is keeping Fort Hood as the center of armored units, rather than scattering them throughout the country."[18]

This move to Fort Hood by CCA, 1st AD, was completed in May of 1959, and by September that year the unit began a concentrated training program that ended in the spring of 1960 when all units were tested. This was followed by Exercise Big Thrust, a field exercise conducted at Fort Hood. CCA at this time became part of the Strategic Army Corps (STRAC), units dedicated to mobility, shock action, and firepower. Shortly after it finished training and testing in the spring of 1960, CCA that summer was committed to support of the R.O.T.C. summer encampment at North Camp Hood.[19]

Another task given CCA, 1st AD, in 1960, because it was the only armored element in STRAC, was the testing of the Army's newest battle tank, the M-60. This had an operating range of 250 miles, and the extensive use of aluminum parts reduced weight, allowing more armor plate to be used in vulnerable spots. Other features included wider treads, increased fordability of streams, and greater ground clearance for rugged terrain. Its major weapon was a 105mm gun. The M-60 was put through cross-country, highway, and secondary road tests by a hand-picked crew of 40 men, then in August was taken to Jack Mountain for range firing. In September it was first used in a tactical test that was witnessed by Major General Edward G. Farrand, then commander of Fort Hood. Eventually the M-60, Main Battle Tank, would become a standard weapon for the Army in Europe and for forces in the North Atlantic Treaty Organization (NATO).

That same year of 1960 CCA, 1st AD, also was assigned five new M-113 armored personnel carriers to test for the next 40 days. Because the M-113 utilized aluminum parts to a great extent, it weighed only 22,000 pounds, compared to 41,000 pounds for the M-59 which it was to replace. It also was shorter, lower, and narrower than the M-59. This made the M-113 transportable by air, and it could be air-dropped to troops in the field. It carried 13 men, had a range of 200 miles, and a top speed of more than 40 miles per hour.[20]

Cuts in the Army's budget in 1959 was what had caused the 1st Armored Division's only surviving unit on active duty, CCA, to be returned to Central Texas in September because Fort Polk was being closed. Another result of this same budget cut was the deactivation of III Corps at Fort Hood on May 5, 1959.[21] The remainder of that year, as well as during most of 1960, all elements of the United States Army—artillery, armor, and infantry—had to work within tight budgetary constraints to maintain combat readiness. This also was a time when new missiles were being developed and tested as adjuncts to ground troops: the Nike-Hercules, the Nike-Ajax, and the Hawk were operational in batteries at sites where Army units were stationed, giving Air Defense Artillery the capability to destroy enemy aircraft and missiles as well as deliver tactical nuclear warheads. Meanwhile, the Nike-Zeus was under development and hopefully would be able to defend against enemy ballistic missiles.[22]

In the presidential campaign of 1960, John F. Kennedy campaigned against the incumbent Republican administration, in part, on the basis of the deterioration of the Armed Forces' ability to defend the nation. He promised to rebuild the Army, Air Force, and Navy to greater strength as the country faced the aggressiveness of the Soviet Union.

Frank W. Mayborn was the civilian most responsible for the location of Camp Hood in Central Texas. In the fall of 1942 he enlisted in the Army and completed the Tank Destroyer Officers Candidate School at Camp Hood. (*Temple Daily Telegram* Photograph)

General A.D. Bruce was the first commander of the Tank Destroyer Center. He is shown here with Colonel Oveta Culp Hobby (center), a native of Killeen who was commander of WACS in World War II. (*Temple Daily Telegram* Photograph)

Ruins of the old Beverly Stage Station, once operated by the G.W. Blackwell family on land that became part of the Camp Hood artillery impact range. This photo, taken in 1942, shows a soldier learning tactics at the Tank Destroyer Center. (U.S. Army Photograph)

"Seek, Strike, and Destroy," the Tank Destroyer's slogan, was at the Camp Hood Gate during World War II. (U.S. Army Photograph)

The halftrack, this one equipped with a 57mm gun and operating on a Camp Hood range in 1942, was one of the early weapons used by Tank Destroyers. (*Temple Daily Telegram* Photograph)

Training on the range at the Tank Destroyer Center. Here a soldier prepares to throw a grenade. (U.S. Army Photograph)

A view of Post Headquarters and Headquarters Avenue in 1942. (U.S. Army Photograph)

The trainees of both the Tank Destroyer Center and the Infantry Replacement Center trained at this Camp Hood obstacle course. (*Temple Daily Telegram* Photograph)

Comedian Red Skelton paused to have his picture taken with WACS during his visit to Camp Hood on July 8, 1943, to entertain troops. (U.S. Army Photograph)

An entrance into the caves at West Fort Hood where atomic weapons were stored. This complex now is used by the Training and Experimentation Command (TEXCOM). (U.S. Army Photograph)

A demonstration of the effectiveness of the bazooka. (*Temple Daily Telegram* Photograph)

This photograph catches the impact of a bazooka shell. (U.S. Army Photograph)

"Nazi Village" in March of 1943. Note the flag with a swastika over "Gestapo Headquarters." (*Temple Daily Telegram* Photograph)

The vehicle on the right was the first truck used by the Camp Hood Exchange. This photograph was taken in 1942 in front of Camp Hood Exchange Warehouse 30. (U.S. Army Photograph)

This photograph, taken in 1943 and labeled "Night Party," shows dismounted Tank Destroyers at work. Note the "sticky grenade" in his right hand and the Molotov Cocktail in his left hand. (U.S. Army Photograph)

Dismounted Tank Destroyers learning their craft by attacking a mock Japanese tank. (*Temple Daily Telegram* Photograph)

One of the atomic weapons stored at West Fort Hood in the late 1950s and early 1960s was the Davy Crockett Atomic Projectile, an infantryman's hip pocket nuclear weapon. (U.S. Army Photograph)

The sign at the entrance to Fort Hood was changed in mid-1954 when III Corps moved to the post. (U.S. Army Photograph)

Launching an Honest John rocket at Fort Hood. (U.S. Army Photograph)

At ceremonies marking the 12th anniversary of the First Armored Division at Fort Hood were (L to R): Representative W.R. (Bob) Poage, Major General Bruce Clarke, commander of the post and the division, Representative O.W. Fisher, Brigadier General Carl A. Phinney, Colonel Charles M. Lagow, Frank W. Mayborn, Lieutenant Colonel Morgan Roseborough, Guy Quirl, and Lieutenant Colonel Relle W. Adams. (*Temple Daily Telegram* Photograph)

Mounted MPs patrolling the ranges of Camp Hood in 1948. L to R: PFC Manuel C. Guillen, Cpl. Roderick B. Becken, PFC James C. Goss, MSgt. Russell Belcher, PFC Harry Machywka, Cpl. Robert Elsey, and PFC Arthur Hmbura. (U.S. Army Photograph)

During the 1970s most of the buildings dating from World War II were replaced with modern, permanent structures. (U.S. Army Photograph)

Sarah McClendon (center, rear), Washington correspondent for the *Temple Daily Telegram*, chats with III Corps commander Lieutenant General George P. Seneff, Jr., and publisher Frank W. Mayborn. (*Temple Daily Telegram* Photograph)

Frank W. Mayborn receiving the Commander's Award for Public Service on April 22, 1985, from Lieutenant General Walter Ulmer. (*Temple Daily Telegram* Photograph)

Present on July 31, 1985, when Gloria Young (center) received the Meritorious Civilian Service Award were (L to R): General Shoemaker, Lieutenant General Fisher, Lieutenant General Powell, Lieutenant General Saint, Roy Smith, and General Cavazos. (*Temple Daily Telegram* Photograph)

Troops at Fort Hood learning to make maximum use of the Apache helicopter. (U.S. Army Photograph)

Van Fleet Hall, the new III Corps headquarters building at Fort Hood. (U.S. Army Photograph)

*Commanders of The Base*

Major General A. D. Bruce
April, 1942 – April, 1943

Major General Orlando Ward
May, 1943 – March, 1944

Brigadier General W.R. Nichols
March, 1944 – July, 1944

Colonel B.F. Delamater, Jr.
July, 1944 – April, 1946

32

Major General John L. Leonard
June, 1946 – July, 1946

Major General John M. Devine
July, 1946 – October, 1946

Major General L.S. Hobbs
October, 1946 – August, 1947

Major General J.G. Christiansen
September, 1947 – June, 1949

Major General Albert C. Smith
June, 1949 – October, 1950

Major General W.B. Palmer
November, 1950 – December, 1950

Major General Bruce C. Clarke
January, 1951 – April, 1953

Major General L.L. Doan
April, 1953 – July, 1953

Major General William S. Biddle
October, 1953 – April, 1954
August, 1957 – March, 1959

Major General Hobart R. Gay
April, 1954 – October, 1954

Major General Thomas L. Harrold
October, 1954 – June, 1956

Major General William N. Gillmore
June, 1956 – August, 1957

Major General Earle G. Wheeler
March, 1959 – March, 1960

Major General E.G. Farrand
April, 1960 – June, 1961

Major General W.H.S. Wright
July, 1961 – March, 1962

Lieutenant General Thomas W. Dunn
April, 1962 – October, 1963

Major General H.J. Jablonsky
November, 1963 – January, 1964

Lieutenant General Harvey H. Fischer
January, 1964 – February, 1965

Lieutenant General Ralph E. Haines, Jr.
March, 1965 – April, 1967

Lieutenant General George R. Mather
June, 1967 – September, 1968

Lieutenant General B.E. Powell
September, 1968 – July, 1971

Lieutenant General G.P. Seneff, Jr.
July, 1971 – September, 1973

Lieutenant General Allen M. Burdett, Jr.
September, 1973 – March, 1975

Lieutenant General R.M. Shoemaker
March, 1975 – November, 1977

Lieutenant General Marvin D. Fuller
November, 1977 – January, 1980

Lieutenant General Richard E. Cavazos
January, 1980 – February, 1982

Lieutenant General Walter F. Ulmer, Jr.
February, 1982 – June, 1985

Lieutenant General Crosbie E. Saint
June, 1985 – June, 1988

Lieutenant General Richard G. Graves
June, 1988 –

Once Kennedy was elected and his choice for Secretary of Defense, Robert S. McNamara, was installed in office, the Army was called on to show what it could do. One of the first of these tests was at Fort Hood. Dubbed Exercise Thunderbolt, this was the first joint Army-Air Force field maneuvers conducted in the United States. CCA, 1st Armored Division, the STRAC unit, was pitted against a mock aggressor force in an exercise that involved tactical air missions, bombardment with (simulated) nuclear weapons, and then conventional attacks by land forces.[23]

This testing by mock combat seemed a prelude for the real thing when what was called the Berlin Crisis erupted. In the summer of 1961 when Soviet leader Nikita Krushchev ordered American, British, and French units out of Berlin within six months, President Kennedy went on national television to explain how close the country was to war and to ask that Congress fund a military build-up. When the Berlin Crisis began, the 36th Infantry Division, a Texas National Guard unit, was involved in its annual two weeks of active duty at North Camp of Fort Hood, and thus its work assumed a greater urgency. Another unit that usually trained at Fort Hood, the 49th Armored, also a Texas National Guard division, was called to active duty in October of 1961 and was assigned to a reactivated Fort Polk, Louisiana.[24]

The Berlin Crisis also had a direct impact on Fort Hood. In August came word that the 2nd Armored Division would change its mission from training to combat preparedness, that it would be brought to full strength, and that it should be ready for any wartime need by December that year. Also, III Corps was reactivated on September 26 and given a full complement of men, and their intensive training to bring the entire unit to combat readiness began immediately.[25]

On February 15, 1962, Pentagon officials announced that III Corps was one of two units being assigned to the U.S. Army Strategic Army Corps (STRAC); the other was the XVIII Airborne. STRAC's mission was to be ready for immediate deployment into combat whenever dictated by the security needs of the nation. The component units in III Corps as a STRAC command were the 2nd Armored Division, stationed at Fort Hood; the 4th Infantry Division, headquartered at Fort Lewis, Washington; the 32nd Infantry Division, part of the Wisconsin National Guard; and the 49th Armored Division, part of the Texas National Guard.[26]

Assigned command of III Corps when it was reactivated was Lieutenant General Thomas W. Dunn, and he also took charge of Fort Hood from Major General W.H.S. Wright, the commander of the 2nd Armored who had been post commander since June of 1961 at the retirement of Major General Edward G. Farrand. General Dunn, born in Fort Worth in 1908, was a West Pointer, class of 1930, and had seen combat in the Pacific during World War II and in Korea during the conflict there.[27]

All this activity brought the troop strength at Fort Hood to some 40,000 men, and base housing could not handle the influx of dependent families. The shortage of rental property in Killeen, Copperas Cove, and even Lampasas quickly became "critical," a problem compounded by the construction of Interstate Highway 35 (I-35) through Bell County; the influx to Central Texas of construction workers on this road meant there was little housing to be had in Belton or Temple.[28]

By year's end there were many rumors circulating at Fort Hood. The major one was that the 2nd Armored Division would be sent to Europe and that the 1st Armored Division would be reactivated. The *Temple Daily Telegram* reported on December 15, 1961, that officials in the Pentagon were studying the possibility of bringing the 1st AD back into existence at full strength. On January 3, 1962, came confirmation of this story when President Kennedy ordered the famed 1st Armored to be reactivated at Fort Hood. CCA would form the nucleus of the new command, which was to become combat ready as quickly as possible. This meant that the Texas National Guard's 49th AD could be released from federal service and the men returned to their homes from Fort Polk.[29]

Assigned command of the 1st AD was Major General Ralph E. Haines, Jr., a self-admitted "Army Brat" and a member of the Military Academy's Class of 1935. Prior to World War II, Haines had service as a horse cavalryman at Fort Bliss and in the Philippines. When the war started, Haines and his family were on the next to the last boat leaving before the Japanese conquest. "It was a traumatic experience to go from horses to tanks," Haines later would say. "I rode in tanks initially in boots, breeches, and spurs. I found they [tanks] moved a bit faster and took the spurs off." After a distinguished combat record,

Haines attended the Armed Forces Staff College, the Army War College, and the National War College, then had a tour of duty in Europe before arriving at Fort Hood in 1960 as assistant commander of the 2nd AD. It was his task to oversee a new Army concept. This was to put all the equipment an armored division would need in storage in Europe. Should some major emergency arise, only the men of the 2nd AD would have to be airlifted to Europe where they would take the prepositioned equipment out of storage and be ready for combat. Haines was in Europe completing this assignment when he was notified he would take command of the newly reactivated 1st AD, which was to be the first of the Reorganization Objective Army Divisions (ROAD).

Because the 1st AD trained so quickly, it became known as "the young division in a hurry." As General Haines later said, "We were essentially trying out the new division organization. This was a flexible thing where we did away with the old regimental structure and came to brigade structure" (three brigades and a support command). Using Combat Command A (CCA) personnel as a professional cadre, Haines and his staff were assigned young soldiers who had just completed their basic but not advanced training who were to be trained in specialty areas as quickly as possible. The basic weapons of this new ROAD division were the M-60 tank and the AH-1G attack helicopter.[30]

The assistant division commander at this time was Brigadier General Frank Norvell, a graduate of the Military Academy (Class of 1934). Recalling those hectic days in the spring and summer of 1962, after the 1st AD was reactivated, Norvell later would say, "The 1st Armored Division's mission was to train and test. We would go out to the field on Sunday afternoon and get back Thursday morning, then clean up and get ready to go out again the next Sunday. It was constant training." So hectic was the schedule that some of the division's chaplains complained, but the training went forward.[31]

So heroic was the effort to bring the 1st AD up to combat readiness that it was given most of Fort Hood's land area in which to do its work. At first the men started out firing at the platoon level, then at the company level, and finally at the battalion level before getting into a brigade-versus-brigade exercise. "We were fully certified as a strike unit in October," Haines later would comment proudly.[32]

During the first days after the unit was reactivated, a division band was formed, most of its members fresh out of basic training and band training units. Under the baton of Chief Warrant Officer Howard W. Vivian, this musical group formed the 1st Armored Division Jeep-Mounted Band. Literally moving in 17 Jeeps, the 47-piece unique musical group would display both vehicular precision and musical talent and would play before President Kennedy and at numerous rodeos and civic functions in Texas.[33]

In the spring of 1962 the Army had decided that in October that year it would hold a gigantic maneuver in Central Texas to show that the 1st AD was combat ready. This exercise, dubbed Core Shield, would involve two divisions, for which Army officials estimated they would need access to some 2 million acres of land northwest of Fort Hood in Coryell, Lampasas, Hamilton, Comanche, Mills, San Saba, Brown, and McCullough counties. Landowners were asked to sign a five-year lease allowing the Armed Forces to use their land for a maximum of 20 days each fall. Aware that local civilians in the past had been angered when their claims for damages had been paid only after long delays, General Dunn announced at Fort Hood, "All damage claims will be settled as quickly as possible either in the form of cash reimbursement or restoration of damaged items. Claims under $1,000 should take no more than a maximum of 72 hours to process and be settled."

However, by this time many landowners in Central Texas, particularly those in Coryell County, wanted no part of the Army, and many of them refused to sign leases allowing the soldiers to use their land for maneuvers. After several months of negotiations with individual landowners and meetings with them in large groups, Army officials had been able to lease only 32 percent of the needed land for Operation Core Shield. This caused General Paul D. Adams, commander-in-chief of the Army-Air Force Strike Command, to announce cancellation of the giant exercise. Instead there would be limited maneuvers at Fort Hood, dubbed "Three Pairs." This actually would consist of three exercises as each combat brigade of the 1st AD would take the field in an exercise against one combat brigade of the 2nd AD; then each division would send another brigade into the field against its corresponding opponent. When this was done three times, the men of each division would have been involved. Air support for these exercises was provided by the Tactical Air Command. In "Three Pairs," each commanding general and his staff acted as if they had an entire division at their command–a type of "war gaming" that was not entirely satisfactory but which was the best thing possible.

Frank Mayborn editorialized in the *Temple Daily Telegram* about the failure of landowners to agree to this leasing program, "The loser is not the Army but the nation." He continued, "There can be no question but what preparation for defense of the United States and prosecution of the Cold War has been seriously impaired." Immediately he began a letter-writing campaign to Texas congressmen and senators as well as numerous high-ranking Army officers to be certain that no troops were transferred elsewhere as had happened when the Army failed to get the land it wanted in 1955. Mayborn placed the blame for the failure on everybody: the Army, civil service employees, lawyers, landowners, even journalists and newspapers.[34]

While the 1st Armored was being brought to combat readiness, the Berlin Crisis did not end with any dramatic announcement in Washington or Moscow. Rather the six-month deadline announced by Nikita Krushchev came and went, and gradually tensions eased. Then on October 22, 1962, while Exercise Three Pairs was underway, the Cuban Missile Crisis erupted. A visibly tense President Kennedy went on television that day to announce that the United States had photographs showing where Russian missile emplacements were being built in Cuba and that missiles were aboard Soviet ships bound for the Caribbean island nation. He ordered the United States Navy to blockade Cuba and to allow no Soviet ships to reach it. Nuclear war seemed more than possible with intercontinental ballistic missiles carrying hydrogen bombs about to be fired on both sides.

Almost within moments of the president's speech, the tempo at Fort Hood increased to a point of high intensity, for the best information available to Pentagon planners was that the Russians not only had infantry but also armor in Cuba to defend the missile sites. Although the base public information office would release no information, anyone driving by the base could see that dramatic activity was afoot. The 1st Division, Old Ironsides, was alerted for airborne and rail movement, and all its personnel on passes and leave were ordered back to the post. The division went on a 24-hour work schedule as combat equipment

was loaded, affairs were settled, and the men were given immuniza-
tion shots. Trucks and vehicles moved into the barracks area, and
empty train cars arrived at Fort Hood to be loaded with tanks, trucks,
armored personnel carriers, and all the other heavy equipment of the
division. Some of the coaches used to move troops by rail in this effort
were so old that one soldier wrote across one of them in chalk, "Don't
shoot the buffalo from the windows."

Division Commander Haines, with two of his top staff people, was
ordered to fly to Fort Bragg, North Carolina, that same day, and on
arrival was told to be ready to move into Cuba. The plan for this move
was drafted by Haines and his two staff members as they flew back to
Central Texas.

Before 36 hours had passed after the president's televised talk with
the nation, some train cars carrying men of the 1st AD were moving
out by rail, and additional units left at the rate of two and three passenger trains daily. Also, huge Air Force transports were landing at Gray
Army Airfield to load troops of the 1st, and when facilities there
proved inadequate the airport at Temple was used by civilian airplanes
leased by the Army to carry additional elements of the 1st out of
Central Texas. One brigade of the division was taken to Fort Lauderdale, Florida, another brigade along with the Headquarters unit to Fort
Stewart, Georgia, and the third to Savannah, Georgia, in order to be
near Cuba in case of hostilities, although these destinations were not
announced at Fort Hood or Fort Stewart for reasons of security. Officially this movement was declared a STRAC mobility exercise, and
it was completed in two weeks, leading the 1st AD commander, Major
General Ralph E. Haines, Jr., to say, "We know of no previous troop
movement wherein an entire armored division, with its full complement of men, equipment and supplies for combat, was initiated from
a standing start in 24 hours and was completed in a little over two
weeks."

Some of the men of the 2nd Armored were angry that the newly reactivated 1st AD got this assignment—especially after some members
of General Haines' division slipped out at night and added under the
2nd Armored's sign at the front gate of Fort Hood the words, "Texas
National Guard." Members of the 1st were extremely proud that they
were selected for this assignment, and morale stood at an all-time

high. Only about 10 soldiers were AWOL, and there were men coming out of the hospital with their arms or legs in casts asking to be allowed to go. "I never saw a situation like this," General Haines later would say.

Some members of the elements of the 1st that went to Fort Stewart could not be accommodated there and were encamped at the Gulfstream Park Race Track at Hallandale, Florida. The troops at Fort Stewart were put to training on the confidence course, while on the coast of Florida other elements of the 1st were practicing amphibious landings. In the harbor at Savannah, Georgia, the men of Old Ironsides sent there practiced loading and unloading combat vehicles from a berthed LST as curious office workers in downtown Savannah watched from office buildings. Another 1,000 men, part of the 1st Brigade, took part in a mock invasion of Hutchinson Island, a narrow, deserted finger of sand and swamp off the Florida coast.

On November 26 at Fort Stewart, after the Cuban Missile Crisis ended, President Kennedy personally inspected the men of the 1st AD, the Army's newest STRAC unit, and praised it for getting combat ready after being activated just 10 months previously. Three days later General Haines told the men of the division that they would be home for Christmas, words that caused the men to "tear the roof off." This was happy news indeed, for numerous rumors had circulated that the 1st would be kept at Fort Stewart, Georgia, a post in the congressional district of the Chairman of the Armed Forces Committee of the House of Representatives, Carl Vinson, sometimes referred to as the Talleyrand of Georgia. In fact, Chairman Vinson suggested to General Haines that the 1st would be kept there, to which Haines responded, "I'd love for you to get a division stationed here, but this is no place for an armored division. Our tanks just sink down into the gumbo, especially on the eastern side of the reservation where the waterline is at ground level." By Christmas almost all of them indeed were back at Fort Hood (one brigade remained in the Fort Lauderdale area for several more weeks).[35]

Another exercise involving the swift movement of an armored division came in the fall of 1963, but this one was not under the threat of war as had been the case during the Cuban Missile Crisis. In the summer of 1963 there was discussion in the Pentagon about ways to save money. One idea suggested was to move home the troops that were kept in Europe, leaving behind in storage the equipment they would need in the event of war. Should hostilities commence, soldiers stationed in the United States could be flown to Europe and be deployed there in just a matter of hours, take the equipment stored there, and be combat ready. "Operation Big Lift" was the result—the movement of the 14,000 men of the 2nd Armored to Europe in just 72 hours. Once there, they were to participate in a one-week field training exercise in conjunction with the 3rd Armored, which was already stationed in Germany.

Exact and detailed planning was necessary to achieve the split-second timing necessary for this maneuver. The equipment that would be left behind at Fort Hood had to be readied to stand idle for a month, for the men would take with them only their rifles and submachine guns. Involved in the maneuver would be 240 transport planes flying 250 sorties, while another 116 combat aircraft were deployed in Europe to take part in the field exercise that would follow the 2nd's arrival. The transports simultaneously were to be using Gray Army Airfield at Fort Hood, Connally Air Force Base in Waco, and Bergstrom Air Force Base in Austin. In order to achieve the necessary split-second timing to bring together planes and troops at the desired times, a Movement Control Center was set up at Fort Hood to arrange for the buses and trucks needed to move troops from Hood to departure points. The Center also had to take into account the traffic flow at various hours during the day of departure at the various air bases, plan alternate routes to be used in case of emergencies, have stand-by vehicles ready in case of breakdowns, and even consider how many minutes might be lost because of traffic signals between Hood and departure points.

The first plane, carrying Major General Edwin H. Burba, commanding general of the 2nd, departed Bergstrom Air Force Base at three minutes before midnight on October 21. Ten hours and 31 minutes later the C-136 (the military designation of a Boeing 707) landed at Rhein-Main Air Base near Frankfurt. With clocklike precision other planes left Connally and Gray, and the last plane, a C-130 turboprop troop transport, set down at Sembach Air Base, 35 miles from Frankfurt, with the last 58 battle-clad troops of the 2nd, landing just 63 hours and five minutes after General Burba's plane had started down the runway at Bergstrom. Operation Big Lift was a dramatic success.

In November, after the division had been in Germany almost a month, the return to Fort Hood commenced. This time the trip was more leisurely, the planes using 10 days to bring the men of the 2nd AD home in time for Thanksgiving.[36]

Yet another mass movement of troops from Fort Hood came in late May of 1964, this one to compensate for the canceled Core Shield exercise of October 1962 when two million acres could not be leased in Central Texas for maneuvers. Called Desert Strike, this involved some 100,000 men from the Army and Air Force and was staged on 13 million acres in the desert Southwest in California, Arizona, and Nevada. By rail, air, and motor convoy, some 28,000 men and equipment of III Corps and the 1st and 2nd Armored Divisions moved west to the Mojave Desert for the giant exercise. One part of the 2nd AD taking part in this exercise, 1,400 men, had just returned from two months in Germany where they had participated in Exercise Long Thrust X, which involved winter training by NATO forces; immediately after returning to Fort Hood, these men were sent to the heat of the Mojave Desert—which proved a test of their ability to go directly from a winter to a summer climate.

III Corps was the headquarters unit for Task Force Phoenix, one of the two "sides" in this contest, and its troops included men from the 2nd AD, the 1st Logistical Command, the 5th Infantry Division (Mechanized), and supporting units. Commanding III Corps (and Fort Hood) at this time was Lieutenant General Harvey H. Fischer. The other "side," Joint Task Force Mojave, included the 1st AD, the XVIII Airborne Corps, the 101st Airborne, and supporting units. Also involved were some 9,000 Army and Air National Guardsmen along with Air Force units from the 9th Air Force and the 12th Air Force. Supposedly this was a battle between Calonia and Nezona, two mythical nations using atomic weapons in their struggle. The men involved in this exercise were happy to return to Texas, saying they had been in a "hot" war indeed in the Mojave Desert. Fort Hood seemed cool by contrast.[37]

Perhaps it was the success of this effort—or perhaps because cooler heads began to prevail in Central Texas—the Army by late 1964 at last was able to get leases signed without payment of any kind to use land in the vicinity of Fort Hood for maneuvers. Not all landowners would agree to the plan, and thus what resulted was a patchwork of small land leases in seven counties (Bell, Travis, Williamson, Lampasas, Burnet, Blanco, and Coryell). On this land in November, the Army held an exercise dubbed Blue Star I, a series of three-day "map wars" designed to test the skill of III Corps technicians. Lieutenant General Fischer, III Corps commander, said, "Although a relatively small number of troops were involved in Blue Star I, a large land area was essential so that each headquarters would 'experience' factors of distance and time which could not be encountered within the land area on the military reservation." No tracked vehicles were used except command armored personnel carriers hauled on flatbed trailers. Of this exercise, General Fischer later would write, "We are able to deploy headquarters at realistic distances and improve our communications training while conducting meaningful command post exercises."

On December 8, 1964, about 100 of the landowners who had signed leases were brought to Fort Hood as guests of General Fischer, who extended the invitation by way of saying "Thank you" to them and to familiarize them with the Army, its role, and its needs. After a tour of the post, they were hosted at a coffee by officers and their wives, and General Fischer thanked each civilian personally. Afterward they were treated to a display of armored weaponry.[38] Clearly both sides had learned something about the other, and an additional exercise, involving 3,800 troops, was held on this same land beginning on February 1, 1965.[39]

General Fischer later looked back with pride on his effort to achieve greater harmony and understanding between local civilians and the military, writing that he and his staff gave "careful attention...to the community relations program, and the civilian community continued to respond very strongly." Fischer saw this, in addition to rigorous combat training, as being among the positive achievements of his tenure, as well as "making Fort Hood an open post-no more visitors' passes were required. The guards-even the guard-houses-at the entrance to Fort Hood were removed, and anyone could drive on or off the post at will. This was a far cry from the days when every civilian, even the mayor of Killeen, had to leave his driver's license with the

MPs when he came on the post. This change was well received by the command and the local civilian community." And "although not authorized by regulations, a lower four grades club was organized. It was carefully supervised, well received, and assisted in reducing our highway accident rate."[40]

In the 20 years following the end of World War II, Fort Hood had gone full circle. In the late 1940s and early 1950s local civilians had supported the mission of the Army and had been persuaded to give up yet more land for military use with only minimal protest. However, another effort by the Army to expand the area under use by lease had been thwarted, but by the mid-1960s many local citizens again were willing to make their land available through lease.

Little did anyone realize at the time that yet another war was about to get underway, this one far more limited in scope than World War II–and far more divisive in the country.

## Chapter Seven

# No Other Post Like It

THE changing nature of the world was evident at Fort Hood beginning in the summer of 1963 when the orange and white colors of the emblem of the National Aeronautics and Space Administration (NASA) could be seen on the post's ranges. NASA scientists came to Fort Hood that year to begin testing various methods of bringing a space module back from space for an earth landing rather than landing it at sea, as had been the practice to that time. During the first two years of these tests, the NASA scientists used a dummy of the Gemini capsule weighing about 400 pounds rather than the 5,000 pounds of the real capsule. Then in 1965 they began using a full-scale Gemini capsule in their tests.

During these efforts, the model was dropped from a C-119 aircraft flying out of Ellington Air Force Base near Houston. The drop was made from an altitude of 11,500 feet, the goal being to bring it down at one of five prepared landing areas on Hood's ranges. In these tests NASA scientists used a parasail-landing rocket system. The parasail was a parachute steered by radio command to operate motors aboard the capsule; turn motors controlled flap angles on the parachute, thereby steering its direction of drift. Altitude sensors—tubular metal probes 12 feet long—were suspended below the spacecraft. When these hit the ground (ahead of the capsule), they ignited two 6,000-pound-thrust motors in the lower bay of the model; these motors reduced the vertical landing speed from 30 to less than 10 feet per second. The capsule then came to rest on its tricycle landing gear. After numerous tests, the orange and white capsule, dubbed "El Kabong," came to a perfect landing in July of 1965, after which a NASA test engineer told newsmen that if a passenger had been aboard the landing would have given him a sensation of stepping down seven inches. These tests continued for several more years, but the sailwing-rocket arrangement was never used to bring a NASA spacecraft back to earth from space.[1]

By 1965 the United States again was in a war, this one in far-off Vietnam in southeast Asia. The American involvement there had begun when President Eisenhower and then Kennedy ordered a few military advisors to aid and instruct the South Vietnamese as they struggled against infiltration by enemy troops from their Communist neighbor, North Vietnam. Gradually, during the Johnson administration, the number of American troops involved grew so that by 1965 there were more than 150,000 in the jungles of South Vietnam, a number that would increase to more than half a million three years later.

So large did the American commitment to South Vietnam become that a new Selective Service Act had to be passed, and by November of 1965 the residents of Fort Hood and Killeen again would see young recruits and inductees arriving for basic combat training. Involved in this training were III Corps units and the 1st and 2nd Armored Divisions. The first recruits graduated from the eight-week basic training course in January of 1966, and by May that year several thousand young men had completed the course. Some of the trainees remained for advanced schooling while others went to other posts in the United States for additional schooling before heading overseas. In September of 1966, basic training again would get under way, and by the following January another 9,000 soldiers had been processed.

To make the training for those bound for the conflict in Southeast Asia more realistic, a simulated Vietnam village was built on East Range Road at Cowhouse Creek by engineers serving the 2nd Armored Division. This consisted of four thatched huts, called "hooches," a well, and a prison compound. Concealed in the area were entrances to a complex system of tunnels which looked like those in Vietnam, but which were reinforced with concrete pipe for reasons of safety. The village was surrounded by a barbed wire perimeter, a moat, and a steep embankment defended by bamboo punji sticks. The bamboo used to make these sharpened punji sticks was brought from marshlands near Pendleton, Texas. And there were booby traps everywhere—in the hooches, the pitch-black tunnels, and around the entrance. These consisted of trip wires connected to the firing pins of smoke grenades. Troops bound for Vietnam conducted simulated attacks and searches of this realistic village, and in the tunnels they became aware of how deadly was warfare in that far-off Asian land.

During the war in Vietnam the 1st Armored—"Old Ironsides"—assumed unit training missions in addition to its Strategic Army Corps (STRAC) mission. For example, it trained and provided logistical support for the 2nd Battalion, 138th Artillery, Kentucky National Guard, until that unit left for Vietnam in October of 1968. In addition to training men for duty in Southeast Asia, the 1st Armored also sent some of its own units to the battle zone; in 1967 five battalions of the 198th Infantry Brigade left Central Texas for Vietnam. In addition, units from the 2nd Armored Division, which also had a STRAC mission, sent men from its brigades (cavalry, infantry, field artillery, engineering, and the 87th Chemical Detachment) to fight in the Asian conflict.

However, the primary mission for III Corps during these years was to be prepared to move out rapidly to Europe should the Soviet Union or its allies try to take advantage of the American commitment in Asia and attack one or all of the North Atlantic Treaty Organization (NATO) nations.[2]

These were strange and difficult years for the officers and enlisted personnel at Fort Hood, as elsewhere in the Armed Forces. Protests against the American involvement in Vietnam started on university campuses on the West Coast, spread to the East Coast, then came to Middle America and spilled off-campus even to Army towns such as Killeen—although in this off-base community the protest was markedly smaller and quieter than in most other towns adjacent to Army posts. These demonstrations against the war in Vietnam often featured civil disobedience and were marred by shouted obscenities and even violence. Gradually this movement expanded to more than just a protest against the war in Asia. Those involved in the movement began speaking and demonstrating against the "military establishment," the alleged suppression of the rights of women, racism, and laws prohibiting the use of marijuana and other forms of narcotics. When demonstrations were planned in Killeen, it became common for law enforcement officials in Temple, Copperas Cove, Harker Heights, the Bell County Sheriff's Department, and the Texas Highway Patrol to be ready to assist policemen in Killeen if the situation threatened to get out of control. However, the overwhelming majority of Central Texans supported their country and its Armed Forces, and the demonstrations rarely reached such a stage.[3]

At Fort Hood almost all of the men of the 1st and 2nd Armored Divisions continued to do their jobs, preferring to leave the politicking to others. They put recruits through basic at the same time that the two divisions were being stripped of trained men, both individually and in units, who were shipped to Vietnam. These men had to be replaced by inductees and enlistees who had to be turned into combat-ready soldiers at top speed. Fortunately the man commanding III Corps and Fort Hood was the same general, Ralph E. Haines, Jr., who had taken charge of the 1st Armored Division when it was reactivated and built into a combat-ready unit in just months. Promoted to lieutenant general, Haines had taken command at Hood in March of 1965.

During his two years as commander of III Corps and Fort Hood, General Haines constantly was faced with complaints from civilians whose land was leased for maneuvers as recruits were trained to combat readiness. Military claims officers felt some of the claims were excessive as ranchers filed for large sums after wheeled vehicles had driven across grassland, but ranchers complained that their side was not given proper consideration. It was during this period that the helicopter increasingly was the vehicle moving men and equipment during maneuvers, thus laying down no wheel or tread tracks. Nevertheless, ranchers complained of noise pollution which, they said, spooked their animals and led to many problems. Haines' response to this was to work through his Civilian Advisory Committee to win public support, but he also sought meetings with groups in surrounding towns, trying to explain to ranchers the Army's needs and point of view.

Haines continued to work on this problem until March of 1967 when Lieutenant General George R. Mather replaced him as commander of III Corps. Under General Haines' watchful eye, the soldiers at Hood had gone about their duties with professionalism and pride.[4]

General Mather, like Haines, had a distinguished military record. A graduate of West Point in 1932, he had been commissioned a second lieutenant in the cavalry and had seen combat in the infantry in World War II. In 1964 he had assumed command of the 2nd Armored Division at Fort Hood, serving there until 1965, and then he had been commander of V Corps in Europe, a post he held until June 1, 1967, when he came to Fort Hood. General Mather's tenure at Fort Hood was brief, just a year and a month, but it was a time of continued emphasis on training and improvement of physical facilities.[5]

During the time Generals Haines and Mather commanded at Hood, more than a million dollars a month was being spent on construction at Fort Hood to "make it a more permanent base," as resident engineer Arthur Brown stated it. Among the structures completed at this time were Darnall Hospital, several barracks, mess halls, administration buildings, a dental clinic, shops at the post motor pool, and even the air conditioning of some buildings. In addition, much new housing for Army dependents was being built as the post continued to process thousands of men. In 1967 Fort Hood officially encompassed 218,405 acres (341 square miles) because additional small parcels of land had been acquired. By this time it had 3,451 buildings with 13.5 million square feet of enclosed space, and 504 miles of streets and tank roads, all with a total estimated replacement cost of $461 million.[6]

This continued construction at Fort Hood was pleasing to civic leaders in surrounding Texas towns and cities, for the post officially was still considered the home of only the Hell on Wheels division. In short, the Army considered it a one-division post despite the fact that both the 1st and the 2nd ADs were there. All indications, especially the large amount of construction of permanent facilities, indicated that it would receive designation as a two-division post, but area leaders and chamber of commerce officials continued to lobby the Texas Congressional delegation for official confirmation. This came on September 25, 1967, during the celebration of Hood's 25th anniversary. Lieutenant General George R. Mather unveiled an anniversary plaque and announced that Fort Hood had been officially designated a two-division post. This meant it would have an average troop strength of 38,000 and an annual military payroll of $88 million plus an additional $16 million annual payroll for the civilian personnel employed at the base.[7]

In September of 1968, Lieutenant General Beverley E. Powell assumed command of III Corps and Fort Hood. A graduate of the Military Academy, Class of 1936, Powell had begun his service in the field artillery, a distinguished record in World War II, and experience around the world in the post-war years before arriving at Fort Hood.

A foretaste of what he could expect at this post in Central Texas was given him in messages sent by friends in the Army at the time it was announced he was taking command of III Corps; the gist of these was "Congratulations on taking over Fort Head," implying that there was a severe problem with drugs among the men at Hood. However, he also had two friends who wrote him to say, "Fort Hood is the best-kept secret in the Army. You are going to love it when you get there."

Once at Fort Hood, General Powell came to the conclusion that his two friends were correct: the post was "the best-kept secret in the Army," an excellent post that had the terrain and climate to train soldiers, and the civilians in the vicinity, for the most part, were favorable to the Army. There were difficulties at the post with drugs, as there were at other military bases, university campuses, and cities across America at that time. Morale was not what it should have been because the units at the post had been stripped of many of their best men, who were sent to combat in Vietnam; replacing them were draftees, many of them unhappy at being inducted into the Army. As Powell later commented, "The American young man doesn't like discipline. He didn't when I was a second lieutenant, and he didn't like it in the 1960s. But they accept the fact that they are going to have to do their duty, and they go ahead and do a pretty good job."

To help the young men and women in the service at Fort Hood understand their legal obligations, especially in relation to civil laws involving drugs, alcohol, and other off-post activities, General Powell had his Legal Services branch publish and distribute a brochure entitled "Local Laws Affecting Fort Hood Personnel."[8]

It was during General Powell's tenure as commander of Fort Hood that the protest against the war in Vietnam reached its peak. In Killeen there was one coffee house that served as headquarters for the antiwar movement, but this never gained wide support. Powell relied on his Civilian Advisory Committee for help in keeping a lid on the activities of the protesters, and the local newspapers and television stations tended to ignore such activities. Both the national and local protest movements fed on publicity; when the group in Killeen did not receive this, it never grew to serious proportions.

Such was the case when movie actress and protest leader Jane Fonda arrived at Fort Hood from leading a widely publicized demonstration at an Army base in Colorado. General Powell later recalled:

> *After I got a run-down on what had happened there [in Colorado], I told my people that I didn't want a fuss made over her, that I didn't want any photographers there, that I didn't want any officers there. If we had to do anything about her, I wanted one of our NCO MPs to handle it. If she wanted to come on the post and did nothing wrong, let her. But she was to get no special attention....*
>
> *She had a small crowd when she came to the East Gate and was going to hand out anti-war literature on the post. This was against our regulations, and she was informed of that. She was told that if she distributed literature on post, she would be picked up.*
>
> *She made a big show of coming in to distribute her stuff. A sergeant took her down to the MP station where a senior sergeant...told her she was banned from the post for what she was doing. They escorted her off the post, and that was all there was to it.*
>
> *The local media people played it with me. No photographers or television cameras were there. She tried to do a demonstration downtown in one of the parks, but the people in town kind of took the same attitude we did. That was pretty much a flop, and so she left town.*[9]

Despite the small numbers involved in promoting anti-war protests in the Killeen-Copperas Cove area, Powell and his successors in command at Fort Hood until the end of the war in Vietnam in 1973 had to stay vigilant. However, Army regulations strictly forbade having any member of the command gather any type of information or intelligence on the anti-war movement. Thus commanders could not act, only react, a situation so absurd that it tested the fortitude of many good soldiers.

General Powell always felt his major problem as commanding general at Fort Hood was not the protesters, nor was it the lawsuits he faced, an average of about one a month by some group or another unhappy with the military during this period. Rather it was a shortage of funds that prevented his training his men to the extent he wished.

"We couldn't take our tanks out as much as needed; in fact, we couldn't take out any of our combat vehicles as much as we should have, and that caused all kinds of trouble. You can't just take men out and foot drill them all the time. And if we can't train the men, that leaves them with time on their hands, and that causes difficulties."

One answer to this problem was better noncommissioned officers, and at General Powell's orders, with concurrence from 4th Army headquarters in San Antonio, the 4th U.S. Army NCO Academy at Fort Hood became a separate unit. This academy quickly became so well known for its excellence that in August the NCO academy at Fort Sill, Oklahoma, was closed, thereby making Hood's academy the only one for NCOs in the 4th Army. In addition, Hood also became the home of the Fourth U.S. Army Area Food Service School.[10]

In 1969 it seemed that activity at Fort Hood might be curtailed somewhat when the Army announced that Killeen Base, on the west side of Fort Hood, would be closed no later than December 31 that year as an economy measure. Area civic leaders quickly joined with the state Congressional delegation in lobbying the Army to reconsider its decision. However, the final disposition of this part of the base was the result of an old friendship. Fort Hood's commanding general, Beverley Powell, had been a classmate of William C. Westmoreland, Chief of Staff of the Army at that time. That spring of 1969 General Westmoreland called General Powell, and during the conversation Westmoreland mentioned that the Army was considering the establishment of a research, development, and testing unit.

Both men knew that across the years the development of new weapons had become a lengthy process, one where the testers and evaluators, wanting to keep their jobs, could always be relied upon to recommend additional evaluation and testing before any new weapons system could be deployed—and thus new weapons, "particularly in the sensory area" which were needed in Vietnam, were slow in reaching troops in the field. As Powell recalled years later, "What the Army needed to do was to set up in one place an outfit that could take something, check it out, evaluate it, make any needed changes, and then say, 'Okay, we go with it, or we don't go with it and throw it out.'"

Westmoreland said of this proposed new unit, "I'm thinking about a place like Fort Braggs for this unit."

Powell reacted:

> *Westy knew Bragg better than any other post because he had spent more time there. I knew Bragg, too, and I told him it was just half the size of Fort Hood and hadn't a fourth of the training facilities that this place has. He said, "We need a place where we can get camouflage and where we can hide troops. You don't have anything like that at Hood, do you?"*
>
> *I asked him if he had ever been to Hood. He replied that he had during Operation Longhorn [in 1952]. I told him, "You come on out here, and I'll show you what we have."*
>
> *...Just before he arrived, I told the commander of the 2nd Armored to take a brigade of tanks out on the West Range.... When Westy got here, we took him out there in a chopper and I said, "Okay, there's a brigade of tanks down there underneath you. Show them to me." He couldn't find them.*[11]

General Powell achieved the result he wanted. On October 1, 1969, Congressman Bob Poage announced that Killeen Base would be kept open as West Fort Hood and would be the home of the Mobile Army Sensor System, Test and Evaluation Resources (MASSTER). From the start MASSTER was unique in that about half its technical personnel were civilians, the other half military, and they worked cooperatively to build a kind of Army "think tank."

The first major task assigned this new unit was testing night surveillance and information gathering electronic equipment. Later it worked on various types of optics and radar equipment. General Powell's assessment was that MASSTER was an outstanding success: "We got rid of some systems under evaluation that we had been wasting money and time and effort on for years. And we got some new equipment through testing and evaluation much quicker than would have been the case in the old days and into the hands of troops in the field."

Commanding MASSTER from 1974 to 1977 Major General Stewart Meyer, a graduate of West Point, Class of 1943, and a veteran of the Normandy Landing in 1944. After various tours of duty, he was able to complete his master's degree in engineering at the University of Michigan, after which he was in Korea and served two tours in Vietnam. Meyer worked hard to pull together the most technically competent staff in the Army, and it was during his three years in command that MASSTER began looking at how space satellites could be used to facilitate the operations of the Army in the field, especially in the gathering of intelligence. Another accomplishment at MASSTER in which Meyer took pride was working out the new organization within divisions of the Army, particularly of armored divisions, in order to integrate air and helicopter support with ground actions.[12]

On April 1, 1976, MASSTER was reorganized and became the Army Training and Doctrine Command's Combined Arms Test Activity (TCATA) and was placed under the Training and Doctrine Command (TRADOC), which operated out of Fort Monroe, Virginia. MASSTER continued to operate at old Killeen Base which was renamed West Fort Hood. For a time this base technically would remain the property of the Defense Atomic Support Agency, although the elaborate security devices and miles of barbed wire that had surrounded the base to protect the stockpile of atomic weapons were removed. In the late 1970s, when TCATA became so large that it needed additional space, about 100 of its personnel moved underground into the miles of tunnels carved into the side of a rocky ridge. This complex was so large that TCATA personnel would pedal from one part to another of it on bicycles rather than spend so much time walking. Still later the unit was renamed the Training and Experimentation Command (TEXCOM), but its work continued along the same lines as before.[13]

Always the troops at Fort Hood were kept ready, no matter how unusual was the emergency. For example, in late 1970 the hijacking of commercial airliners had become such a commonplace occurrence that the president ordered "sky marshals" to be placed on random flights to discourage this threat. The marshals were charged with detecting and preventing criminal acts at airports and in flight and to deter smuggling and pilferage on American carriers. At first these marshals were drawn from the U.S. Bureau of Customs, but it did not have sufficient manpower to fill the 2,100 slots deemed necessary for the program. Therefore the Customs Bureau began recruiting on military bases, and some 25 Fort Hood soldiers were drawn into the program to "ride shotgun" on commercial flights.[14]

During these changes the men of the two armored divisions at the post continued to train replacements for duty in Vietnam and to keep themselves combat ready. Each year there were major field exercises, many of them in conjunction with the Air Force. For example during fiscal year 1971, which ran from July 1, 1970, to June 30, 1971, there were five exercises dubbed Brim Fire in which troops were airlifted to some point and then were involved in mock warfare. Always the 1st and 2nd kept their men ready for whatever the nation might need.[15]

In 1971 came a major change at Fort Hood when the colors of the 1st AD were taken to Europe to replace those of the 4th AD. The 4th officially was inactivated at this time, but the men and equipment of what had been the 4th simply became the men and equipment of the 1st AD. Taking over the equipment and many of the personnel of what had been the 1st Armored Division when it was at Fort Hood was the 1st Cavalry Division, just returned from Vietnam.

The 1st had been activated at Fort Bliss, Texas, on September 13, 1921, as a true cavalry unit, and it spent its initial years patrolling and protecting the border between the United States and Mexico, trying to stop the activities of bandits and smugglers. During the depression, it trained Civilian Conservation Corps (CCC) workers in addition to its regular duties. Nicknamed the "First Team" by General Douglas MacArthur, the 1st Cavalry Division was dismounted in 1943 prior to leaving Fort Bliss, after which it was organized as an infantry division and began combat on February 29, 1944, in an assault on the Admiralty Islands. That fall the Division spearheaded the landing at Leyte in the Philippines and became the first Allied unit to enter Manila. There followed a period of intensive training as the 1st Cavalry Division prepared to lead the invasion of Japan. After VJ Day, the 1st performed occupation duty for five years in Japan, then made an assault at Po-hang-Do on July 18, 1950, when the Korean Conflict began. Following the landing at Inchon, the 1st Cavalry Division became the first unit into Pyongyang, the capital of North Korea. After the Korean Conflict ended, the 1st was withdrawn to Japan where it stayed until 1957; then it returned to Korea to patrol the Demilitarized Zone for eight years.

The 1st Cavalry Division was reorganized on September 13, 1965, as the 1st Cavalry Division (Airmobile) to bring it into the configuration of the Army's new air mobility concept. Just 75 days later the 1st arrived in Vietnam to fight in that conflict, the fastest a newly organized division had ever moved so far, so fast, and so efficiently. In this conflict in far-off Asia, Army historians would note that this division was the first to move into Cambodia, just as it had been first into Manila, Tokyo, and Pyongyang, thereby showing the truth of their motto: "Fight anywhere, fight anytime, and win!"[16]

A new acronym came to Fort Hood when the colors of the 1st Cavalry arrived from Vietnam to be unveiled at Fort Hood on May 1, 1971. Speaking at the ceremony was General William C. Westmoreland, Army Chief of Staff. The 1st Cavalry had been designated to test a new concept involving a TRIple CAPability (TRICAP) of armor, airmobile infantry, and the Air Cavalry Combat Brigade (which gave rise to yet another acronym, ACCB). The resulting combat unit largely drew its men from what had been the 1st Armored Division. The concept was that this unit would make use of helicopters, armor, and foot soldiers in new and experimental ways, an outgrowth of the Army's experience in Vietnam. This test was conducted in conjunction with MASSTER at West Fort Hood, then commanded by Major General Robert M. Shoemaker, and was intended to point the way the Army would develop in the future.

The old 1st AD had consisted of two armored brigades, a mechanized infantry brigade, division artillery, and support command. Under TRICAP, the 1st Cavalry would have one armored brigade, division artillery, and support units but also would have an air cavalry combat brigade and an air mobile brigade. The TRICAP concept had evolved from the war in Vietnam and was designed to make maximum use of helicopters as machine gun platforms and to move men about quickly. Tanks would be used for shock on the ground, Hueys and CH-47 Chinook helicopters would provide troop transport, and either Cobra gunships or Lockheed Cheyennes would be missile helicopter platforms for support. To accommodate this new concept, Fort Hood Army Airfield underwent extensive construction and was enlarged significantly.[17]

Taking command at III Corps and Fort Hood on July 31, 1971, from General Beverley E. Powell was Major General George P. Seneff, Jr., who at the time was commanding the MASSTER project at West Fort Hood. Seneff had begun his Army career as a private in 1936 and then had graduated from West Point. His appointment reflected the new trend in Army warfare, for many of his commands during his 35-year career had been in the field of aviation. And he had qualified as an Army aviator in 1956 in both fixed-wing and rotary aircraft.

Another change coming at this time was the merging of the 4th Army into the newly designated 5th Army, whose headquarters would remain at Fort Sam Houston. The new 5th Army included the states that had been part of the 4th Army–Texas, New Mexico, Oklahoma, Arkansas, and Louisiana – plus what had been in the 5th Army–Illinois, Indiana, Iowa, Kansas, Michigan, Minnesota, Missouri, Nebraska, and Wisconsin. The merged unit was named the 5th Army because in World War II that unit had extensive combat while the 4th was a training and equipment center.[18]

During the years of the TRICAP test, the men of the 2nd Armored Division kept training to keep themselves combat ready. At intervals there were field maneuvers that included additional airlifts as part of "REFORGER." This was a name derived from "Redeployment of Forces to Germany," a NATO trilateral agreement in 1967 which stipulated that Army and Air Force personnel were to be redeployed to alternate bases in the United States but would remain committed to the defense of NATO.[19] There also were major maneuvers at Fort Hood, such as the Gallant Hand 72 and Gallant Hand 73.

Meanwhile, Central Texans were seeing and hearing many innovative ideas being tested in their midst under the aegis of TRICAP. For a time they heard the roar of dune buggies, and then it was helicopter-delivered motorcycles. Brigadier General Jack Hemingway, deputy commander of the 1st and then transferred to MASSTER, later would recall how refreshing it was to serve in this TRICAP division because any idea with seeming merit was pursued vigorously.[20] Because of this testing of innovative equipment and concepts, the organization and doctrine of the Air Cavalry Combat Brigade (ACCB) were accepted and adopted by the Department of the Army. TRICAP testing ended on February 20, 1975, at which time there were dramatic changes in the 1st Cavalry, which was named the Army's fourth armored division; it consisted of a 1st Brigade of two tank battalions and a mechanized infantry battalion; the 2nd Brigade (which had been the 4th Brigade) and consisted of an armored cavalry squadron, a tank battalion, and a mechanized infantry battalion; and the 3rd Brigade, composed of a tank battalion and two mechanized infantry battalions. In addition, the 1st Cavalry had division artillery and a support command.

Simultaneously the 6th Cavalry Brigade (Air Combat) was activated and placed under the direct command of III Corps. It consisted of a headquarters unit, an attack helicopter squadron, an air cavalry squadron, the 55th Signal Company, and the 34th Support Battalion.

Another major change occurred in the spring of 1975 when the 2nd AD was authorized to form a 4th Brigade. This was unprecedented and made the 2nd the first armored division in the Army to have four brigades. The unit was designated the "Phoenix Brigade" and soon grew to its authorized 3,800 men, making the 2nd AD the Army's largest division with 19,000 men. When the colors of this unit were presented, the brigade commander, Lieutenant Colonel James R. Groves, said its mission was to "be ready to fight victoriously anytime and anywhere." Not all members of the 2nd were at Fort Hood, however, because the 3rd Brigade was ordered to Germany, the move to be completed by June, in order to begin a rotational deployment there.[21]

There also was a change of post and III Corps commanders at this time. Lieutenant General Allen M. Burdett, Jr., who had succeeded George P. Seneff, Jr., in command of the post in late September of 1973, was promoted to command of the 5th Army, headquartered at San Antonio, which had replaced the 4th Army as the next level of command above Fort Hood. Born in Washington, D.C., in 1921, General Burdett had graduated from the Military Academy in 1943 and then commanded a rifle company in Europe during World War II. Various duty stations followed, including two tours in Vietnam, one with the 1st Cavalry and the other with the 101st Airborne.[22]

Replacing General Burdett as commander at III Corps and Fort Hood on March 11, 1975, was Robert M. Shoemaker, who was promoted to lieutenant general shortly after assuming the post. A graduate of West Point, class of 1946, Shoemaker had served three tours in Vietnam, and he had been at Fort Hood since 1970 as Chief of Staff at III Corps, commanding general at MASSTER, and commanding general of the 1st Cavalry Division.[23]

During General Shoemaker's two and a half years in command of III Corps, the Army, as he saw it, was playing "catch-up" by trying to build permanent facilities on the post and tear down the World War II "temporary" structures." At the time he took command, half the soldiers were still living in wooden barracks, relics of the World War II temporary construction at the post. Moreover, all units' headquarters were in wooden buildings. Usual Army policy in building better facilities on a post followed a pattern: first, get the troops out of temporary structures, then upgrade utilities, and finally work on buildings for unit headquarters. Such was the pattern followed by Shoemaker and his successors; not until 1989 would a new III Corps headquarters building be completed.

In connection with upgrading the post, both in terms of facilities and long-range Army needs, officials in Washington in 1975 had determined that additional land would be needed. Information about this proposed expansion had been tightly held in Washington and at III Corps Headquarters by General Burdett, Shoemaker's predecessor. When Burdett learned that Shoemaker was to replace him as III Corps commander, he said, "Bob, we ought to delay this [change of command] until mid-March. That will permit me to get this land business out of the way." Shoemaker was surprised, for he had not heard about any proposed expansion of the post.

Unfortunately for General Shoemaker, the "land business" was not "out of the way" when he took command. On March 3, 1975, Texas Senator John Tower told Sarah McClendon, Washington correspondent for the *Temple Daily Telegram* that the Army wanted to expand its acreage at Fort Hood in order to hold multi-brigade and division-size maneuvers. A large part of the 217,000 acres already owned could not be used for exercises because the majority of this land had been an artillery range for so many years. Before these acres could be used in maneuvers, they would have to be cleared of all unexploded rounds, a task that was almost impossible and thus would expose soldiers to the risk of great injury or death.

When at last the Army announced its hope that Congress would authorize expansion, officials explained that the intent was to take an additional 60,000 acres, all in Coryell County on the west side of Fort Hood. This would require an expenditure of some $36.5 million in order for the Army to buy the land. As explained by General Shoemaker, a "fair market value" would be paid to each landowner before any land was taken, and landowners would have a year to move after title to their acres was taken.[24]

The public outcry was instantaneous and large, although most officials in area chambers of commerce and the housing industry cautiously supported whatever the Army wanted. An officer at the Temple branch of one mortgage company wrote publisher Frank Mayborn:

> *I think that most people in Central Texas recognize the tremendous influence of Fort Hood on our economy. For those who do not, they should review the situation in the early '60s when one division was moved from Fort Hood. At that time, Killeen, Copperas Cove, Harker Heights, and Nolanville and even Gatesville could have been bought for about 30 cents on the dollar. Many businesses were unprofitable, unemployment was a serious factor, many homes stood vacant and home foreclosures were a daily occurrence. This slump condition continued until Fort Hood regained its two division strength.*
>
> *Now that there is strong opposition to the need for Fort Hood expansion as expressed in Gatesville property owner meetings, I believe the news media in all its forms should actively support what is best for most of Central Texas.... For our part, we need to promote Fort Hood all possible [sic], be thankful for its presence and let our congressmen and senators know what our majority thinking really is.*
>
> *Least of all, do we need elements that might effect strength reductions at Fort Hood. God save the King if a division were removed permanently for the second time.*[25]

Frank Mayborn's *Temple Daily Telegram, Killeen Daily Herald*, and KCEN-TV tried to educate the public about the Army's needs and what Fort Hood meant to the area's economy, and General Shoemaker held several meetings with people in the affected area to answer their questions. Nevertheless, the 250 landowners whose land would be taken responded by forming "OUR LAND OUR LIVES: A Coalition For Human Rights." This organization was totally opposed to an increase in the size of Fort Hood, and it provided spokesmen for every forum at which the expansion was discussed. Moreover, the coalition proved surprisingly sophisticated in the political arena, sending spokesmen to walk the halls of Congress and buttonhole members of various committees to express opposition to the expansion.

The situation grew increasingly heated, especially when those opposed to expansion received coverage from national television networks and major metropolitan newspapers. The Vietnam-era of hatred for the Army had not yet faded, and there were some residents in the area who recalled the displacements of the past. General Shoemaker tried in every way possible to show the Army's viewpoint, going out to speak to any gathering that would invite him. It was his feeling that only about one-fourth of the 300 owners affected had a real emotional attachment to their land and did not want to sell at any price. Others were willing to sell at the right price, but this group was not nearly as vocal as those who loved their land. No matter how much General Shoemaker tried to explain the Army's needs, those people refused to budge.

Publisher Frank Mayborn summed up the frustration of those who could see the Army's viewpoint when he wrote that there indeed had been heartache for those displaced in the past, but there also should be concern for young soldiers who needed the training they could get on this land and for the thousands of people whose economic support came from Fort Hood; "Their well being should be of equal concern," wrote Mayborn, "to those who are suffering displacement of land when considering any change or limitation upon the training at Fort Hood which could possibly have any future repercussion upon the civilian economy supporting the Army."[26]

This fight lasted almost two years, ending after Congress turned down the Army's request on the ground that it had failed to show sufficient need for the land. Obviously the Army did need this land, but getting it was politically unrealistic. Therefore in November of 1976 Harold L. Brownman, Assistant Secretary of the Army, said the Army would not ask Congress for additional land at Fort Hood in the Fiscal Year 1978 budget pending a "new and comprehensive review" of training requirements. The issue was dead, although General Shoemaker continued to insist that more land was urgently needed at Fort Hood for the training of soldiers there.

If Fort Hood could not be expanded, either because of opposition by landowners or else owing to the high political cost, Army officials at Fort Hood decided the area used for maneuvers could be enlarged another way. In August of 1978 soldiers began removing unexploded shells from some 8,000 acres of the impact area–"dedudding" was the word used. This land then became "dual purpose." It simultaneously was considered a live-fire area as well as usable for maneuvers. Eventually some 24,000 acres was cleared, increasing the land on which maneuvers could be conducted to 154,000 acres.

However, "dedudding" was a slow, costly process, taking about a month to clear sufficient land for maneuvers. Therefore it could be used only when the need for additional space for maneuvers was most pressing. Ideally, the Army needed a larger area on which to train its men, but the time for such expansion had passed; no longer was it politically feasible to exercise the right of eminent domain and take additional acres.[27]

If some Central Texans did not want the Army to expand its land holdings at Fort Hood, they certainly did not want to see the military presence in their vicinity reduced. In April of 1979 rumors circulated that the Army might move TCATA, the unit which had replaced MASSTER at West Fort Hood. TCATA (and MASSTER) had tested many of the Army's new weapons during the 10 years it had been at West Fort Hood. It was TCATA, for example, which was testing the XM-1, scheduled to replace the M-60 as the basic battle tank. The XM-1 had a low profile, making it less vulnerable to a hit. It also was faster and had more armor, and it carried a 120mm gun.

Fearful that the Army might move TCATA elsewhere, area communities in Central Texas banded together to prepare joint reports that involved both military and economic reasons why the facility should be kept where it was. These reports, prepared professionally, were hand-carried to Washington to be presented to Congressional leaders, high military officers, and the Secretary of the Army. Not until December 19, 1980, was a decision rendered, and it was favorable to Central Texas. Not only would TCATA be kept at West Fort Hood, but also its scope and responsibilities would be broadened.[28]

One of the major tasks General Shoemaker tried to accomplish during his tenure as commander of III Corps and Fort Hood was a rebuilding of the non-commissioned officer corps. During the War in Vietnam, most of the veteran NCOs had pulled two and three tours of combat duty, and many of them had been wounded or killed. To replace them, privates and corporals had been promoted faster than usual ("Shake and Bake NCOs" was the term used to describe them). Every officer knows that the backbone of the Army is its NCOs, and by the mid-1970s there were too few good ones left to see to the training of the enlisted men, many of whom had no great interest in being good soldiers. The majority of the lower ranks at Fort Hood at this time were two-year draftees, many of whom, after their basic training, had gone to Vietnam and then had returned to the United States with only a few months left to serve. Their major interest was in getting discharged and returning to civilian pursuits.

Nor was the officer corps in good shape at this time. Most junior officers had gone through an R.O.T.C. program at some university, getting a commission at graduation. After a few months' advanced training, they were posted to Vietnam, and the result for units such as those at Fort Hood was that officers at the company level rotated far too fast. General Shoemaker later would recall that in 1970, when he came to Hood as Chief of Staff, he made a survey which showed that the 300 company-level units at the post had averaged five commanders each in the past two years.

By the time General Shoemaker became III Corps commander in 1975, the draft had ended, and the Army had reorganized as an all-volunteer force. He found junior officers were still overcompensating for their inexperienced NCOs, thereby compounding command problems because senior officers thus had to do the work of junior officers. Thus a major part of the training at Fort Hood during Shoemaker's tenure was to upgrade the NCO corps so that junior and senior officers could return to performing their own duties. In the process the men of III Corps again became able to perform what General Shoemaker perceived to be their primary job: be ready at a moment's notice to move out to reinforce NATO forces—or, in a broader sense, to do whatever the nation asked of them.[29]

Late in 1977 General Shoemaker was promoted to the position of Deputy Commanding General of the U.S. Armed Forces Command (FORSCOM) at Fort McPherson, Georgia (the unit which supplanted the old Army Ground Forces; III Corps and its divisions were part of FORSCOM). On November 30, 1977, General Shoemaker relinquished command of III Corps and Fort Hood to Lieutenant General Marvin D. Fuller. He came to Central Texas after serving two years as Inspector General of the Army. Born in South Dakota in 1921, Fuller had enlisted in the Army Air Corps in 1942 and was commissioned when he graduated from Aviation Cadet training. He then served as a bombardier in Europe. After World War II, he was discharged and went to college, then was commissioned in the Regular Army in 1949. In the years that followed, he served in several posts and capacities, including a long combat stint in Vietnam.[30]

Just as General Fuller took command at Hood late in 1977, the Army began to reassess the innovations that had been made in the 1st Cavalry Division in 1975 and decided to test a new configuration in what was called a Division Restructuring Study (DRS). After 18 months of planning, high-ranking officials in Washington had determined that Army units should be tailored to the capabilities of new weapons before these were in the hands of soldiers, weapons such as the XM-1, the main battle tank being developed for use in the 1980s. This would be the first time in 20 years that the Army looked at the possible restructuring of the make-up of a division. Conducted exclusively at Fort Hood, the test was designed to compare the current organization of mechanized and tank battalions to like units under a newly proposed organization. All three brigades of the 1st Cavalry were involved in this restructuring, but just after a few short months came an announcement that the restructuring was "too ambitious."

On January 16, 1978, came orders that only the 2nd Brigade was to continue under the new configuration, the other two brigades returning to their former organization. To test the concept in mock battle, the 2nd Armored's 4th "Phoenix" Brigade took the field against the 1st Cavalry's 2nd "Blackjack" Brigade in September of 1978. There were no permanent results of either the exercise or the proposed new structure for Army divisions, for the 1st Cavalry returned to its old plan of organization.[31]

No matter how a brigade was organized, either in the 1st Cavalry Division or the 2nd Armored, the schedule of training to keep the men combat-ready continued, limited only by military budgets that did not keep pace with the rapid inflation of the late 1970s. One program involving the men at Fort Hood was "Brigade '75," in which battalions from Fort Hood's two armored divisions went to southern Germany for six-month periods to train with NATO forces. For a time this program was scrapped because of the cost of transporting units from Texas to Europe, but President Jimmy Carter ordered that an entire mechanized infantry brigade, composed of volunteers from the 2nd AD, be permanently stationed in northern Germany to offset the end of the program. In August of 1978 the last contingent of troops departed Fort Hood for Germany under the terms of Brigade '75, and that fall more than 1,000 families of men in that part of the 2nd AD selected for permanent duty in Germany began packing to move to Europe. The new post was at Garlstedt, located about 30 miles from Bremerhaven on the North Sea. This move to Germany was completed by September of 1979; there the unit was designated the 2nd AD (Forward), and at Fort Hood, to save money, the 4th "Phoenix" Brigade was inactivated. This left the 2nd AD with two brigades at Fort Hood and one in Germany.[32]

In looking back on his time as commander of III Corps and Fort Hood, "Red" Fuller later would write:

> Seldom thought of as noteworthy, the most significant "happening" was the deceptively simple fact that our training permitted III Corps to remain in the combat-ready posture required to ensure mission accomplishment. This status was demonstrated from time to time by our deployments to Germany in support of NATO exercises.
>
> The other significant activities of the period of my command were the wholesale revamping of the Fort Hood firing range system, the development of a documented method for the systematic oversight of resource utilization and a program designed to improve the effectiveness of our automated Management Information System. The oversight system was later to serve as the basis for an Army-wide regulation spelling out the manner in which all Army installations would husband the resources allocated to them.[33]

Fuller also had come to the conclusion that not all the concessions made in the area of discipline during the changeover to an "all-volunteer Army" had been good. The end of the draft and the advent of the all-volunteer Army meant that there had been frequent attitudinal surveys to determine how soldiers, both male and female, felt, how they wanted to be treated, and what they thought of various military bases. Officers were taught to try to keep their men happy and to stress reenlistment, to earn respect instead of demanding it solely on the basis of their rank.

Fuller decided what was needed was a return to an emphasis on basic discipline, saying to one of his brigade commanders, "Let's get hold of these guys." Once again Fort Hood echoed to the calling of cadence at 30-minute morning drills. The idea was to get the enlisted men accustomed to following orders and to get the NCOs accustomed to being in front of their men and taking charge. There were stringent inspections, also intended to enforce discipline as well as raise standards. By the time Fuller left Fort Hood, there was a marked change in the military posture of the troops there, while his updating of the master plan and implementing many of the things in it had done much good for the post itself.[34]

By mid-1978 many civilian experts on the military capabilities of the United States were criticizing the administration of President Jimmy Carter, saying that spending on the Armed Forces had been cut too deeply. In an attempt to counter the groundswell of criticism, the president's political handlers had him stage well-publicized visits to several military installations, including Fort Hood. Months of work went into preparations for Carter's two-hour tour of the post on June 24. The president observed a live-fire training exercise at Blackwell Mountain involving both Army and Air Force units, but he was not treated to a firing of Redeye and Chaparral missiles; both were under a moratorium owing to malfunctions that had occurred at other posts. "If nothing else," Carter said when he was ready to depart, "it was worth the expenditure of funds [on these maneuvers] just for my own education."[35]

During the 1970s the training of National Guardsmen at North Fort Hood continued to be a major activity each summer. Each spring troops from South Fort Hood would be sent north to prepare the area for the Guardsmen who swarmed across the area during the hot months of summer. Then in the fall the area would be "mothballed" for another winter. The facilities at North Camp largely were temporary World War II structures, and the Guardsmen were billeted in tents. In 1978 Congress appropriated funds for the building of permanent facilities at North Camp for the training of Reserves and National Guardsmen, but, as always, financial constraints meant that these facilities would be austere. This project, called Annual Training and Mobilization facilities, also would see some use from troops of the Regular Army. In addition, construction also began in 1978 on a permanent National Guard facility called Mobilization and Training Equipment Site (MATES) costing some $2.7 million; this building, primarily a maintenance facility, was located on an 82-acre site and opened in the spring of 1980.

Thanks to these and other improvements, North Fort Hood through the decade of the 1980s would continue to be a major training post each summer for Army Reservists and National Guardsmen. During the busy months of May, June, and July, National Guard and Army Reserve units from across Texas would come to Fort Hood for training, but even more would come from a dozen and more states: Missouri, Minnesota, Oklahoma, Arkansas, Iowa, Mississippi, Illinois, Alabama, Arizona, Louisiana, Wisconsin, California, and Delaware. Most of these would be combat units, but North Fort Hood and even the main Fort Hood base would be used to train some administrative units. Only by coming to Fort Hood could some National Guard regiments have all their men together at one time, for most Army bases were too small to accommodate them.

While these National Guard and Reserve units were at Fort Hood, they increasingly were subjected to standardized tests that compared their combat readiness to that of troops in the Regular Army. For example, Test 6 gave Army Training Tests (ATTs) to Guardsmen and Reservists from Tennessee, Kentucky, Arizona, and Texas at the same time they were administered to analogous units in the 2nd Armored Division. As a result of these tests, the Army began sending teams out to work with the Guard and Reserve units in their home towns as well as close coordination with them during their annual two-week stint at North Fort Hood.[36]

And always the combat training continued. In January of 1979 a brigade of the 1st Cavalry went to Germany on REFORGER '79, the first major NATO winter exercises in many years. In addition, the 1st Battalion of the 41st Infantry, 2nd AD, was also ordered to participate in the REFORGER exercise on a no-notice (emergency) deployment basis to test its readiness for sudden moves. This meant that planes of the Military Airlift Command would be at Robert Gray Army Airfield to pick these men up just 96 hours after they were notified to be ready to leave.

By this time the Army had developed a new way to get armored units from the United States to a potential combat zone in Europe in record time. All the weapons, ammunition, vehicles, and supplies needed by the two armored divisions at Fort Hood were stockpiled in Europe in secret hideaways under a concept called "Prepositioning of Materiel Configured to Unit Sets," or POMCUS. This was done in order to be able to get divisions in the Army of the Continental United States (CONUS) to Europe within ten days, thereby quickly address-ing the imbalance of NATO versus Warsaw Pact forces. NATO actu-ally has more manpower in Europe than the Warsaw Pact Nations, but it would be much easier to move fully equipped divisions from the western Soviet Union than from the United States. POMCUS was the answer for the Allied forces. During REFORGER maneuvers, units from CONUS have tested their ability to move their men to Europe quickly, get their prepositioned (POMCUS) equipment, and then move out to join American and Allied forces in the field. This theory meant, as described in *Newsweek*, that III Corps had become "doomsday cavalrymen" ready to charge off to NATO's rescue at a moment's notice.[37]

The REFORGER exercise of 1982 proved that this concept worked. Once in Europe and in possession of their tanks, other vehicles, heavy equipment, ammunition, and supplies, the men of III Corps spent two weeks on the move, both night and day, fighting under conditions similar to those that might be encountered in World War III. In this situation the 17,000 men taken to Europe in 1982 proved themselves ready for whatever was needed.

In addition to the annual REFORGER exercise, maneuvers on the Fort Hood reservation were almost constant, as in "Rolling Thunder IV" in May of 1980 that pitted men of the 1st Cavalry as an aggressor force and the two brigades of the 2nd Armored in defensive positions. Another major exercise was Hardened Steel II, conducted in January of 1981, which saw 10,000 members of the 2nd AD in the field.[38]

Well might ranking Army officers welcome the 1980s, for the previous decade had been one of great social and political upheaval in the United States. The war in Vietnam had ended in 1973, and the unrest and demonstrations associated with it had ceased. But the social changes that had accompanied it left many problems. The radicals had failed to win legalization of narcotics, but the recreational use of drugs had spread into the Army as it had in society in general. With increasing frequency there would be stories in local newspapers of arrests for drug sale and use both on the Fort Hood reservation and in surrounding towns—even in area high schools, junior high schools, and elementary schools.

These were the same years when demands for women's rights grew, and the Army was not immune of the feminist movement. During World War II the members of the Women's Army Auxiliary Corps had performed secretarial, clerical, nursing, and motor pool duties. In the postwar years, the role of women soldiers had gradually expanded. Then came the 1970s, and women in the Army began moving into jobs previously thought to be the exclusive domain of men. By January 1, 1980, there were 2,544 women soldiers at Fort Hood, seven percent of the total strength of the post. They were prohibited by law from serving in combat units, but they were involved in such diverse jobs as the military police, driving heavy duty construction equipment, and working in intelligence and communications units.

By the late 1980s women would be moving closer than ever to combat assignments, at least in their training. "I don't really feel any different than anyone else would," says Warrant Officer 1 Portia Dublar. "There's no different treatment." Such were her comments when she became the first qualified aircraft armament maintenance technician working on Apache helicopters in the Army in early 1989. "Wherever we [the soldiers of her unit] deploy, I'll go."[39]

At the close of 1977 all but 16 of the Army's 377 military specialties—all of those clearly combat related—were open to women officers and enlisted personnel. According to Secretary of Defense Harold Brown, women had become "full partners in our national defense, with full opportunities to progress with their male counter-parts." A nine-month study had concluded that women could make up as much as 35 percent of many combat units without changing unit performance. Increasingly this change could be seen at Fort Hood as women soldiers performed their duties in the same combat fatigues and boots as the men, not the skirts and starched blouses of the old Women's Army Corps.[40]

Another evidence of the changing nature of the Army which began just at the end of the war in Vietnam was what General William C. Westmoreland liked to call "Adventure Training." This meant an innovative approach to training in the new volunteer Army, training which was both challenging and fun to the soldier. One example of this started in 1972 at that part of the Lake Belton Reservoir included within the limits of Fort Hood. Soldiers were taken in small groups to the reservoir and shown the proper way to go up and down the face of almost-sheer cliffs some 150 to 175 feet high. Other forms of adventure training came into use when the proper equipment became available and qualified instructors were found.

Moreover, many work details which had caused soldiers to grumble for innumerable decades became a thing of the past as civilian contractors took over what once had been the work of soldiers. For example, in the Army of the 1980s, mess halls except those in combat units increasingly were run by civilians, freeing soldiers from KP (kitchen police), peeling potatoes, and similar dreaded chores. And there were other signs of change as chain fast food stores, such as Burger King, came to Fort Hood under the auspices of AAFES (Army-Air Force Exchange Services). Credit cards were accepted at the Post Exchange and the Post Commissary and all their branches, and anti-smoking campaigns came to the fort for reasons of health. However, there never seemed to be sufficient affordable housing for civilian dependents despite continued building both on and off post.[41]

Taking command of III Corps and Fort Hood in January of 1980 was Lieutenant General Richard E. Cavazos, a native of Texas and an R.O.T.C. graduate of Texas Tech University in Lubbock. He was a veteran of combat in Korea and Vietnam and had first come to Fort Hood in 1953—and was furious at this assignment. At the time he "was an infantry officer going to an armored post, and I thought it was the end of the world." He found this three-year tour of duty at Hood "the most formative period of my life." He returned to Central Texas in 1975 as Assistant Division Commander of the 2nd AD, then had commanded the 9th Infantry Division at Fort Lewis, Washington, from 1977 until his return to Hood as III Corps commander.[42]

General Cavazos was a close student of history, and he understood that for the Army of the 1980s the helicopter was becoming increasingly analogous to the tank. He knew that at the beginning of World War II the French had actually had more tanks than the Germans but had scattered them throughout their Army rather than massing them for battle as did the Germans; the result was the Nazi *blitzkrieg* in which divisions of Panzer tanks wrought massive destruction. Therefore Cavazos wanted to change Army strategy of putting a few Apache helicopters in each unit; rather he wanted them massed. This concept could be tested at Hood thanks to the presence there of the 6th Cavalry Brigade (Air Combat).

The 6th Cavalry Brigade had been activated at Fort Hood on February 21, 1975, as the first active, separate air combat cavalry brigade in the Army. Armed with the AH-64A, an attack helicopter dubbed the Apache, the 6th developed the doctrine and tactics for attack helicopters, including gunnery, nap-of-the-earth flying techniques, and operations during adverse weather and nighttime. Once again Fort Hood was the home of tank destroyers, for a major role for the Apache was finding and destroying enemy tanks. The 6th Cavalry completed its Apache training in 1986, showing it had mastered the battlefield requirements of mobility, firepower, and communications, and then the following year the brigade began a five-year training and testing program at Hood for all future Apache units.[43]

Fort Hood proved an ideal place for training soldiers to make innovative uses of helicopters, as well as other types of aircraft, because it had an ideal climate that allowed training almost every day of the year. Moreover, its isolation from major population centers and the patriotic attitude of most Central Texans meant there were few complaints about noise. During the 25 months General Cavazos commanded at Fort Hood, this became the center of the greatest concentration of military aviation in the United States. In addition to 40 battalions using the Apache there, the Air Force was sending giant C-5s as well as speedy F-4s to practice "touch and go" landings at Robert Gray Army Airfield, while C-130s practiced at two assault landing strips constructed at Hood by Cavazos' engineers.

All this activity would lead to the establishment of the Apache Training Brigade at Fort Hood on July 14, 1984. Designated the AH-64 Task Force Headquarters, it was charged with the responsibility for planning, programming, training, and fielding advanced attack helicopter battalions for the Army. Taking the nickname "Attack Warriors," the Apache Training Brigade has pioneered the combined use of the Apache, Blackhawk, and OH-58 helicopters in battlefield conditions.[44]

Cavazos did such an outstanding job in Central Texas that in February of 1982 he was promoted to full general and transferred to Fort Benning, Georgia, to command FORSCOM. Succeeding him as III Corps and Fort Hood commander was Lieutenant General Walter F. Ulmer, Jr., a native of Maine and a graduate of the Military Academy, Class of 1952. Like almost every other Army officer serving in the 1950s, 1960s, and 1970s, he had seen service during the wars in Korea and Vietnam, and he had been commandant of cadets at West Point for two years. He first had come to Fort Hood in 1977 as assistant commander of the 2nd Armored, and in 1982 he returned to Central Texas after commanding the 3rd Armored in Germany.[45]

The XM-1, later renamed the M-1 Abrams, had first come to Fort Hood to be tested by TEXCOM in the late 1970s. By the time General Ulmer took command of the post this new tank had become a commonplace sight in units of the 1st Cavalry and the 2nd Armored, and by mid-1984 the changeover to the M-1, Main Battle Tank, had largely been completed in both divisions. It was in this period that construction funds were available for a division headquarters building for the 1st Cavalry, new hangar facilities, an expansion of Darnall Army Community Hospital, new modular complex barracks for the soldiers, new motor pools and shop facilities, new simulator training buildings, a totally new range complex complete with remote controlled moving targets for live fire, and numerous other smaller construction projects. In Fiscal Year 1984, for example, Fort Hood received $68.5 million for construction at Fort Hood.

Also during General Ulmer's tenure at Fort Hood, the contingency

plans for Reserve Components were upgraded, and there was emphasis on Corps-wide tactical training using simulations as well as field
exercises. Moreover, there was work on creating a command climate
in which motivated individuals could be trained to execute the Army's
newest tactical doctrines. General Ulmer espoused and implemented
a "power down" approach to leadership, meaning that his leaders
should delegate responsibility to the lowest possible level of capable
leadership, and, second, that leaders should be held accountable for
whatever was delegated. The intent was to foster and build bold,
dynamic, risk-taking leaders needed in time of battle.

Another major change came in 1983 with the announcement that
the units at Fort Hood would be reorganized under a plan labeled
"Division '86." This called for the post to receive 250 new tactical
systems, including the M-2 Bradley fighting vehicle and the multiple-
launch rocket system. The Bradley would prove controversial, and
there were those in 1986 who opposed replacing the Jeep with the
Hummer, a high-mobility multipurpose vehicle. And always there
were maneuvers, including annual REFORGER exercises in Germany in which the 1st Cavalry and 2nd Armored were involved. For
example, in 1983, the 1st Cavalry participated in a REFORGER exercise
that began in the Netherlands; thereby it became the fist American
combat division to enter Holland since World War II.

Almost every month the base newspaper, the *Sentinel*, as well as the
*Killeen Daily Herald* announced that one unit or another would be on
maneuvers in the Mojave Desert, in Honduras, in North Carolina and
that MPs or intelligence officers or helicopter units would be training
at Hood. The goal was to keep the men prepared for everything from
a terrorist attack to nuclear war–and everything in between.

Moreover, the personnel at Fort Hood always have to be ready to
change the type of training given to new members of the 1st Cavalry
or the 2nd Armored–or to update the skills of seasoned veterans–in
order to meet the defense needs of the United States. For example, the
last two decades have seen an increase in urban guerrilla warfare, and
soldiers have to be ready to meet this challenge. It was for this purpose
that St. Elijiah, a replica of a European village, was built to train for
Military Operations in Urban Terrain. This 32-building, $7.8 million
facility, built on a wooded hilltop in an isolated corner of the post,

contains hotels, a school, stores, homes, two gas stations, and a police station, each as authentic as possible. There even is a four-foot sewer to teach subterranean search techniques.

During a one-week training course at this facility, whose signs are in German and whose streets are strewn with rubble and the burned-out hull of cars, the trainees, ranging from sergeants to captains, climb, run, crawl, roll, and rappel through every part of the town. The goal is to teach the 40 members of each class the skills they need to survive in such an environment. The intent is not to destroy a city or to kill the friendly population there, just to flush out and destroy the enemy wherever they may be hiding. There even is some emphasis on using some of the techniques of the guerrillas themselves, such as how to make and throw Molotov cocktails. A specialty of the training in this village is teaching how to check for booby traps. Those who graduate from this course are expected to pass on what they have learned at St. Elijiah to the soldiers under their command. A sign of the changing times in the Army is the fact that women NCOs go through this combat training in exactly the same way as do the men.[46]

The work of the Army, whether in garrison duty, in training, or on maneuvers, has always been filled with hazard. Soldiers off duty occasionally drink too much and have accidents, helicopters crash, men drown in amphibious exercises, and live ammunition occasionally explodes unexpectedly. Thus across the years there have been sad announcements of men being wounded or dying—but that always has been part of the price to be paid to keep America strong and free.

During the 1980s the size of the post varied slightly as small amounts of land were transferred (or traded) for civilian use, but basically the size of the reservation remained at approximately 217,000 acres. The book value of the land and improvements rose to $700 million, and the payroll at the post for the 40,000 soldiers and 4,500 civilian employees rose toward $1.5 million a day and then by 1986 to more than $1 billion a year. Every annual budget passed by Congress contained construction money for the post, some of it military construction and some of it for housing and related facilities; for example in 1984 the funds appropriated for construction at Fort Hood totaled $75 million.[47]

On June 11, 1985, General Ulmer retired from active duty after 33 years of service to become president of the Center for Creative Lead-

ership in Greensboro, North Carolina, turning over command of III
Corps and Fort Hood to Lieutenant General Crosbie E. Saint. Coming
to Hood from command of the 1st Armored Division in Germany,
General Saint, called Butch by his close friends, had been born at the
Military Academy at West Point where his father was an instructor. He
was commissioned in 1958 after graduating from the Military Academy, and like others of his generation, he was a veteran of Vietnam.
Interspersed between two tours of duty in that war were four tours of
duty in Europe, holding every job from platoon leader to division
commander before assuming command of III Corps.[48]

Immediately obvious to General Saint was the dramatic changes at
Fort Hood and its area towns in the years between 1971, when he had
first come to Central Texas as a major in the 1st Cavalry to serve six
months at the post. He recalled Killeen as being a "bar outside the gate
kind of place," but by 1985 it had become a respectable city complete
with mall and national chain stores. Fort Hood likewise had changed,
many of its World War II barracks replaced by permanent structures
and its training facilities improved and upgraded.

During his years as commanding general, Saint encouraged his
troops to become more familiar with new, improved weapons that
were coming on line. To accomplish this, he had his staff develop the
range operations in ways that would challenge "not only the machines
but also the people. Good people like a challenge." His third major
objective was to improve the housing conditions of his soldiers off the
post: "We had some knock-down drag-outs over inadequate housing
and how much they [off-post landlords] could charge soldiers who
couldn't afford it."As Saint recalled that effort, "I was trying to establish a more reasonable dialogue between the post-toasties and the
townees." Finally, he put as much of the resources at his command as
possible into developing a simulation center where both active and
reserve officers could do high-level staff work. He, like other high-
ranking Army officers, regretted that additional land had not been
acquired at Hood because of the costs involved in moving his men to
the National Training Center at Fort Irwin, California, for division-
level maneuvers—a center that might well have been at Hood had
additional land been acquired. He even suggested that as land came on
the market within the area needed to expand Fort Hood that it be

bought, with no heat placed on anyone to sell, and that as it was acquired it could be used for command posts during maneuvers. However, this idea was not accepted in Washington.[49]

General Saint received his fourth star before leaving to assume command of the 7th U.S. Army Training Command and of U.S. Army Europe. When he departed on June 17, 1988, for his new post, he left III Corps and Fort Hood in the hands of one of his classmates at West Point, Lieutenant General Richard G. Graves, who had previously been in combat in Vietnam and who had held staff positions in both the 1st Cavalry and the 2nd Armored. Among his other accomplishments was earning a master's degree in political science at the University of Indiana and completing most of the work on a doctorate of philosophy. He came to Hood from duty as Deputy Chief of Staff for Operations and Plans at the Pentagon.[50]

General Graves, like General Saint and his predecessors, found that Fort Hood was far more than just a two-division post. In addition to the two armored divisions, the 1st Cavalry and the 2nd Armored, it also was home to several additional brigades, including TEXCOM, started in 1969 as MASSTER, and the 6th Cavalry Brigade (Air Combat), formed in 1975. These are brigades whose primary task at Fort Hood is to assist in the training of the men of the two armored divisions there. These include the 13th Corps Support Command, abbreviated 13th COSCOM. Activated in September of 1965, this unit supports the men of III Corps in almost every area of supply and services, including engineering construction, maintenance of vehicles and aircraft, finance services, field services, smoke generation,and decontamination. Moreover, it trains technical service units to provide these combat support services. With a strength of some 6,000 men, 13th COSCOM is the third largest unit at Fort Hood, and they try to live up to their motto, "Service to the Soldier."

Also at Fort Hood is the 3rd Signal Brigade, activated on September 17, 1979, to install, operate, and maintain III Corps and area communications systems as well as to provide terminal communications facilities to echelons of III Corps Headquarters. In 1988, when the 3rd Signal Brigade fielded the Mobile Subscriber Equipment, it proved itself able to provide field commanders with reliable, rapid communications. In addition to this service, the brigade also is involved in planning for all communications contingencies as well as proposing new field equipment or new applications of old equipment.

The 89th Military Police Group, activated on March 15, 1966, in Vietnam, provides general military police support in both the III and IV Corps zones. Its task is to command, coordinate, and control the operations of its military police battalions as well as to provide a Provost Marshal staff section. In the late 1980s the brigade had only two battalions on active duty, the 720th at Fort Hood and the 716th at Fort Riley, Kansas, but it was ready to draw on National Guard battalions to bring it to full strength should the need arise. Because of the role the brigade played during the Tet Offensive of 1968 in Vietnam, it adopted the motto, "Proven in Battle."

Yet another unit at Hood, this one providing active, multidisciplined intelligence services to the III Corps commander and all units at the base, is the 504th Military Intelligence Brigade. Activated in April of 1978 as an Army Warfare Intelligence Brigade, the 504th can trace its history to the 137th Signal Radio Intelligence Company in World War II and was organized into its present configuration in October of 1985. Headquartered at West Fort Hood, this unit has the ability to collect, process, and analyze human, signal, and imagery intelligence.

The 31st Air Defense Artillery Brigade, which had service in World Wars I and II before being deactivated in 1977, was given new life on April 1, 1988, at Fort Hood. Its new task was to provide low and medium altitude air defense protection to the III Corps and its combat units. Basically this unit uses missiles–the Hawk, Chaparral, and Capstone–to accomplish its purpose, and thus it has components to provide maintenance for motors, missiles, ordnance, and communications related to these weapons.

Also on the post are several units performing limited service functions. Among these is the Medical Department Activity (MEDDAC) part of the Health Services Command at Fort Sam Houston which is charged with providing health care at Fort Hood, including sanitation, occupational health, industrial hygiene, radiological hygiene, and the prevention and eradication of disease-carrying organisms. The Criminal Investigation Command, Fort Hood District, Third Region is charged with investigating crimes committed by members of the Army or against the Army in 117 counties in Texas. Detachment 14, 5th

Weather Squadron, actually part of the Air Force's Air Weather Service, provides primary weather support for III Corps and Fort Hood from its headquarters at Robert Gray Army Airfield, with a limited observation section at Hood Army Airfield. The 47th Ordnance Bomb Disposal Squad is at Hood to detect, identify, recover, defuse or render safe, evaluate, and dispose of unexploded ordnance, both foreign and domestic; not only does it provide this service to Fort Hood, but also to neutralizing and removing hazardous ordnance or homemade bombs in 78 counties in Central Texas. Finally at Fort Hood is Red Thrust, a FORSCOM command whose purpose is to train units to duplicate the formations and tactics of Soviet forces during field exercises. Formed in 1982, it has trained the "opposing forces" each year at the National Training Center and is there each quarter to give training, advice, assistance, and retraining as needed, thereby insuring realism in FORSCOM maneuvers and exercises.[51]

In commanding all units at Fort Hood, General Graves, like General Saint and his predecessors, had the task of keeping the men of the 1st Cavalry and the 2nd Armored divisions in top combat readiness while simultaneously facing a bewildering array of new problems. Few World War II commanders could have foreseen the day when there would be negotiations with base civilian employees, but such became the case in the 1980s. The American Federation of Government Employees had a local in Killeen, and it negotiated with base officials over work issues on a regular basis.[52]  General Graves also was expected to host high-ranking foreign Army visitors, such as Marshal Sergei Federovich Akhromeyev, the top military leader of the Soviet Union who came to Hood in July of 1988, as well as any congressman or senator who happened to be in the area for a "photo opportunity." Simultaneously he had to work with civic leaders in Killeen and other surrounding towns to get better housing at reasonable rates, for increasingly the soldier of the 1980s was married and had a family.[53]

Another issue of the 1970s and 1980s, one causing many problems for General Graves and his staff, has been the use of narcotics both by soldiers and civilian workers on the post, which, in turn, has caused greater problems of crime on the military reservation and in surrounding communities. In the new Army of the 1980s the III Corps commander indeed has multiple roles to play; he is expected to be a soldier, a leader of soldiers, a logician, and a tactician as well as a diplomat, a public relations expert, a labor negotiator, and an orator able to keep Rotarians, Kiwanians, and other service club members awake at dozens of meetings a year.

In his many speaking engagements to civilian groups, General Graves likes to draw an analogy between soldiers and firemen:

> *I see myself and our business as kind of like a big fire department. The bigger the city, the bigger the fire department. No one wants to have a fire, and as long as there is no fire the people...usually don't pay a lot of attention to the fire department. But they expect their fire department to be trained and competent. When a fire does occur, they don't expect the fire truck to break down en route to the fire. They expect their firemen to be alert, available, and ready, and they want them to arrive at a fire, be competent, and put out the fire quickly with the least amount of damage.*
>
> *They don't expect their firemen to get into an argument at the fire station about whether the fire is a moral fire or an immoral fire. When a fire comes, we fight the fire. I'm trying to make certain that our people are as competent as they can be to fight the fire.*
>
> *We are not going to do away with fires by doing away with the firefighters. I'm trying to prepare soldiers to fight, survive, and win the next war should we have one.*[54]

In the face of the many changes that have taken place in the world in the last two decades, there is much that remained the same. Every year new recruits arrive to be trained in the ways of the Army, the cadence calls of their instructors booming across the sunburnt Texas earth and the rolling thunder of the explosions of their shells echoing off the hills. Always there are green troops to be indoctrinated in the ways of battle through maneuvers in the field and exercises around the world. Old-timers have only to look up at the newest helicopters or at the points where new tanks and personnel carriers are parked to know that they must update old skills. Every summer North Camp has to be readied for Army Reservists and National Guardsmen coming for their brief stints of training. This new Army is trying to live up to the recruiting slogan it uses on television. It wants every man and every officer to "be all that you can be."

# Chapter Eight

# The Changing Nature of "R and R"

WHEN Army officials announced that a major Army post would be built in Central Texas, there was worry among some civilians. Everyone knew that soldiers did not train 24 hours a day 365 days a year. The human body and mind were not capable of such sustained work, and thus the men would be given time off even in that era of frantic mobilization. Every evening during the work week there would be some men free, and many would get weekend passes. Moreover, when the base was first being built, recreational facilities had a low priority. Thus those men given a pass, with nothing to do on the post, would go to nearby towns–and there was fear about what the impact would be.

There were those in some communities around Camp Hood who preached that the arrival of so many young men, freed from the restraints of family supervision, would bring moral decay. There would be drinking, and decent young ladies might be endangered. It was pointed out that, as Shakespeare had noted in *As You Like It*, soldiers were "full of strange oaths" and "quick in quarrel." Bankers were warned that they would be doing business with people whom they did not know, and there would be losses from forgeries and hot checks. Many people worried there would be an increase in the number of criminals in their area because bootleggers, prostitutes, and gamblers would flock to the area to lure these young men into sin and fleece them out of their monthly pay, small amount though it was.

Quickly such fears were put to rest, as noted in an editorial in the *Killeen Daily Herald* of September 18, 1942. The men of Camp Hood, the editorial commented, must be different from those at other bases, else "we have been misled" in thinking they would be rowdies who would cause trouble. "Camp Hood boys...are a quiet, gentlemanly, well-behaved bunch of young men," he wrote, continuing:

> *Surely soldiers [elsewhere in the Army] do not measure up to the*
> *standard of Camp Hood men. From General [A.D.] Bruce down*
> *through all of the ranks to the privates that it has been our pleas-*
> *ure to know and talk with..., the friendly helpful disposition has*
> *been manifested and we have left [the base] each time more*
> *determined in our mind that those fellows, every one of them, are*
> *men, real he men.*

The writer of that editorial concluded, "Is Camp Hood different, or is Killeen just lucky?"[1]

Almost immediately after Camp Hood was created, there was a quarrel between its commander, General A.D. Bruce, and Mayor T.H. Minor. According to town legend, Minor was incensed that the Army had taken one half the land in Killeen's trade area, and when General Bruce came to town to talk about ways local civilians could help the Army, the mayor testily told him, "General, you run the camp and I'll run the town." Perhaps as a result of General Bruce's disfavor, Killeen never was able to get a Defense Area designation, which would have allowed it to get lumber for new housing, and the town did not grow significantly during World War II.[2]

During the war, soldiers on leave from Camp Hood, a few traveling by private automobile but most on public buses or the train, hurried through Killeen and Belton to reach Temple. Civic leaders in this city cooperated fully with General Bruce, the Chamber of Commerce calling Temple the "Gateway to Camp Hood." Realizing the economic benefit to their community, members of the Temple Chamber of Commerce organized a vast recreational program for the soldiers. What had been the town Y.M.C.A. building was turned over to the United Services Organization (USO); the Temple Y.M.C.A. facility had been the only one in Texas with its own swimming pool, and this became available to soldiers. The Temple USO also had a dance hall, badminton courts, 20 assorted games, a bowling alley, and rooms for reading and writing.

Lonely soldiers flocked to the Temple USO in record numbers, which tried to find rooms for them in private homes so they would not have to go back to the post when they had overnight passes. The lonely soldiers especially loved dances, and one was held at the USO almost every Friday and Saturday night with a live orchestra playing. The music popular during the war years was the type that encouraged dancing; for example, the top 10 songs in September of 1943 were:

1. "Sunday, Monday and Always."
2. "Paper Doll"
3. "In My Arms"
4. "Pistol Packin' Mama"
5. "People Will Say We're In Love"
6. "You'll Never Know"
7. "In the Blue of the Evening"
8. "I Heard You Cried Last Night"
9. "Put Your Arms Around Me"
10. "Say A Prayer for the Boys Over There"

On one occasion there were 515 soldiers at a USO dance, so many that not all those who wanted to get on the dance floor could do so.

A special feature of the Temple USO was the barbecues it organized, the Chamber of Commerce supplying the barbecue. Another feature was a weekly birthday party for all soldiers having a birthday that week; the local Eastern Star chapter donated the cakes for this function. At Thanksgiving and Christmas the Temple USO recruited local families to take soldiers into their homes for a meal. For example, in November of 1942 the USO had a campaign in Temple to "Share Your Thanksgiving Dinner," and more than 1,600 soldiers were fed a home-cooked meal that day.

This was still an era of segregation, and black soldiers found it especially difficult to find something to do while on a pass from Camp Hood. They even had difficulty getting away from the post because of the Texas "Jim Crow" law that required them to sit on the back seat of the bus. Eventually this was modified at Fort Hood so that blacks loaded from the rear of the bus forward while whites loaded from the front to the back. For blacks serving their country, Temple organized a black USO whose programs matched those of the white USO.

The success of the USO program in Temple was evident by the statistics that resulted. From July 4, 1942, to July 1, 1943, 87,657 letters were mailed from the Temple USO, which had found rooms for 9,277 service men during that time. By October 23, 1943, it could claim to have served 595,672 soldiers in one way or another.[3] In addition to the USO, the Red Cross had a canteen in Temple where soldiers could get free doughnuts, coffee, sandwiches, and fruit.

So many soldiers crowded into Temple looking for something to do that there rarely was an empty seat at any of the six movie houses in town no matter what film was being shown. Others went to one of the three softball diamonds at Baker Field where ball games seemed to be continuous; still others went to Temple public parks where there were community events going on nightly. In addition, there was a public swimming pool west of the Santa Fe depot which stayed open from spring to fall. A tennis court and outdoor pavilion, sponsored by the "Home Towner" campaign and the Gridiron Club and located near the USO building, were in constant use, as were a carnival and amusement center on the city courthouse square sponsored by the American Legion and the city recreational department. Almost every weekend the Municipal Auditorium had a professional wrestling card with five percent of the gate going to the city recreational fund. Black servicemen had a softball field at Avenue E and Eighth Street, and there was a separate amusement park for them.[4]

There were those businessmen in Temple and other cities near Fort Hood that operated establishments that Army officials did not want the troops to frequent. From time to time Camp Hood commanders would find it necessary to place some establishment "Off Limits," meaning it was illegal for any military personnel to enter the place so named. For example, the Temple Hotel at 114 $^1/_2$ S First Street was declared off limits on June 12, as was the Riverside Swimming Pool one mile east of Belton on Highway 81. Businessmen found that having an establishment placed off limits caused a severe drop in business, and most made immediate efforts to restore themselves to the Army's favor. For example, when the Carnival Grounds in Killeen was placed off limits on March 7, 1944, its owner immediately made changes, and on March 10 the off limits designation was removed from his establishment.[5]

There were similar efforts to make the servicemen at Camp Hood welcome in Gatesville, Copperas Cove, and Lampasas. In each of these towns the local churches made an effort to get servicemen invited to homes for Sunday dinner, and movie theaters in each town were overrun at every showing. Lampasas went even further by donating its Hancock Park, a recreational facility of 150 acres, to the government. This had a swimming pool, bath house, dance hall, concession and assembly buildings, and 12 guest cottages. For the duration of the war it was operated by the Special Services Office and the Post Engineer at Camp Hood.[6]

Privates making only $21 a month (more during the latter part of the war) did not always have the 70 cents needed to ride the bus round-trip to Temple, and thus the completion of recreational facilities on the post was especially welcome. By November of 1942 there were three major post exchanges completed and opened along with 12 movie theaters (that could also be used for lectures), three swimming pools, a nine-hole golf course, several tennis courts, dozens of baseball diamonds, a football field, and three bowling alleys.[7] Completed in January of 1943 was Building 4410, a sports arena which troops promptly dubbed "The Cracker Box" because of its small size; this was the post gymnasium and had only enough room for one basketball court (also used for volleyball and badminton), and there were ping pong tables as well as space for weightlifting on a stage. In addition, classes were taught at the base gymnasium, and movies were shown there. (This facility became known as the Old Ironsides Sports Arena after the 1st Armored Division was reactivated at Hood in 1957.)[8]

One activity popular in almost every unit at Camp Hood—as in every unit in the Armed Forces at that time—was voting for a favorite "Pin-Up Girl." Usually this was for some current movie starlet, but soldiers could enter anyone they wished. During World War II the woman most often voted a favorite Pin-Up Girl by servicemen was swimsuit-clad Betty Grable, but these contests were not always taken seriously—as shown by the men of Headquarters Company, 648th Battalion, at Camp Hood in August of 1943. In the semi-finals of the vote in this unit, such familiar movie stars as Katherine Hepburn, Dorothy Lamour, and Joan Crawford were eliminated, and in the finals Betty Grable received only seven votes. Declared the "Pin-Up Girl" for the company, with 121 votes, was a three-month-old boy named Dickie Ruppert from Fairgrove, Michigan, whose picture appeared in local newspapers just before the vote was taken. The election judges, after counting the ballots, raised a question of legality inasmuch as young Ruppert was a boy, and they referred the issue to a committee. Its members immediately announced that Ruppert was the winner and sent him a telegram bestowing the title "Mr. Pin-Up of 1943" on him.[9]

Absolutely necessary at Camp Hood was a post exchange (PX) where soldiers could buy both necessities, such as soap and razor blades, and luxuries, such as cigarettes, candy bars, and soft drinks. The first PX on the post, located at North Camp Hood, was hastily opened to serve the men there. Its counters were pieces of plywood thrown across sawhorses, and it sold cigarettes for $1 a carton, candy bars at 4 cents each, and soft drinks by the case at 3 cents per bottle. The first PX at South Camp was furnished slightly better and was located in the headquarters complex, but its prices were identical to those at North Camp.[10]

Equally important to the officers and soldiers at Camp Hood in those first years were the service clubs. The officers assigned to the post established their first Open Mess on the roof of the Kyle Hotel in Temple. Once construction at the camp reached the point that everyone moved there, an Officers' Open Mess opened on Headquarters Avenue directly across the street from Post Headquarters. This 1942 facility would continue to serve until 1959.

For enlisted men there were three service clubs where they could go to listen to records or the radio, write letters, and get snacks, beer, and other refreshments. The first to open was the North Fort Hood Service Club, which was for men training in that area. Beginning service in 1942, it would continue in use until 1955 at which time it shifted to summer use only by National Guard troops and Army Reservists during their annual two weeks' training. The second enlisted men's service club was the one opened at South Camp on Brigade Avenue (in what later would become the Entertainment Center). It discontinued service there in 1959. And there was the 162nd Street Service Club, which was destroyed by fire in 1955.

During World War II, all three of these service clubs for enlisted men served only beer with 3.2 percent alcoholic content, and they were open from 5 p.m. to 10 p.m. on weekday evenings, 12 noon to 10 p.m. on Sundays. All bottles of beer purchased in these establishments were uncapped at the time of sale, and they had to be consumed on the premises.[11]

Keeping the men informed about activities at the post was the *Hood Panther*, a newspaper put out by the Public Information Office. At first it was small, for no government funds could be used to print it and newsprint was scarce during World War II. Gradually, however, it would become more professional, opening its pages to advertising so it could become larger. Later, in the postwar years, the paper's name would be changed to the *Armored Sentinel*, and it would grow in excellence to the point where many soldiers at the base read no other paper.

Another way some soldiers kept themselves informed and entertained was by going to the base library, which opened in 1943 with few books, no recordings, and a minimum of personnel. Located on Headquarters Avenue, it provided a place where men on the post who wanted reading material, either for entertainment or self-education, could get it. For eight years this one library would serve the entire post as it gradually added to its holdings. However, it did begin getting books to units in the field with three mobile units in September of 1943.[12]

The men who came to Camp Hood during World War II, either as volunteers or draftees, were from a generation for whom the movies and radio were the major form of entertainment. During the depression-ridden 1930s, the number of movie tickets sold each week soared to 80 million and more, and elaborate theaters, rivaling Turkish palaces in their opulence, were built. Even in tiny Killeen the one theater there, the Sadler, created an illusion of romance and make-believe with its plush seats and colorful, cool interior. The movie theaters at Camp Hood could not compare with civilian counterparts, but the soldiers who patronized the base theaters got two hours of escape for their 10-cent admission.

The other form of escape was the radio. Every barracks boasted at least one radio, and even the smallest receiver could receive Frank Mayborn's KTEM from nearby Temple with ease. Bigger sets could pull in signals from far-off Dallas or Fort Worth or San Antonio or Austin, and listeners could be thrilled by stories about crime fighters or entertained by comics and comedians. This was the era of the big band, and the music of Glenn Miller, Tommy Dorsey, and Wayne King and ballads rendered by Bing Crosby and the Andrews Sisters flooded the airways.

But for the men at Camp Hood, there was an added treat. The USO regularly brought top film stars, radio personalities, musicians, sports figures, and other entertainers to military bases, allowing the men to see these people in person. Perhaps the best-known name in the history of USO entertainment of servicemen, Bob Hope, came to Camp Hood on April 20, 1943. Already a star of dozens of movies, Hope had a weekly radio show that was extremely popular, and that night he broadcast it live from Central Texas. Coming with him to do the show were Francis Langford, Skinny Ennis and his orchestra, Jerry Colonna, and Vera Vague. That night's show was considered one of the biggest entertainment spectaculars at Camp Hood during World War II.[13]

Another comic star of movies and radio coming to Hood was Red Skelton. He played to capacity audiences during shows at both North and South Camps in 1943. At one point he asked an impromptu question that almost brought the show to a total standstill with laughter when he asked a soldier wearing only a helmet liner, "What did you do? Eat the turtle out of him?"[14]

One of the first Hollywood starlets to visit Camp Hood was Joan Blondell, who came in March of 1943 to make a personal appearance in connection with the USO road show, "Hellzapoppin." A popular musical group, Fred Waring and his Pennsylvanians, came to Hood on February 18, 1944, for a show. That night they honored the men of the Tank Destroyer Center by playing and singing songs selected by the troops, songs such as "Every Night About This Time," "When You're a Long, Long Way From Home," and "Touch of Texas." Waring and his Pennsylvanians performed these hits on the NBC radio program, "Chesterfield Time," a popular show sponsored by the cigarette of that name.[15]

Not meant as entertainment but rather as education was a broadcast done from Camp Hood in 1943 by Lieutenant Burgess Meredith. Already a star of movies and the stage, Meredith was serving in the Army's Public Information Office and did a broadcast on a show known as the "Army Hour" in which he described the training at Camp Hood's Tank Destroyer Center.[16]

Two of the all-time great sports figures of the 20th century were at Camp Hood on December 6, 1943, to put on an exhibition of boxing. These were world heavyweight champion Joe Louis and an up-and-coming welterweight named Sugar Ray Robinson. They performed before 5,000 soldiers in the post field house and gave lectures on physical fitness. Lewis, then the heavyweight idol of the nation, sparred with Corporal Bob Smith for three rounds, while Robinson, who at the time already had won 188 consecutive professional fights, clowned and danced around the ring with Private Jackie Wilson.[17]

Also coming to Camp Hood were others whose names were not well known at the time but who would go on to achieve renown. Training in the 899th Tank Destroyer Battalion at Fort Hood in 1942 was Lieutenant Will Rogers, Jr., son of the great humorist star of vaudeville, radio, and motion pictures; Rogers left Camp Hood in January of 1943 to take a seat in Congress, to which he won election in November of 1942 (and later he would star in several movies and host a national television show).

Also at the post during the war was Jackie Robinson, who later would become the first black to break the color line in professional baseball. Robinson in the early 1940s had gained some fame as a great college athlete who had lettered in four different sports at U.C.L.A., but in 1943-1944 he was just another lieutenant at Camp Hood.

Robinson had completed Officers' Candidate School at Fort Riley, Kansas, and as morale officer for black troops there he fought against segregation and discrimination. Transferred to Camp Hood, he found Texas laws at this time were even more discriminatory than those in Kansas. On July 6, 1944, knowing that the Army had issued orders ending segregation on military buses, he refused to move to the back of a commercial bus even after ordered to do so by military police and the base provost marshal. He was court-martialed for insubordination, but the trial judges ruled he had acted within his rights.[18]

When World War II ended, so did the USO-sponsored parade of Hollywood stars and radio personalities at Camp Hood. However, with the arrival of the 2nd Armored Division in 1946 came something new, a base football team that played college and military teams. During the war, when the draft took most young men away from colleges and universities, football fell on hard times. Some universities tried to make up a roster with those classified 4-F (unfit for service). Others played freshmen just turning 18 before they were drafted. A fortunate few schools had contracts with the Navy's V-5 and V-12

program, and the Navy allowed the men studying in these programs
to participate in football. Thus there were relatively small and unknown universities with football teams that won major bowl games
during this period. Moreover, there were some military bases that
fielded football teams that competed with major university teams during
the war years. Camp Hood was not one of them.

Then in 1946 the 2nd Armored Division was stationed at Hood, and
General John M. Devine, the commander of the unit, decided the
division could field a team in that era when military units had more
time for recreation. The week before the season opened, the Hell On
Wheels team, called the "Wheelers," had a scrimmage against the
Louisiana State University Bengals, a team which the year before had
won seven and lost two. Unfortunately for the Wheelers, the quarterback for the LSU team that year was Y.A. Tittle, a passing quarterback
destined for Hall-of-Fame greatness in the National Football League.
Another player for the Bengals that day was Alvin Dark, who would
become famous as a professional baseball player and manager. According to a newspaper account of the scrimmage game on September
20, 1946, no score was kept but "The collegians ran rough-shod over
the tankers."

However, General Devine still had hopes that his Wheelers might
have a winning season.  On September 23 he wrote Temple publisher
Frank Mayborn:

> One of the reasons for pushing the football team at Camp Hood
> this year was in the hope that the team might be good enough to
> arouse some interest outside the Camp itself, and perhaps build
> up an enthusiastic following in Temple where we will play our
> home games. Our season opens next Saturday and invitations
> have gone out to representative groups of citizens in surrounding
> towns. In order to start things off right we have asked these
> people to meet us at the Kyle Hotel before the game and have a
> drink, to get in the proper mood to watch the football game....
> How good our team will be of course we do not know, but we have
> high hopes. We have a considerable number of former football
> players on our squad and it is just possible that we might turn out
> a winning combination.[19]

What General Devine did not realize was how good most college teams would be that year. Immediately after World War II, the National Collegiate Athletic Association (NCAA) had ruled that men who had been in military service had not lost any eligibility. Collegiate athletic ranks thus were filled with men older, stronger, and more mature than the 18-to-22-year-olds who normally were on athletic teams. Therefore the Wheelers faced excellent competition even when playing teams not normally football powerhouses.

On September 28 the Wheelers played their first game with Woodson Field in Temple serving as the home stadium. Their foe that day was Southwest Texas State Teachers College, and when the final gun sounded the score was 0 to 0. A week later the Wheelers lost to the University of Houston 32-7, then on October 12 they dropped a contest with the Pensacola Navy Fliers by a score of 26-2. On October 19 they managed a come-from-behind victory against a team from Camp Campbell, Kentucky, by a score of 13-7. The rest of the season was extremely disappointing as the Wheelers lost to Fort Benning 45-0, to Southeastern Oklahoma State Teachers College 20-0, and to Navarro Junior College 7-0.[20] The post never again fielded a team.

In the years just after World War II, as the pace of military activity slowed, so few soldiers were at Camp Hood that providing for their recreational needs was easily handled on post or in nearby towns. Then came 1950 and the announcement that Hood would become a permanent post with a second division activated there, which meant that once again the base would swarm with young men who needed something to do, young men with considerable discretionary income. They would have a strong economic impact on those communities that welcomed them, which publisher Frank Mayborn recognized in an editorial in the *Temple Daily Telegram* of April 16, 1950:

> *Not the least of the problems either brought or reemphasized by Fort Hood's permanent status is that of soldier recreation. Central Texas communities, Temple included, did a good job on that during the war, primarily through the USO but with a considerable amount of local initiative, too.*
>
> *Since the war, there has been a natural decrease in interest in such activity. That shouldn't have happened, but it has followed*

*every war ever fought.... In Temple, for instance, the old YMCA
building which housed the USO activity has been turned over to
the city recreation department....*

    *Fort Hood has stated its willingness to cooperate in practical
ways in an adequate soldier program here, and can be of great
help. The army is offering to meet the civilian community more
than half-way.*

    *...It is certainly plain for anyone to see that we had better be
getting at it. If we don't solve this problem soon, it may be too
late. People–and the fact that soldiers are people is the whole
basis of this–form the habit of going certain places, as is known,
and those habits are hard to break. Finally, the soldiers of Fort
Hood are going where they think they are wanted, and where they
can enjoy themselves most at the least cost. We owe them something more than the opportunity of coming here to spend their
money.*

The people of Temple did get behind this effort, making the men of
Fort Hood so welcome that many of them came to that city to go to
movies and shop. Many of them would choose to live there, renting
apartments, duplexes, and houses in that city, driving to the post each
morning and home each evening, because they liked Temple so well.
Only as Killeen grew and civilian attitudes in the town changed did it
begin to compete for these dollars.

    When Fort Hood became a permanent post, the Army made a tre-
mendous effort to see that adequate housing on the post was available
for the dependents of the troops stationed there. Across the years
congress would appropriate money to build additional base housing or
to upgrade existing quarters on an irregular–and often stingy–basis.
By the 1980s there would be more than 5,000 quarters available to
personnel at Fort Hood; these were assigned by rank and grade among
eligible personnel, but always there was a waiting list. The Family
Housing Office has made the best of what has been available to it,
referring those unable to secure quarters on post to the Off-Post Re-
ferral Office; its task has been to counsel those who rent in nearby
communities and attempt to see that they get adequate quarters at reasonable rates.

There also was a major effort at Fort Hood in the postwar years to provide recreational facilities on the base so the soldiers there would not have to drive long distances, mostly during hours of darkness, to find something to do. In the late 1940s and through the decade of the 1950s the roads around Fort Hood were being improved by the Texas Highway Department to eliminate spots where wrecks occurred with too great a frequency, but auto makers were building cars with greater horsepower and speed; the result was that too many soldiers were killing themselves in auto wrecks as they tried to drive to Dallas or San Antonio while on a weekend pass. Thus Army officials wanted to provide more types of entertainment at Fort Hood to encourage the men to stay there after hours on weekdays and weekends.

In fact, the effort to keep the troops entertained on the base began even before the announcement that Hood would be a permanent post. In 1948, when the decision was made to begin switching from temporary to permanent buildings, the first structure constructed was a new post theater. This was made possible because base officials were able to secure $2 million from the Army and Air Force Motion Picture Service Fund, created by diverting to it a small percentage of admission fees paid by servicemen at theaters and service clubs at bases around the world. Costing $325,000 and seating 1,006, Camp Hood Main Theater (Theater No. 1) was dedicated on May 25, 1949, by Major General A.D. Bruce, then deputy commander of the 4th Army.[21] Also financed out of the $2 million secured from the Army and Air Force Motion Picture Service Fund was a Post Stadium capable of use for baseball or football; it was made of reinforced concrete and seated 4,560. Other facilities constructed with this money included the first nine holes of a permanent 18-hole golf course, three swimming pools, five baseball diamonds, including the main post diamond with bleachers to seat 3,000, and 17 tennis and volleyball courts.[22]

Officials at Fort Hood subsequently were able to get additional unappropriated funds for construction of recreational facilities, and these dollars were used in ways that increased soldier satisfaction. For example, an extensively remodeled Fort Hood Exchange was reopened by Major General William S. Biddle, commander of the 1st Armored, at a ceremony in 1954. This enlarged and updated the old post exchange, located at Headquarters Avenue and 50th Street, giving it new departments, air conditioning, new lighting and counter fixtures, and, for safety, a fire sprinkler system. Work then began to add a cafeteria, beer bar, shoe repair service, laundry, beauty parlor, and barber shop at the exchange, and, across the street from the Post Theater a gas station and garage were constructed and opened.[23]

Built in this same period with non-appropriated funds was the Academic Drive Service Club, which opened in 1952. It was in the eastern part of South Camp and was intended for use by military police troops and new units moving to that area. As Fort Hood grew after it became a two-division base, the post exchange system was enlarged until it was operating more than a dozen retail stores, five "groceterias," and a score of snack bars and cafeterias, some devoted to serving beer and pizza, others to hamburgers, and still others to different menu specialties. There even would be several Fort Hood package stores for those wanting alcoholic beverages.[24]

For officers at Fort Hood, there was the Officers Open Mess, usually referred to as the Officers Club. The first such facility opened in 1942 on Headquarters Avenue directly across from Post Headquarters and served until April of 1959 when a new Officers Club was dedicated at the corner of 20th Avenue and 24th Street. At the time it featured the latest comforts and conveniences: air conditioning, three dining rooms, game room, bar, ballroom, lounge, cafeteria, snack bar, and swimming pool.[25]

Across the years this facility would be refurbished, but by the mid-1980s it no longer was one of the better clubs in the Army. For this reason it was closed just after New Year's Day in 1982 and would remain shut for 11 months for a $4.3 million renovation that included increasing its floor space, new furnishings, and new fixtures. The funds for this work came from club profits and a loan, not from any appropriated funds, and allowed it to expand its membership to 5,000.[26]

The first Non-Commissioned Officers (NCO) Open Mess was opened in Building 325 in February of 1947, but because all enlisted men could use this facility the NCOs on the post still did not have a place exclusively for them where after hours they could buy a hamburger, get a beer, shoot pool, or just relax and listen to the radio. For this reason a new NCO Open Mess was dedicated in 1958; located near the intersection of South Avenue and 37th street, it had a dining room, stag bar, cocktail lounge, couples' lounge with color television, and a swimming pool along with a ballroom where dances could be held. Also on the corner of South Avenue and 37th Street, and supervised by the NCO Open Mess, was an Enlisted Men's Club.[27]

Then came 1959 and the opening of Fiddler's Green, an $800,000 enlisted men's service club located on 162nd Street. This was built under an Army-wide plan for modernizing service clubs. It had rooms devoted to listening to stereo music, pool, table tennis, color television, card playing, jam sessions, reading, and writing. There was a large ballroom with a stage, full lighting facilities, and dressing rooms. Major General William S. Biddle, III Corps and Fort Hood commander, cut the ribbon at opening ceremonies for Fiddler's Green on March 14, 1959. The name for the facility was chosen after a contest during which some 3,000 names were submitted in a post-wide contest. The winning name came from an Army legend which holds that Fiddler's Green is a cool, refreshing meadow dotted with shade trees and crossed by laughing brooks, and to this paradise go retired cavalrymen and horse-mounted artillerymen. This facility has remained one of the best at any Army post in the world thanks to periodic renovation.[28]

Fort Hood also had scheduled activities for those soldiers who wanted to be challenged physically. Even during World War II a golf course was built. At first this was only a nine-hole course, but later it was enlarged. Later there would be two 18-hole courses—Clear Creek, located just west of the main installation, and Anderson, located near the East Gate; adjacent to Anderson is also a driving range. There are two 24-lane bowling facilities at Hood, Bowlers Green and Albee Lanes, while the Post Roller Rink on 37th Street has a skating program for all ages. Abrams Field House features an indoor Olympic-size pool, and there are seven other swimming pools scattered around the base. At Lake Belton there are beaches, pavilions, a boat dock, a fishing dock, and furnished cottages, and Sherwood Forest Archery Range is in that vicinity with an active Fort Hood Archery Club. Those who are interested can learn to water ski, sail a boat, or rent small craft for pleasure or fishing at the Boat Dock, and anchored there is the *Terry Queen Party Boat* which can accommodate as many as 22 people for day or night parties. In more recent times the Special Services branch has used the Belton Lake Recreation Area for 10-kilometer "Fun Runs" and other types of activities for a generation of troops and their dependents more attuned to physical fitness than was the case in the past.[29]

Soldiers have an intimate acquaintance with firearms, and thus it was natural for a Rod and Gun Club to be organized. Located on Pilot Knob Road, it became a gathering place for sportsmen, and at that facility a snack bar, lounge, game room, skeet range, dog kennel, and picnic area with barbecue pits were built. In 1978 the skeet range at the Rod and Gun Club was the site for the 4th annual Forces Command (FORSCOM) shooting championship, and those who entered from Fort Hood represented their club well.[30]

Almost from the first day an Army post was opened at Camp Hood, some of the officers and men stationed there viewed it as a hunter's paradise. Not until August 25, 1943, was hunting permitted on firing ranges and other camp land not in use, and three days later came an order saying that during the 1943-1944 season hunters would have to limit themselves to a bag limit of 10 mourning doves daily and 10 quail daily, 30 per week.

Hunting at the post was improved thanks to new Army regulations in 1963. Under these, Fort Hood hired a civil service employee to head up a Fish and Wildlife Section. Through sound conservation practices and carefully controlled hunting, this section gradually built a hunters' and fishers' paradise on Fort Hood's 217,000 acres. Some of the methods that were used included food plots and stock tanks specifically built to supply food and water to game animals—and it worked, for the white-tail deer population soon increased to more than 10,000. Wild turkeys initially were stocked at Hood in 1958 with 200 domestic birds, and the following year 80 wild toms were brought from the King Ranch in South Texas. Each year there is a census of the 11 types of game animals native to Fort Hood, and the hunting permits sold for their cropping by the Fish and Wildlife Section are carefully monitored. Organized for avid hunters who also like to ride was the Hunt and Saddle Club, while those who wanted only to ride could join the Montague Riding Club.[31]

Fort Hood also developed first-rate facilities for those interested in various hobbies. The Skills Development Center, located in Building 3 on Headquarters Avenue, has areas devoted to leather crafts, lapidary, pottery, print-making, drawing, weaving, painting, sculpture, photography, and jewel making. A Ceramics Shop is in Building 235 on Battalion Avenue, a Woodworking Shop in Building 236, a Fort Hood Crafts Shop at West Fort Hood, and four shops for auto repair and tuning conveniently located around the post.[32]

Less traditional were clubs at Fort Hood for those interested in flying and skydiving. In 1959 a group interested in proficiency in flying organized the Fort Hood Aero Club with membership open to military and civilian employees. Members were able to earn a private pilot's license and then could rent one of the club's 12 aircraft for personal use. The Skydiver's Club was formed in 1960 for those interested in that sport. New members received extensive ground training until they qualified to jump, and every Saturday the members would aim for a drop zone at the corner of Georgetown and Elijah roads (northwest of the main cantonment area).[33]

There even were organized activities and clubs for the children of Army personnel at Fort Hood. The Dependent Youth Activities (DYA) office provides a full program of youth sports for boys and girls, such as soccer, football, baseball, basketball, wrestling, and cheerleading. Special activities available to young people on the post, in addition to Boy Scouts and Girl Scouts, are gymnastics, karate, the Dolphin Swim Club, a rifle club, and the Adventure Club. There also is a DYA Summer Recreation Program of arts and crafts, indoor and outdoor games, drama, nature programs, and special theme events.[34]

In the post-Korean War period, the type of activities desired by young men and women serving in the Army began changing, and thus Fort Hood's Special Services branch had to organize new types of activities to stay relevant. Opened in 1956 was the Fort Hood Little Theater, built with non-appropriated funds, and it offered a wide variety of entertainment for post personnel and their dependents. Among the early productions were notable plays such as "Paint Your Wagon," "Harvey," and "Detective Story." The actors, actresses, and behind-the-scenes workers in these plays, amateurs giving of their time and talent, grew in ability and soon were noted for their extremely professional sets and prize-winning performances, even of plays as demanding as those by Shakespeare. For example, at the annual 4th U.S. Army Drama Contest, held in 1963, the Fort Hood Little Theater production of "Blood, Sweat, and Stanley Poole" won first-place honors.[35]

When Fiddler's Green, the Enlisted Men's Club, opened in 1959, the old Brigade Avenue Service Club was closed, and the building was turned over to the Entertainment Section of Special Services. Renovated and refurbished, it became the Fort Hood Entertainment Center and began offering a monthly jazz session called "Jazz On The Rocks" that featured local combos. Attendance at first was small, but as word spread about the quality of the offerings the crowds grew to standing-room-only. Then, as musical tastes changed, the Center offered "Shindig," a twice-monthly show featuring rock 'n roll performers, local groups and vocalists, and even an occasional comedian. For other tastes there was the monthly "Folkfest" which featured a Country and Western music group made up of Fort Hood soldiers. And the Entertainment Center showed its versatility by offering "Showstop," a variety program taken to different areas of the post with a portable stage called the "Show Wagon." Finally, soldiers with musical ability but no wish to play before an audience could check out instruments and have private sessions in rooms at the Entertainment Center.[36]

Each division at Fort Hood had its band that played for major reviews and other formal functions, and both have given occasional concerts for entertainment. In addition, these often have played in surrounding towns to create a favorable impression about the Army. Moreover, both division bands also formed a chorus, as, for example, the "Stouthearted Men of the 1st Armored Division Chorus." Started in 1962, the group took its name from the Old Ironsides theme song, "Stouthearted Men." Growing to some 50 singers, the chorus developed a repertoire that included military and popular favorites as well as a number of hymns, and it would appear to sustained applause both on and off post at numerous functions.[37]

The new Army of the postwar world demanded soldiers far more educated than their counterparts of the so-called "Old Army." To help those troops who wished to further their schooling after regular working hours, a Fort Hood Education Center was established. At first it offered little more than a few correspondence courses from the United States Armed Forces Institute (USAFI) along with a General Education Development (GED) test that would enable anyone who had not completed high school to get a certificate equal to a diploma. However, in the 1950s the Army gradually realized the benefit to it from helping soldiers who had even less than high school work, and the Education Center eventually employed civilian teachers to instruct at the elementary level. In addition, the center offered testing and counseling to help soldiers recognize potential areas where they might want to study as well as Military Occupational Specialty (MOS) libraries where soldiers could learn more about their Army specialty and hasten promotion.

Gradually the Education Center expanded its offerings upward as enlistment standards were raised. Coming into the new Army were soldiers who wanted to get college-level work, even to earn sufficient credits to get a college degree. At first the Education Center offered correspondence courses from dozens of universities and colleges across the country, most of them at reduced rates for military personnel. However, there was a need for on-post courses, and the Army contracted with Mary Hardin-Baylor College (later renamed the University of Mary Hardin-Baylor) to offer classes at Fort Hood with the Army paying three-quarters of the cost.

And it was the Army that helped make possible the opening of Central Texas College, a public junior college in Killeen. When General Ralph E. Haines, Jr., took command at Fort Hood in 1965, a major topic of discussion in Bell and Coryell counties was the possibility of this institution of higher learning. General Haines suggested that greater support for getting a favorable public vote on creating this college could be had by locating it just south of Highway 190 almost exactly on the Bell-Coryell county line on land that belonged partly to Fort Hood and partly to the Air Force (dating from the days of Gray Air Force Base). Haines, believing that more than 50 percent of the students at this proposed junior college would be soldiers, was able to get the acreage needed for it declared excess military property and deeded over to the public institution.

When Central Texas College opened in Killeen in 1967, hundreds of military personnel flocked to it to further their education at little cost (because the State of Texas allows those in the Armed Forces to attend its public institutions of higher learning at in-state tuition rates). Central Texas College offered both associate degree programs as well as numerous vocational-technical courses. Working closely with those troops enrolling there has been the Fort Hood Education Center, which through its on-base instruction at the high school and university level, through correspondence courses, and through coordination with off-campus junior college offerings has made it possible for thousands to further their education while serving their country.[38]

Aiding efforts at education and self-improvement at Fort Hood, as well as providing a form of entertainment, has been the base library system. The single library opened in 1943 was able to serve the needs of the post in the immediate postwar world, but when Hood became a two-division permanent base there was need for expansion. In 1951 the first branch library was established at the old hospital in the western cantonment area. When Darnall Army Hospital opened in 1965, the hospital library branch moved there, and its "truck" could be seen moving through the halls and into rooms to allow bed-ridden patients the opportunity to select reading material.

In 1955 the library opened what it named the Academic Branch on the outskirts of the Wainwright Heights housing development. However, the name was changed to Branch No. 2 in 1965 because some patrons thought the word "academic" meant the branch handled only textbooks and materials related to school work. Branch No. 2 contained the first collection of children's books on the post because it was nearest to housing and school areas.

Eventually the base library system would expand to serve all areas of the post–and in ways no librarian ever considered in previous years. By the 1980s there were four base libraries: Casey Memorial Library on Battalion Avenue, Academic Drive Library (the old Branch No. 2), the West Fort Hood Library, and the Hospital Branch Library. The system had built its collection of fiction and nonfiction to tens of thousands of volumes, but it also had begun to stock records, audio tapes, compact disks, and video tapes, all available to post personnel and dependents as soon as–or, in many cases, faster than–nearby public libraries have them.[39]

Also intended to serve an educational function were the museums opened on the post. During World War II there was a Tank Destroyer Museum, located near 24th Street and Park Avenue in Classroom 19 and open daily under the direction of curator W.T. Tardy. Next to open was a museum for the 2nd Armored Division. It was created in 1949 but not recognized officially until 1963, and five years later it moved to a permanent home in what had been a post theater building during World War II. The 2nd Armored Division Museum specializes in artifacts of the men of the "Hell on Wheels" division during World War II, and it has maps of all the campaigns fought as well as examples of the weapons used in each of them. A special section in this museum was set aside to honor General George S. Patton, Jr., who commanded the unit during World War II; a prized exhibit is one of his winter coats. Another special exhibit is an early Sherman tank with a full cast hull (rather than welded), and near it is an M-103, the largest tank ever adopted by the Army.

The other museum on the post is the one maintained by the 1st Armored Division. The men of Old Ironsides could visit this to see the history of armored warfare and the development of individual soldiers from the time of horse cavalrymen to their modern mechanized counterparts. Much of the credit for creating this museum belongs to Major General George Ruhlen, who personally donated many of the articles on exhibit. One of these was the vehicle he used during reviews of the 1st Armored at Fort Hood: a World War II halftrack which he had salvaged from a vehicular graveyard in Chicago; called "88 Bait" because of the way it attracted fire from German tanks armed with an .88 caliber cannon, this halftrack and hundreds of others just like it carried troops of the 1st Armored into battle during World War II.

Also at the 1st Armored's museum were many different weapons. The oldest was a mace (spiked club) dating from about the year 1500. Another antique weapon, a crossbow from the 18th century, closely resembled a crossbow used by the Viet Cong during the war in Vietnam. Modern weapons, such as the M-60 machine gun, were on display alongside the mace. Also in the museum were flags from East Germany and the Viet Cong as well as a tattered banner once carried by men of Battery C, 1st Battalion, 6th Artillery, the first American unit to fire a shot in World War II. All the uniforms worn by men of the 1st Armored were displayed on mannequins, while pictures showed what conditions were like for soldiers from different eras. The museum's most famous donor was Walt Disney, who gave a saddle used by a cavalryman during the Indian Wars. The museum for the 1st AD moved to Germany when the division moved there in 1971.

Today there still are two museums at Fort Hood. The 2nd Armored continues to display relics of its heritage in Building 418 on Battalion Avenue, while the museum originally built by the 1st Armored, located in Building 2218 on Headquarters Avenue, now houses memorabilia of the 1st Cavalry Division. Named the First Team Museum, it has been updated with exhibits ranging from those about the days of cavalrymen in the Indian Wars to others about the war in Vietnam. From tanks in the parking lot to uniforms, weapons, insignia, and maps, it tells the story of the different wars in which the 1st Cavalry Division has been involved. As with the 2nd AD Museum, the purpose of this facility is to collect, preserve, and exhibit objects significant to the history of the division in order to train soldiers and educate the general public.[40]

Serving the health needs of the soldiers at Fort Hood during World War II and afterward was a hospital that consisted of a series of one-story barracks connected by covered walkways. Opened in 1942, this served until the construction of Darnall Hospital in 1965. A five-story, modern facility with 285 beds, Darnall did not have large wards as had been the case previously; in the new facility, the largest ward contained only six beds, and most had only four. Included in it were Red Cross offices, a chapel, a library, a post exchange, a coffee shop, a barber shop, and a dining room. It was located away from noisy parts of the post, yet was close to troop and dependent housing areas. After it was built in 1965, the post hospital gradually would be enlarged as would dental facilities on post.[41]

Religious services for the men on the post were provided by Army chaplains when the first troops arrived there in 1942, and soon chapels were constructed at several locations. These were temporary structures which proved inadequate to the needs of the modern Army, and a program to construct permanent chapels began in the 1950s. Thirty years later the post has 18 chapels convenient to both troops and to dependent housing areas. Serving in these are dozens of Army chaplains representing Catholic, Protestant, and Jewish faiths. Those wanting instruction in any religious faith can get it at the Religious Education Center, while the Fort Hood Marriage and Family Clinic is sponsored by the chaplains at the post to help soldiers and their dependents in times of family crisis.[42]

During World War II and in the years that followed, the officers and soldiers at Fort Hood could avail themselves of all the usual types of after-hours entertainment—and some not so usual. The number of name entertainers coming to Fort Hood under the auspices of the USO slowed dramatically with the end of World War II, but occasionally there would be a visit by someone whose name was well known. For example, in 1966 motion picture star Burt Lancaster made a quick visit to the post to see his son, Jim, then a 19-year-old recruit undergoing basic training. Another entertainer who came to Fort Hood was singer and motion picture star Pat Boone, but his visit in 1971 was to witness for his Christian beliefs, not to entertain troops. And sports figures continued to visit the post, men such as Willie Davis, a great defensive end for the Green Bay Packers; he was at Hood in June of 1966, just after his team had won the Super Bowl the year before, to show films of the 1965 grid season at service clubs and sports facilities.[43]

The celebrity who caused Army officials the greatest headache was at Fort Hood not as an entertainer nor as the holder of a high political office nor yet as a sports hero, but rather as a light truck driver in a tank unit of the 2nd Armored Division. On March 28, 1958, Elvis Presley, whose gyrations and singing style had caused pandemonium among teens during the previous three years, arrived on post. A pop culture figure whose incredible popularity defied interpretation, Presley was drafted into the Army and underwent basic training at Fort Chaffee, Arkansas. After he completed basic, officials at that post heaved a sigh of relief as the rock and roll star departed for Central Texas aboard an Army bus with other trainees.

His arrival could not be kept routine, so a press conference was arranged for radio and newspaper reporters who clamored to cover the event. When Presley came off the Army bus at 5:00 p.m. that day, reporters surged forward to shove microphones at him and shout their questions. Eventually Army public information officers were able to restore order, and they issued an announcement which stated that after this initial press conference, "Pvt. Presley will be treated exactly as all trainees are treated. Nothing is to interfere with his training while he is at Ft. Hood."[44]

Newsmen respected the Army's wishes, and Presley, while on the post, was secure from shouted questions by prying reporters and the cameras of photographers. For the months he was at Fort Hood, post switchboard operators learned to intercept the telephone calls that came from Presley fans from across the United States and foreign countries, and every day three or four bags of mail were delivered to his barracks.[45]

There were problems outside Fort Hood caused by Presley's presence. After his initial eight weeks of training, followed by a two-week leave during which he went to Memphis, Presley returned to Central Texas and rented a house for his parents on Oak Hill Drive. After hours at the post he would leave the base by chauffeur-driven limousine and stay at this house until he was due back at the base at 11:00 p.m. each evening. Soon his parents' yard was filled with teen-age girls waiting for the singer to arrive, and at sight of his limousine they would begin screaming and shrieking. Presley eventually began to get out of his limousine on Highway 190, climb the embankment, and go through back yards to reach the back door of his parents' home. As one neighbor commented, "We just always felt so sorry for him. He was always hounded."

While Presley was in Central Texas, he had a chauffeured limousine for his parents' use, but personally he drove a small, inauspicious car when running errands in town. Yet wherever he went, he had little privacy. For example, the First National Bank of Killeen had a walk-up sidewalk teller's window, and Presley would come there to do his banking business. When he parked and walked up to the window, a crowd would gather around him outside, and bank president Roy Smith would become aware of Presley's presence because all his tellers would gather at the sidewalk window.[46]

Sergeant First Class William C. Fraley, Presley's platoon sergeant in Company A, 37th Armor, later said that the trouble he had while the singer was in his unit "wasn't his [Presley's] fault. It was caused by the people who came to see him." Fraley recalled that Presley was "above average" as a trainee, that he was "a good soldier," and that he was "a real fine fellow."

An official letter was sent from officials at Fort Hood to the port of embarkation when Presley departed on September 29, 1958, for duty in Germany after 25 weeks in Central Texas; this warned Public Information officers at the port of embarkation to expect a storm of reporters coming there to cover the event. This letter said that the singer had "showed outstanding leadership traits from the start, and a fine attitude toward his service obligation." When Presley departed for Europe, one witness was reported to have said of him, as could have been said of every other young man finishing his training at Fort Hood, "Well, he's a soldier now."[47]

Just as the training and recreational facilities and activities at Fort Hood changed in the years following World War II, so also did living conditions on the post as the Army sought to make career service more attractive. In 1970-1971, for example, travel restrictions for soldiers were eased, and bed checks were eliminated except for those undergoing punishment. At the same time, on orders from Army Chief of Staff General William C. Westmoreland, mess halls began serving beer and short order foods in addition to traditional full meals; soldiers could get a hamburger and beer for lunch or dinner rather than the usual Army fare at Fort Hood mess halls.[48]

During the war in Vietnam the word "coffeehouse" entered the popular vocabulary as a meeting place for students and "hippies," and some young soldiers at Fort Hood, when off post, were attracted to them. In fact, officials at Fort Hood grew concerned that some of these coffeehouses in Killeen were being used to recruit soldiers to the antiwar movement. In response to this, chaplains at the post planned a coffeehouse of their own. Partitions were torn out of Building 912, creating a large room filled with tables featuring candle light, and on the walls were paintings by post artists. One 8 x 12 foot painting was used as a backdrop for the stage. Named the Woodshed Coffeehouse, it immediately had standing-room-only crowds. Open from 7:00 to 11:00 p.m. on Tuesdays and Thursdays, the Woodshed, like other coffeehouses, featured folk singers who would render songs requested by members of the audience, who often were asked to join in the singing. Later the name was changed to the Dialogue Coffeehouse, reflecting its changing nature; it became a place where serious discussions were held as positions were taken and defended, and the pros and cons of major events of the day were argued. Still later, in a different building, there would be a Cabaret Music Hall for those who wanted this type of entertainment.[49]

Riding horseback was both a Texas tradition and a part of the Army's heritage, and the two came together after the 1st Cavalry was ordered to Fort Hood and the Horse Platoon was formed. Actually such a unit had been proposed even before the 1st Cavalry arrived. In 1970 Lieutenant Sam Dack of the 2nd Armored, who owned a horse he kept off-post, decided it would be a colorful idea to have a cavalry color guard. First he convinced his commanding general the idea had merit, then the commanding general of III Corps, and finally General Bruce Palmer, the Vice Chief of Staff for the United States Army. However, money to finance such a unit could not be found. Then in 1971 Lieutenant General Seneff, then III Corps commander, decided that the unit could be justified on the basis of the interest it would stir in the Army, especially after it was announced that the 1st Cavalry was coming to Fort Hood. Construction began in December on the first 16 stalls, and the first horses arrived in February and March of 1972. A platoon then was organized with eight volunteers, soldiers who would use the exact equipment and follow the same drills as had been used in the horse cavalry. Later the number of men and horses in the unit grew toward 20.

Their first show was at Tulsa, Oklahoma, and was a great success. The reputation of this unit quickly spread, and soon the First Cavalry Horse Platoon became a popular attraction at area rodeos, parades, the Texas State Fair—even in distant states such as California, New Mexico, Arizona, Arkansas, Kansas, and Missouri. Part of the standard contract signed by the Horse Platoon and those who wanted it to perform was that no admission could be charged on the sole basis of the Horse Platoon's performance. The officer in charge of the unit in 1973 concluded that it "has done a tremendous amount to re-establish the image of the Army here in the Southwest."[50]

Another sign of changing times was the new name given the old Special Services Branch: the Morale Support Activities Division. Morale Support Activities showed its willingness to encourage the formation of new clubs and to support new activities when a sufficient number of soldiers at the post indicated an interest. For example, under the auspices of Morale Support Activities, a Fort Hood Dirt Riders Club was organized, and it built and operated a motocross trail on which motorcycle dirt riders could compete. Similarly, a Fort Hood Dragway was opened on Railhead Drive beside Prichard Stadium;

drag races at this facility were supervised by professional crews using electronic lapse timing and signal equipment. For yet others there was the Sports Car Association which tried to host some type of event every other weekend. And for youngsters–and some not so young–there was Go-Kart riding at Sadowski Parade Ground. Those owning their own Karts could drive them, while those without could rent Karts.[51]

A longstanding form of recreation at Fort Hood was travel in tour groups to places of entertainment, such as Six Flags Over Texas in Arlington, to historic sites, such as the Alamo at San Antonio, or to sporting events, such as Southwest Conference football games. Miss Adele A. Zukas, post service clubs director, pushed these tours in the 1950s and 1960s and fought for reduced rates for service men and women. By the 1970s there was a gradual change in the type of sporting event that soldiers wanted to see during tours organized by Morale Support Activities; increasingly it was professional football in Dallas or Houston or big league baseball at Arlington Stadium or the Astrodome. By the 1980s, professional basketball was a major attraction on the sporting scene, and tour buses would leave for Dallas, Houston, or San Antonio for these events. And by the 1980s old-timers could only shake their heads in wonder at tours organized to take soldiers and their dependents to Durant, Oklahoma, where they could gamble at a giant bingo palace built and operated by the Choctaws.[52]

The soldiers who came to Fort Hood in the 1980s had grown up playing electronic games at video arcades in shopping malls, games that frequently featured knights from the medieval period on their crusades. This gave rise to a phenomenon on university campuses across the nation known as the Medieval Fair, and when a sufficient number of soldiers at Fort Hood formed a Society for Creative Anachronism and expressed an interest in such an activity, Morale Support Activities listened. The first Medieval Fair was staged in 1983, and soon it developed into an elaborate celebration of what the program in 1985 termed a "time of romance and splendor." Unusual games at the Fair in 1985, staged at West Fort Hood, included Jacob's Ladder, King of the Log, and Hunker Houser. Another activity called "smooshing" involved teams of four or five tied to long 2-by-4s that then tried to run an obstacle course. Members of the Society for Creative Anachronism dressed in knights' costumes and staged mock combat between themselves, while wandering minstrels entertained everyone with music. Booths featured arts and crafts for sale, while the Fort Hood Community Theater performed "The Lion in Winter."[53]

By the 1980s Morale Support Activities could brag that under its auspices there were more than 250 different types of recreational and sports activities underway at Fort Hood. These ranged from the usual baseball leagues in summer to some 30 tournaments annually through its Sports Branch. Whatever a soldier wanted in his or her off-duty time, Morale Support would try to provide it on base–from completing a high school or college diploma to jousting in a medieval tournament. Meanwhile, Killeen had grown to approximately 70,000 residents, and soldiers from the post could shop in modern air-conditioned stores carrying the latest goods, bowl in local bowling alleys featuring the latest equipment, go to movies at theaters featuring several screens, skate at local rinks, or just hang out in the food court at the local mall. A four-lane access-controlled Highway 190 provided easy access to nearby Interstate 35 which would carry them to Temple in just half an hour or in about an hour to Austin, grown to 600,000 and able to provide all the recreational facilities of a big city. The soldiers at Fort Hood no longer were isolated in rural Texas.

# Chapter Nine

# Friendship
# and Mutual Support

FORT Hood was born in a time of American desperation. Prior to the official dedication of the post in September of 1942, the United States had suffered the humiliation of Pearl Harbor and the fall of the Philippines. During this same year, however, American Naval forces had fought the battles of the Coral Sea and Midway, and Marines had begun the assault on Guadalcanal. Less than two months after the dedication of the fort, the Army would make landings on the coast of North Africa, and the tide of battle would begin to change. Almost all Americans were united by this conflict, and thus support for Fort Hood, its men, and its mission was virtually unanimous in Central Texas. On the post itself, there were far-sighted commanders who understood that this support could slip away if not cultivated properly, especially when the war ended and the sense of national urgency passed. Yet with or without widespread public support, Fort Hood would bring dramatic change to more of Central Texas than just what happened within its 217,000-acre confines.

The most immediate and obvious impact of Fort Hood was on the towns surrounding it. Prior to 1942 and the creation of the post, Bell and Coryell counties had largely been rural and agricultural. There were few towns of any size in either county, Temple the largest at 15,000 and Belton second followed by Gatesville. Both Killeen and Copperas Cove were little more than villages, and other towns that would grow up in the area were nonexistent at that time. Underpinning the local economy was row-crop farming and hardscrabble ranching. Each spring area farmers secured credit at area banks and stores for seed, food and clothing, and then everyone–townspeople and farmers alike–prayed for good weather and good prices. When the cotton was harvested, ginned, and sold or cattle were rounded up and sold to be slaughtered, farmers and ranchers settled their accounts for the year and hoped they had not gone farther in debt.

Although it was apparent only to a few far-sighted Central Texans, this old way of life already was dead when World War II began. The Great Depression of the 1930s along with mechanization had already begun a dramatic transition that spelled doom for those operating small farms. The change was apparent in places like Copperas Cove, which lost population between 1930 and 1940. Towns all over Texas found themselves with two alternatives–they could shrivel up and die, or they could join the cutthroat, dog-eat-dog competition for industry, any kind of industry, to keep young people from fleeing to big cities where they might find employment.

All this changed in an instant in Central Texas in the spring of 1942 when the government began taking land for Fort Hood. Approximately half of Killeen's trade area was bought, and 300 families were moved. Some local merchants hoped that a new market had been created, one not tied to the weather and the price of cotton and cattle. Yet the change seemed a disaster to those farmers and merchants tied to the 160,000 acres that became the original post. Most of the farmers moved elsewhere and used the money eventually paid them to start over. Implement dealers in town along with the operator of the public scales and those who owned cotton gins, seed houses, mills, and corn shellers had to find new ways to make a living.[1]

Growing out of the old Killeen, population 1,263 in the census of 1940 and little changed by 1942, was what one journalist correctly called "the city Hitler built." By the late 1980s Killeen had an estimated 70,000 people[2], making it easily the largest city in Bell County and the area immediately around Fort Hood. Two-thirds and more of this population consisted of military personnel and their dependents, while 95 percent of the business in many stores in town is done with military people. The local school district has received tens of thousands of dollars in federal funds to help cope with the growth, just as federal dollars helped build streets and improve the water and sewer districts. One of Killeen's biggest industries has been building houses and apartments for these soldiers, the thousands of civilian employees, and their families to occupy, and facilities had to be built in which they could shop. In 1970 the Mid-Town Mall opened, an indoor wonder that drew shoppers to its air-conditioned comfort. Then in 1981 Killeen Mall opened; much larger, featuring modern department stores as anchors, it quickly became the shopping center for Killeen, while the old downtown area deteriorated badly.[3]

Killeen also has become home to a significant international community. The census of 1940 listed only six "foreign-born" residents, but by the 1980s those born outside the United States comprised approximately 10 percent of the population. Koreans came to the town in significant numbers in the early 1950s, followed by a number of German war brides returning with soldiers involved in Operation Gyroscope in 1957 and since that time. Then beginning in the early 1970s came a wave of Vietnamese refugees seeking opportunity, and Killeen began to take on a cosmopolitan air with restaurants serving dishes containing things that old-timers thought inedible. The census of 1940 had a zero under the classification for black Americans, and that likewise has changed as both the Army and Killeen integrated in the 1950s. Today blacks comprise about the same percentage of the population in Killeen as they do in the United States as a whole.

Killeen indeed has changed from what one soldier in 1943 called "a little cowboy town," adding, "You couldn't walk too fast [through Killeen] or else you would be out of town." At that time there were only two saloons in Killeen, and both preferred not to cater to military personnel. Only a few soldiers stopping in for a drink meant that the entire supply would be consumed, and there would be none left for locals. Forty years later a Killeen businessman, asked about the noise of helicopters and cannon firing on the nearby ranges, noted the large amount of money spent in Killeen by soldiers and added, "I can put up with all the helicopters and loud explosions for that kind of [financial] boost."[4]

By the late 1980s Killeen had a major suburb immediately adjacent to it on the east. This totally new town, two miles east of Killeen when it started, was located on what had been a hog farm owned by Pinckney R. Cox and Harley Kern. A water district was incorporated in 1955, and two years later Cox began subdividing and selling lots. In September of 1960 those who had built homes circulated a petition calling for incorporation of what they called Harker Heights, and the vote was favorable. Three years later Harker Heights officially became a city, and in the next two decades it grew rapidly as a bedroom community for Fort Hood. On July 1, 1984, its population was 8,444.[5] Almost immediately adjacent to Harker Heights on its east, but not a suburb to it, is Nolanville with its population of 1,726. This was a community dating from the 1850s but which never grew to any size until the coming of the Army in 1942.[6]

Likewise booming because of Fort Hood was Copperas Cove, located just west of Killeen on Highway 190 in Coryell County. In 1940 this was a community of only 356 people, a decline in numbers from the previous census because Farm-To-Market roads and automobilies allowed area residents to speed into bigger towns to make their purchases. When the Census Bureau released its revised estimates of population for July 1, 1984, Copperas Cove had grown to 21,097, making it the largest city in Coryell County. In addition to providing housing and shopping facilities for many of Fort Hood's military personnel and civilian employees, especially those at West Fort Hood, Copperas Cove also had attracted some manufacturing.

A major factor in the growth of all three of these towns came in 1971 when Temple publisher Frank Mayborn was able to win a designation for what officially was called the Killeen-Temple Standard Metropolitan Statistical Area (SMSA). This was a designation awarded by the Federal Office of Management and Budget; a necessary factor in being designated an SMSA was a contiguous metropolitan population of 50,000 or more. This designation had emerged in the late 1930s, and three decades later it had grown to have great significance. Mayborn, as he tried to bring industry to his hometown, found that business and industrial leaders shied away when they found that Temple was not an SMSA. If he could gain that designation, Temple would be included in directories used by businesses thinking about relocating, and this would make Temple eligible for many additional types of federal grants and loans.

However, Mayborn knew that a population of 50,000 was years away for Temple. Even if Temple and Belton were considered contiguous, they would not reach a joint population of 50,000 until the 1980s. What he needed, Mayborn concluded, was a slight change in the definition of an SMSA. He decided that the Office of Management and Budget should consider Temple, Belton, Harker Heights, Killeen, and Copperas Cove, along with other towns in between, as contiguous, making a "Killeen-Temple SMSA" of more than 150,000 people. In 1968 he organized a committee to pursue this goal, and in 1971 Secretary of Commerce Maurice Stans informed Mayborn that a change in the rules of what constituted an SMSA had been made and that the Killeen-Temple SMSA had been approved.[7]

Almost immediately builders in Killeen and Copperas Cove, where a housing shortage had existed for years, were able to get loans and begin erecting large blocks of apartment houses. Also, this enabled chamber of commerce officials in both cities to woo and win industrial relocations in their communities. As Killeen's historian, Gra'Delle Duncan, noted, this designation as an SMSA was "like being tapped with a magic wand."[8]

Although located farther from Fort Hood than Killeen, Copperas Cove, and Harker Heights, Temple likewise profited from this large Army base to its west, although to a much lesser extent. There were some soldiers who preferred that their families not live in the immediate vicinity of the post, and they would rent apartments and homes in Temple. Moreover, many of them shopped in Temple, at least until the modern Killeen Mall opened in 1981. By the census of July 1, 1984, Temple had become the second-largest city in Bell County, behind the booming Killeen, but still could count 45,044 residents.[9]

Not growing at the same pace as other cities in the vicinity of Fort Hood was Gatesville, the seat of Coryell County. From 1942, when it numbered approximately 3,500 residents, Gatesville by July 1, 1984, had reached only 6,931,[10] making it second in size to Copperas Cove in Coryell County. Gatesville benefitted economically from the post only during summer months when Army Reservists and National Guardsmen came to North Fort Hood to train, but because the town was small most of them drove past it to Temple or Waco to spend their off-duty time and dollars. Gatesville's economic underpinning would not be the Army but rather prisons operated by the Texas Department of Corrections.

Almost from the founding of Fort Hood, one problem confronting commanding officers at Fort Hood has been the so-called "brass pickers," thought to be headquartered in Gatesville. These were civilians who illegally went–and still go–onto the military reservation to pick up discarded brass shell casings. These can be sold for scrap metal at a good price. However, these brass pickers, called the "Gatesville Gang" by some military officials, endanger themselves by going out onto the firing ranges to pick up fragments of exploded shells–and even to take unexploded shells. In so doing, they endanger themselves, just as they constitute a major danger as they take their booty through Gatesville and other towns. And more sophisticated thieves in one night have rolled up a mile or two of telephone or electric wire to be sold for its copper or aluminum, thereby disrupting activities on the post. Still other civilians in the area have come onto the range to rustle the cattle grazing on the post.[11]

By the mid-1970s it had become obvious to almost everyone in Killeen, Copperas Cove, and Harker Heights that their economic prosperity depended on the military. Thus when Army officials decided they needed more land, city fathers, chamber of commerce officials, and civic clubs in these towns were unanimous in their support. However, in Gatesville there was no enthusiasm about the proposed expansion of the post. The "Our Land, Our Lives" organization that fought this expansion was centered in Gatesville, and it battled the Army's effort to expand the post to a standstill (see Chapter Seven). During World War II the Army found Central Texans more than cooperative and ready in all instances to assist in every way possible in keeping relations between the troops at Fort Hood and their civilian neighbors on a happy plane. However, when the fighting ended in 1945, some civilians no longer were willing to overlook sources of friction. Except in time of war, many Americans traditionally have had an anti-military bias.

Late in 1946 officials in the Pentagon realized that some formal mechanism was needed to promote harmony between civilians and military personnel at Army bases in the United States, and orders were issued that in each military district the commanding officer would form an Army Advisory Committee. Early in 1947, General J.M. Wainwright, commander of the 4th Army, complied with this directive. His first move was to seek the names of community leaders near each major Army post in his command and ask them if they would be willing to serve on an Army Advisory Committee. After receiving favorable responses from most of those he asked to serve, he issued an order to his post commanders which stated:

> *It is of the utmost importance that Army Advisory Committees be organized promptly in order to promote good-will [sic] between the Fourth Army and communities in this Area. Community relations are becoming increasingly important to the entire Army, particularly since the expiration of the Selective Service Act.*[12]

Accompanying this order was a "Recommended Program Outlining the Organization, Missions, Functions and Procedures" for these committees that bluntly stated their purpose:

> *(1) Reporting those things which hamper our Army Policy.*
> *2) Assisting in the correction of adverse conditions through bringing to light underlying causes and making the correct facts known.*
> *(3) Advising the Army on all community attitudes which are based on adverse reaction to our National Defense policies.*
> *(4) Providing channels for the dissemination of information and policies of the Army in a manner which the public will understand.*[13]

Elected chairman for the Advisory Committee for Fort Hood was Frank Mayborn, publisher of the *Temple Daily Telegram*, and he looked for leaders in other towns around Fort Hood to help with this effort. In Killeen, that man was Roy Smith.

After working in banking and as a bank examiner for the Federal Reserve Bank in Dallas, then serving in the finance division of the Navy, Smith arrived in Killeen in 1946 as owner of the First National Bank. He had heard that people in Killeen did not like the military, and as a signal that he would work for change he arrived in the little town wearing his Navy uniform. "I came knowing this was a military town and that we had to depend on the military for our business," he later said. Thus when he was approached to join the Military Affairs Committee, he gladly joined.

Just after Smith arrived in Killeen, he had lunch with Frank Mayborn, and they agreed that local squabbles should be put behind them
in order for all towns in the area to grow. As Smith recalled their conversation, they agreed that it would be to the benefit of all area civilians
to work together and help Camp Hood grow and become permanent.
If that happened, the two men said, there would be opportunity for
everyone to prosper along with the Army. Thus Smith worked with
Frank Mayborn, and they were joined by Roy Sandeford of Belton, Ed
Rhode of Copperas Cove, and other area leaders. In addition, Frank
Mayborn knew exactly the person to call when special help was needed.
As Roy Smith recalled, "Mr. Mayborn knew everybody. He knew
whose button to push. And he pushed them. Many times he would call
me and say, 'Roy, so and so can be a big help.'" The Military Affairs
Committee had frequent meetings, usually once a quarter, and it worked
with Fort Hood personnel to keep relations between civilians and
soldiers harmonious.

One of the first areas addressed by this committee was recreation
for off-duty soldiers, but the major problem across the years was
housing. Always there was the need for more and better housing at
reasonable prices for soldiers and their families. Each year the commanding general would have members of his staff brief the Military
Affairs Committee about the amount of dollars in the federal budget
for Fort Hood. Then there would be exhortations by the general and
his staff for the civilians to persuade local utilities to lower the deposits
required of soldiers to get service turned on, as well as to get better
treatment of military personnel in business establishments in Killeen
and surrounding towns.[14]

By the time of the Korean War, this first civilian advisory committee
had lapsed into inactivity, although Mayborn continued to give public
relations advice and assistance to the commander of Fort Hood during
this period. Moreover, he, Roy Smith, and others who had joined the
Military Affairs Committee in 1947 were instrumental in helping the
Army acquire additional land in 1953-1954 and achieve other Army
goals in the area.[15]

Not until 1963 was a new Civilian Advisory Committee for Fort
Hood formed, this one by Lieutenant General T.W. Dunn. It consisted
of local civic leaders, most of them the same as had been on the

previous committee, and staff officers who met quarterly with General Dunn "to discuss the handling of personnel problems, housing facilities, traffic violations in the different areas, and any other subject that should be resolved with the civilian communities." This would promote "continued firm, friendly, and just relationships." A formal constitution was drafted for this committee, which continued in effect after General Dunn was replaced by Lieutenant General Harvey Fischer and he in turn by Lieutenant General Ralph E. Haines.[16]

Great social changes took place in Central Texas during the 1950s and 1960s, changes which had a dramatic impact on both civilians and soldiers. For example, on the agenda of the meeting of the Civilian Advisory Committee on September 19, 1963, were such topics as integration of area schools, integration of area recreational facilities, "equality of treatment and opportunity for Negro military personnel," and the local housing situation for black soldiers.[17] Other topics covered across the years involved everything from upcoming maneuvers to local highway needs, from flooding of local creeks to the abuses of slum lords, from opportunities for civilian employment at the post to coming construction projects, from coordination of fund-raising efforts on behalf of Community Chest (United Fund) organizations to plans for Armed Forces Day activities.[18]

When General Haines departed Fort Hood to become Vice Chief of Staff of the Army, he disbanded the Civilian Advisory Committee in order that his successor could appoint his own body. Lieutenant General George R. Mather did name a new committee, as did subsequent commanders of III Corps and Fort Hood. Some of them had regular meetings with this body, while others met only infrequently with it. The name of the group changed from Army Advisory Committee to Civilian Advisory Committee, but always the intent was the same: to promote harmonious relations between Army personnel and the surrounding civilian communities.

General Crosbie E. Saint later commented that he never saw his Civilian Advisory Committee as a "puppet," but rather as a "two-way street. I would tell them the things we intended to do, things not yet announced, and then say, 'What kind of questions have you got?' And they'd ask all the hard ones." Crosbie's attitude in these sessions was, "I won't get mad if you won't get mad." His attitude always was, "You guys tell me why I shouldn't do this, why this is not good for the soldiers or good for the town." At other times he would say to them that the Army was a security company and the stockholders were the public; thus the Civilian Advisory Committee "ought to have a say in what we are doing." In short, his goal, like that of other commanding generals, was "to make them part of the solution." In discussing his relationship with his Civilian Advisory Committee, General Richard Graves expressed the same thought but in different words: "We're trying for fairness on both sides, making sure that soldiers are treated with fairness and that they treat the business people right."[19]

Likewise promoting harmony and understanding between soldiers and civilians in Central Texas were chambers of commerce in every nearby town. Each had a committee, whether named "Military Affairs," "Military Relations," or "Military Activities," whose task it was to promote goodwill on both sides. Moreover, it was these committees which alerted their respective bodies when political action was needed. For example, when Operation Sagebrush was announced in 1955, with Army threats to close Fort Hood and move all the troops there to Camp Polk, Louisiana, there was a howl of protest from every chamber of commerce in the area, all of them trying to bring congressional pressure by letter, telegram, and delegation. Each year at appropriations time, these same committees worked to promote increases in the annual budget, both for the Army and for military construction. Killeen was not alone in recognizing that "What was good for the Army was good for the local economy. " What was said of this community in 1962 could equally have been said about other towns close to the post; that year an editorial in the *Killeen Daily Herald* stated the case succinctly in recalling the old days when agriculture began to die and, along with it, rural towns in Central Texas:

> *Killeen was in a unique position. It had Fort Hood.*
> *Every progressive community is interested in economic diver-*
> *sification and naturally Killeen would look kindly toward more*
> *industry. But the city's major economic bulwark is Fort Hood*
> *and because of this our industrial foundation doesn't have to*
> *mortgage the city's soul to save its economic life.*
> *So—how does such a community as ours say thank you to Fort*

*Hood? The answer is very simple.*

*We first recognize the fact that our growth–among the greatest of any non-suburban city in Texas–is the direct result of the presence of Fort Hood. Then, we direct all our efforts to 100 per cent co-operation with this font from which our blessings flow.*[20]

Thus it was in the interest of both townspeople and Army officials to promote harmonious relations between the two sides and to work to ease tensions as they arose. Assisting greatly in this effort was retired Brigadier General Frank Norvell, who in 1964 became City Manager of Killeen, a position he held for many years. A constant source of friction for him was Avenue D, a street in Killeen where there were merchants catering to the baser needs of soldiers. Army officials complained and declared certain businesses off limits to soldiers, and the city fathers of Killeen worked within the law to try to close the worst offenders. For many years the city police patrolled the area in company with MPs, there with only the legal authority to "assist" the police. By the early 1980s, as General Cavazos noted, "There was a clean-up of Avenue D, but it never was cleared up entirely."[21]

Another source of difficulty was landlords in Killeen who were trying to "get every cent they could out of the troops" for quarters that were little more than slums. The Killeen Chamber of Commerce worked hard to persuade local landlords to keep up their rental properties and to make them available at reasonable rates. Perhaps even more a cause of complaints from soldiers at Fort Hood were some used car dealers in surrounding towns who specialized in high pressure salesmanship of junky cars that seemed to stop running the minute they were driven off a lot. When General Beverley Powell retired from the Army, he became associated with the Fort Hood National Bank, and as a member of the Killeen Chamber of Commerce he visited a number of these used car dealers to talk with them. "To my surprise," he later commented, "the worst used car dealers, the ones causing the most trouble, were retired non-commissioned officers."[22]

Another duty of chamber of commerce committees, whether at Killeen, Copperas Cove, Belton, Temple, or Harker Heights, was to seek out those Army personnel who were retiring and to sell them on staying in Central Texas. Gradually there grew in every town in the area a substantial number of retired Army officers and men, so many that in September of 1965 the State of Texas issued a charter to a group in Killeen known as the Organization of Retired Military (ORM). Soon the group spread to other towns in the area, then in the region, and finally across the nation, encouraging military retirees to register and vote, to participate in civic programs in their community, and to lobby for military preparedness and veterans' rights.[23]

Likewise seeking to support the Army has been the area chapter of the Association of the United States Army (AUSA). Started in the mid-1950s, this organization admitted both civilian and military members in what was described as a voluntary, educational, nonprofit organization of American citizens who manifest their interest in a strong United States Army by

> *actively supporting an organization established to contribute its full resources to advance the security of the United States. Its purpose is to foster, advocate and support the legitimate role of the United States Army and all of its components as an integral part of a sound national defense for our country.*[24]

The Central Texas chapter of this group was organized on January 16, 1957, with Brigadier General R.H. del Mar as president.

By 1966 the Fort Hood chapter had a membership of more than 4,000 drawn from seven local communities and from every unit on the post. Three times a year they gathered, usually at the Fort Hood NCO Club, and each year they sent a large delegation to the annual national meeting in Washington, D.C. The Fort Hood AUSA chapter also promoted patriotic observance of national holidays, and a special goal was establishment of a museum at Fort Hood. The Fort Hood chapter received national attention when one of its founding members, Frank W. Mayborn, was given a Certificate of Achievement at the annual meeting in 1969 for promoting excellent relations between the Army and the people of Central Texas.[25] Ten years later, in 1979, Mayborn again was honored by the AUSA, this time with its General Creighton W. Abrams Medal for his "significant contributions to the U.S. Army over an extended period."[26]

Yet the relationship between military personnel at Fort Hood and area civilians has been far from one-sided. As the *Killeen Daily Herald* noted in an editorial on the occasion of the post's twenty-fifth anniversary, "Our civil-military relationship, in fact, has become very special [with an] atmosphere of friendship and mutual support."[27] Always there was someone from Fort Hood when a speaker was needed for a luncheon program; always there was a division band available for Christmas parades or summer rodeo festivities. Every year tens of thousands of dollars were collected for the Community Chest (United Fund) for Killeen. It was Engineers from the post who built the first dam to begin the Nolan Creek flood control program, and it was Fort Hood that donated the land on which Central Texas College was built.[28] Yet there was more, much more, that soldiers from Fort Hood did not only for Central Texas but also for the entire state and region.

One of the first major disasters in which personnel from Fort Hood aided civilians was the explosion of the *S.S. Grandcamp* and the *S.S. Flyer* at Texas City, Texas, in 1947. More than 500 people died, and the city was left stunned at what had happened. Twenty-five cooks from the 66th Tank Battalion and the 41st Armored Infantry Battalion traveled to Texas City, set up Army mobile kitchens, and fed dazed survivors and tired rescue workers. Also, there were 10 radio operators from the 1st Armored Division in Texas City with military radio sets to provide communications for the city.[29]

Another example of the compassion of Fort Hood soldiers came in the spring of 1953. Shortly after General Bruce Clarke had transferred to command I Corps in Korea, he wrote friends at Fort Hood that local Korean people were "helplessly caught in the war's back-lash" and were suffering bitter hardship during the winter because of poor and inadequate clothing. Quickly some 1,400 pounds of clothing were collected at the post and sent to Korea where General Clarke had it distributed at the village of Posan-ni.[30]

This also was the year of the tornado in Waco. On May 18, 1953, a twister roared through downtown Waco with widespread property damage and loss of life. Within hours there were 200 men and 31 vehicles and pieces of heavy equipment from the 16th Armored Engineer Battalion, 1st Armored Division, in Waco from Fort Hood clearing away the debris. This unit began work at the city square and worked a quadrant bounded by Franklin Avenue, the Brazos River,

Washington Avenue, and Third Street. In this area the Army engineers put 210,000 miles on their vehicles' odometers as they moved 26,000 cubic feet of wreckage and recovered 14 bodies. The men of the 16th worked four straight days, much of it in driving rain, with little or no rest. Also helping at Waco were the Post Engineers, a communications team from the 141st Signal Company, a detachment from the 123rd Ordnance Battalion, a team from the 1st Quartermaster Battalion, and men from Combat Command B of the 1st Armored Division.

That same day of May 18, 1953, another tornado hit downtown San Angelo, Texas, and the Officers' Wives Club of the 4th Tank Battalion gathered three truckloads of food, furniture, and clothing to be sent there.[31]

That same year of 1953 men at Fort Hood helped in another deadly situation. Early that summer two children were killed at Brownwood, Texas, when a 37mm high explosive shell they found detonated. This shell, and many others like it, came from the hills and ranges of nearby Camp Bowie, a post deactivated at the end of World War II. In five days a two-man team from Fort Hood found 225 shells that were supposed to be duds—like the one that had exploded and killed the two children. The year before men from Fort Hood had found and defused 350 of these killers. Brownwood authorities were not alone in calling demolitions experts from Fort Hood whenever some explosive device was found, especially old shells and other forms of war souvenirs, even old blasting caps and other types of explosives having nothing to do with the Army. Calls regularly come to the post from the police in surrounding towns and cities.[32]

Four years later in April, Killeen was hit by a flash flood that killed three people and inundated parts of the city. Troops from Fort Hood aided in the evacuation and rescue work, directed traffic, sandbagged buildings, and rescued many stranded by the rising waters. And when the waters receded, these same troops used bulldozers, dump trucks, and picks and shovels to clear away the debris left behind. A hundred men from the 24th Armored Engineer Battalion along with Company D of the 46th Engineer Battalion were on hand to fill sand bags and stack them around Hillandale Hospital to divert the surging water. Helicopters from the 504th Aviation Company performed reconnaissance work and rescued one person trapped in his car and about to be swept away.

During this catastrophe there were several acts of quiet heroism. For example, a young boy was clinging desperately to the porch of a house surrounded by water. A soldier threw him a rope; then when it was tied securely, the soldier climbed hand-over-hand to the house, put the youngster on his shoulders, and then climbed back across the swirling water to safety. Another family had climbed atop the kitchen table in their home, and the water was almost at table top when soldiers burst into the home to take them to safety.

On May 12, 1957, another flood hit at nearby Lampasas. A wall of water 10 feet high hit the city after levees on Sulphur Creek overflowed, destroying $5 million in property and killing at least five people. Five buildings, including a church, school, and hotel, were destroyed as were 38 homes. Another 48 homes were damaged. At Fort Hood clean gasoline tanks were filled with potable water and rushed to the area along with communications equipment. Engineers from the 46th Engineer Battalion came to help with the cleanup, while other officers and men directed traffic. Left behind in the wake of the flood were tons of debris, spoiled food, and dead animals, and the soldiers used bulldozers, cranes, and shovels to clean the area.[33]

That July of 1954 came a flood in the Rio Grande Valley that swept away bridges at Laredo and Eagle Pass. The Bridge Company of the 16th Engineers, 1st Armored Division, built a treadway bridge between Laredo, Texas, and Nuevo Laredo, Mexico, while another group of Fort Hood engineers replaced a strand in a broken highway bridge between Eagle Pass, Texas, and Piedras Negras, Mexico. Field kitchens and water purification units went from Hood to the two affected areas and helped on both sides of the border.[34]

The Army's help in Central Texas did not always come after a disaster, at least when it came to North Nolan Creek. This stream normally was peaceful and sluggish but after a major rain could jump its banks to threaten property and life–as it did in 1957. In the late 1950s the men of the 46th Engineer Battalion began building dams along North Nolan Creek, a process that continued for years. One dam was dedicated on December 5, 1961, and others had appropriate ceremonies when they were completed.

However, Nolan Creek could not be tamed easily. On September 18, 1964, it jumped its banks in a flash flood that damaged some 52 trailer homes and made 102 families homeless. Five-ton wreckers came from the 2nd Armored Division's Support Command to Killeen to move trailers from along the creek, and cots and blankets were provided for those who were evacuated. Eight months later, on May 17, 1965, 9.5 inches of rain fell in just a short time, and winding Nolan Creek again ravaged through parts of Killeen. Some 250 people had to be evacuated from houses and trailer homes in Killeen, and another 100 homes in low-lying parts of Belton were flooded. There was heavy damage to streets in Killeen, Belton, Nolanville, and Harker Heights, and nine cars of a Santa Fe Railroad train were derailed between Killeen and Nolanville. Army units from Fort Hood again assisted, both in cleaning away the debris and taking care of the homeless.[35]

In 1961 Hurricane Carla ravaged the Texas coast, causing millions of dollars in property and crop damage. The hardest hit area was at Galveston, Freeport, Port Lavaca, Palacios, Corpus Christi, and Houston as well as smaller communities in this area. Once again the troops at Fort Hood swung into action to help clear up the devastation once the storm had passed. On September 9, while the storm was still raging at its height, the 502nd Aviation unit of the 2nd Armored Division began a series of relief flights that would continue without interruption for two weeks. Blankets were flown from North Fort Hood to a refugee center in Houston where thousands had fled from the coastal area. Some of the planes involved in these flights took off and landed in winds gusting to 50 knots. At the same time the men of the 502nd also flew search missions for a private plane that had gone down somewhere between Corpus Christi and College Station.

On September 13, after the storm turned inland, disaster teams left Fort Hood. These were the men of the 501st and 502nd Aviation Company, the 46th Engineer Battalion, the 141st and 142nd Signal Battalions, and the 1st Quartermaster Battalion. During the emergency Army pilots from Fort Hood flew 10,000 pounds of emergency equipment, including serum needed to prevent the spread of disease, into Freeport; they searched for dead and strayed cattle from area ranches; and they took supplies wherever they were needed. Some of the engineers were called on to erect a bridge between Corpus Christi and the University of Corpus Christi, which had been isolated on an island when the regular bridge washed out.[36]

These are but a few of the disasters to which the soldiers of Fort Hood have responded. Whenever there is suffering anywhere within range of the base, the men and women serving at this post have been ready to take their equipment, their knowledge, and their compassion to the troubled area to minimize suffering and speed recovery. A good expample of this was MAST, an acronym for Military Assistance to Safety and Traffic. First authorized by congress in 1970, this program gradually spread as funding was made available, reaching Central Texas in 1972.

Under this program, Army air ambulance helicopters would operate within a 100-mile radius of Fort Hood, not in competition with civilian ambulance service but rather in those instances when a critical time factor was involved and the location of the emergency made the use of a helicopter more feasible than ground transportation. Loaded with medical supplies and a medic and flying at speeds of 120 miles an hour, these helicopters were involved in many unusual situations. For example, it was a MAST helicopter that brought a horseback-riding accident victim out of a remote area near San Antonio. Other MAST evacuees included the victims of many traffic accidents, some skiing accidents, and a few snakebites, even an occasional train wreck.[37]

Other ways whereby soldiers from Fort Hood have helped civilians in times of trouble are many and varied. They and their equipment have been used in "clean up and fix up" days in Killeen, Copperas Cove, and Harker Heights.[38] They have loaded their bulldozers, dump trucks, and heavy earth-moving equipment onto planes and flown to New England to help northeastern states plagued by snowstorms, fighting snowdrifts and ice to aid residents imprisoned by winter storms.[39] And they have used their human energy and their equipment to battle forest and grass fires not only on their own range and in the immediate area, but also in distant parts of the country. For example, in 1988 during the great fire that ravaged Yellowstone National Park, men from Fort Hood were there risking their lives to save this national treasure from greater damage.[40]

Some situations in which the soldiers at Fort Hood have given their help have not invoved an emergency, either real or potential. Rather there have been many times when the men and women on the post wanted to donate their time and labor in order to brighten the lives of youngsters in the region. For example, in April of 1973 a platoon from the 8th Engineer Battalion, 1st Cavalry Division, quietly began work at Camp Tahuaya, one of two camps operated by the Heart O' Texas Council of the Boy Scouts of America. For two months these men labored, removing 1,500 cubic yards of silt from the bed of the camp's small lake to make it usable for canoe and boat training, building a 525-foot culvert to redirect the stream that caused the lake to overflow regularly, and erecting two 20 x 6 foot shower-bathroom facilities. The men of a different platoon of this same engineering battalion worked at Camp Hope near Fort Worth, a facility that provided recreational and rehabilitation opportunities for mentally retarded children. This group renovated existing facilities, built a storage shed, and laid a concrete apron around the camp's swimming pool.[41]

About all that was needed to get the service people at Fort Hood involved in a project was to show that it would benefit youngsters in some way. This is why the gathering of toys at Christmas has been an on-going effort at the post. Each year the drive begins in November to gather toys, and these are distributed in surrounding communities to youngsters who otherwise would not know the joy of the season, most of them never knowing that a nameless soldier from Fort Hood was their Santa Claus.

Frank Mayborn, the civilian most responsible for the location of Fort Hood in Central Texas and who in the late 1940s fought hard to get the post made a permanent Army facility, kept a file showing the economic impact it had on the surrounding area. These figures, updated annually, showed the acreage of the post, the number of men serving there, the number of civilian employees on the post, the number of dependent families on the base and in surrounding towns, and the amount of money coming to Central Texas annually as a result of the post's location.[42] These included the figures released annually by the Public Information Office at the post as well as area chambers of commerce and politicians wanting to take credit for everything good in the region. What these show is that Fort Hood has been a good neighbor. As Mayborn editorialized in 1965 on the occasion of Fort Hood's 23rd anniversary:

*Central Texans know and recognize the need for a fluctuating military population at Fort Hood, and nothing short of complete disarmament in the world—a most unlikely prospect, obviously—can change that.*

*But we have learned to live with this fact, and still remain thankful and proud that this area plays such an important role in the nation's defense establishment. Further, as Central Texas has expanded and progressed in other economic areas, the impact of thinner ranks at Fort Hood is more easily absorbed.*

*So the outlook remains rosy. The tremendous investment in Fort Hood's physical plant will continue, troop strength will grow, and the post will provide more and more jobs for permanent civilian employees.*

*The news is definitely good from our good, good neighbor, Fort Hood.*[43]

Mayborn's words would remain true during the post's second quarter century in Central Texas—Fort Hood indeed has been a good neighbor.

# Chapter Ten

# Toward the 21st Century

FORT Hood has been a primary force in the growth of Central Texas, helping move its surrounding area from a sleepy economic backwater to a vital and growing region. Roy Smith, longtime president and chief executive officer of the First National Bank of Killeen, commented in 1989 that the main reason that city along with Harker Heights and Copperas Cove had grown so tremendously was because they provided "the necessary housing for Fort Hood" and because of Army retirees who had settled in the area. "Industry has been hard to come by" in this part of Central Texas, he acknowledged, because of two major impediments: the transitory nature of much of the work force in the area, and because "we are off the mainstream"; Killeen is 18 miles west of I-35 and has few cars just passing through to bring travelers' dollars to the local economy.[1]

The Army easily can be identified as the major reason Central Texas has grown and prospered, and this prosperity has rippled out across the Lone Star State. As the largest single employer–with the largest payroll–in Texas, Fort Hood has been a stabilizing influence in the economy of a region often suffering from drastic fluctuations in petroleum and agricultural prices. In the summer of 1989, expenditures at Fort Hood were at an annual pace of approximately $1 billion a year. There were 38,991 military personnel at the post along with 14,458 on-post family members, and in surrounding communities were 24,939 retirees and 42,359 off-post military family members.[2]

More important to the United States, however, has been Fort Hood's contribution to the military defense of the United States. What began in World War II at a dark moment in the nation's history as a place to train Tank Destroyers has changed as the nation's needs have changed.

In 1944, for example, part of the post was given over to training replacements for the Infantry and another part to basic training for recruits. With war's end, an armored division was assigned to the post, but the military population declined sharply during America's postwar rush to demobilize. Then in 1950, with the onset of the Korean Conflict, Fort Hood for a time was home to two armored divisions, and III Corps moved its headquarters there.

The late 1950s saw another American effort to demobilize, and Fort Hood again was reduced to being a one-division post. However, early in the 1960s the Cold War caused America's leaders again to make this Central Texas military reservation a two-division post, and since that time it has been the home of armor as well as a place for pioneering the Army of the future. General Douglas MacArthur might well have had Fort Hood in mind in 1963 when he said: "We must hold our minds alert and receptive to the application of unglimpsed methods and weapons. The next war will be won in the future, not the past. We must go on, or we will go under."[3] It would have been easy for III Corps and division commanders at Fort Hood to lose sight of preparation for the future because they lived in a world of constant pressures about preparedness and training as well as in a time of annual threats of budget cuts–and the anti-military attitude prevalent in some circles in the United States.

Fortunately for the nation, Fort Hood for more than 40 years has had commanders who ignored civilian attacks on the military and the austerity forced on them by Congress. They have kept the future needs of the Army in mind at the same time they have been training troops for the present. And always these commanders have been leaders in innovation. General Ralph E. Haines, Jr., had the task of training the Army's first ROAD division (Reorganization Objective Army Divisions) when the 1st Armored was reactivated at Fort Hood in 1962. In 1969, thanks to the foresight of General Beverley E. Powell, the post became home to MASSTER (Mobile Army Sensor System, Texas and Evaluation Resources), a part of the Training and Doctrine Command (TRADOC) at Fort Monroe, Virginia. The men of MASSTER (and its successors, TCATA and then TEXCOM) have been leaders in conceiving and testing new ideas and weapons just as they have been instrumental in making changes in Army organization, weapons, and technology. Another innovation came to Fort Hood in 1971 when the post became home to the Army's first TRICAP (Triple Capacity) Division with the arrival of the 1st Cavalry; this involved a new organization that brought together armor, foot soldiers, and helicopters in one division.

Across the years of Fort Hood's existence, the soldiers training there have used a variety of weapons. World War II saw the M-3 halftrack with its 75mm gun along with the M-10, M-18, and M-36 Tank Destroyers. By the time the 1st AD was reactivated as a ROAD division, the basic weapons were the M-60 tank, the M-113 armored personnel carrier, the UH-1 light helicopter, and the UH-1G attack helicopter. Today's 1st Cavalry and 2nd Armored Divisions use the M-1 Abrams tank, the M-2 Bradley Infantry Fighting Vehicle,the M-3 Scout Vehicle, the UH-60 Blackhawk helicopter, and the AH-64 Apache attack helicopter. As part of the Army's Training and Doctrine Command (TRADOC), Fort Hood's TEXCOM is a vital unit in the Army's "Architect of the Future," working to perfect what is called the AirLand Battle Future.[4]  These are men dedicated to the principle stated a hundred years ago by Philip James Bailey: "It is much less what we do than what we think, which fits us for the future."

Fort Hood, the largest armor base in the United States, does have its limitations. The major one is its size. Ideally the post should be much larger in order to allow maneuvers pitting one division against another as opposed to today's size which allows only brigade-sized maneuvers. In years subsequent to World War II, General Andrew D. Bruce, commander of Camp Hood during its first critical months, expressed his belief on several occasions that the Army should have taken far more land when the reservation was created early in 1942. The dollars paid at that time for a larger post would have been cheaper than "shipping units to the desert [for maneuvers], wearing out equipment in the process and paying claims for damaged land." The post was enlarged in 1953-1954, but subsequent efforts to bring it to a size that would allow division maneuvers were defeated by barrages of protest from local landowners.

Despite any drawbacks present at the post, General Bruce believed that it had great value to the Army. "Those of us who worked with and at Camp Hood," he later would say, "feel that the post contributed to the armored forces by the further development of the Christie tank treads, in the development of high velocity guns, and ammunition, and in many indirect ways."[5] In addition to the Tank Destroyers trained at Camp Hood during the war, thousands of infantrymen were prepared for combat at this Central Texas post, and additional thousands of recruits received their basic training there. Camp Hood, indeed, had helped win the war.

When Germany and Japan surrendered and peace temporarily returned, Camp Hood might well have been closed, as were many other World War II posts opened at the start of that conflict. However, it survived, in large measure, because of the efforts of some civilians in Central Texas who understood the necessities of the political process. Frank Mayborn, joined by civic-minded citizens and politicians from the region, fought long and hard to get Camp Hood transformed into Fort Hood, to get permanent buildings erected, and to have it declared a two-division post.

However, this political battle never could have been won had not high-ranking Army officers been convinced that the Fort Hood military reservation was the best place in the country for training soldiers for combat. In late 1951, when the newly reactivated 1st Armored Division was in training in Central Texas, its troops were inspected by General J. Lawton Collins, Chief of Staff of the Army, and Lieutenant General LeRoy Lutes, commander of the Fourth Army. To an Armistice Day formation, General Lutes said:

> *I am firmly convinced that General Collins has not seen any setup for the fundamental training of the individual as good as you have at Fort Hood. I am convinced that you have the best arrangements for the training of the individual combat soldier that we have in the country.*[6]

This high praise for the Central Texas post has been echoed by almost every commanding general of the post in the years since General Bruce first arrived in 1942. High on the list of reasons why Hood is such a great place for training is its varied terrain. General Robert M. Shoemaker noted this when he said:

*On the west side of the post is a brigade-sized maneuver area*
*in which rolling terrain is characteristic with wooded and open*
*areas, much like in the mountains. This permits military forces*
*to practice using the terrain the same way they would in the great*
*temperate areas of the world, where there usually is rolling ter-*
*rain. This is truer at Fort Hood than at any post I know of in the*
*United States with a size that is adequate for training purposes.*

*On the east side of the post, on the other hand, it is densely*
*wooded over toward Lake Belton. There are ideal areas for train-*
*ing for war in jungles. This closely wooded area does not have*
*the same vegetation as in the jungle, but it presents the same*
*problem militarily.*[7]

Likewise, Fort Hood's climate is such, as Shoemaker and many
others have commented, that "You can plan training 365 days a year
with a certainty that there will be no more than one or two days a year
when you have to just stop and huddle for survival." And Fort Hood
is surrounded by Texans, a people who, for the most part, are old-fash-
ioned patriots who believe in the need for a strong, well-trained defense force. Finally, Hood is sufficiently isolated from large centers of
population that maneuvers, with accompanying noise from cannon,
bombs, airplanes, and helicopters, do not bring a flood of complaints
from civilians to both the Army and politicians.[8]

Fort Hood indeed has advantages in terrain, climate, remoteness
from population centers, and patriotic people in the vicinity. And in its
almost half-century of existence, those advantages have continued
despite dramatic changes in tactics and weapons.

The future doubtless holds yet more change for the Army, but Fort
Hood seems destined to remain the center of the Army's heavy forces.
As the 1980s drew to a close, Army Chief of Staff General Carl E.
Vuono drafted a policy paper entitled "A Strategic Force for the 1990s
and Beyond" predicated on the probability that most American forces
will be brought home to American soil by the mid-1990s because of
a diminished threat from the Soviet Union and reduced budgets. In this
eventuality, the Army still will have to cope with regional instability,
drug trafficking, and terrorism as well as be prepared to defend American
interests around the globe. In this changed world, the Army will need

to be able to respond to any emergency with strength and speed.

As General Vuono envisions this new force, it will consist of three elements: airborne units that can parachute into remote areas; light infantry divisions capable of being taken to these areas and landed at airstrips taken by the paratroops; and heavy (Army) units transported by ship for sustained operations. Airborne units could respond to international crises, Rangers and light infantry could rescue hostages and conduct counterterrorist operations, while Armor and mechanized infantry would continue to be at the center of the Army's plans for defending Europe and for large-scale combat operations. This plan foresees that armored and mechanized infantry divisions would be headquartered at Fort Hood, Texas.[9]

Yet as the Army tries to envision what will be needed in the future, one thing has remained constant in all the years since farms and ranches gave way to a military reservation in Central Texas. In the late 19th century Rudyard Kipling was too narrow when he wrote in *The 'Eathen*, "The backbone of the Army is the Non-commissioned Man!" In the world of the 1990s, the United States Army must still have good NCOs, but also it needs a great officer corps and superbly trained enlisted men who are tightly disciplined and well-equipped, men capable of rapid deployment to any place around the globe. The skills that a soldier needed in the past are still the skills he needs as the United States approaches the 21st century, and these are being taught at Fort Hood, Texas.

# Notes

## Chapter One: *Land and People*

1. William T. Carter Jr., H.G. Lewis, H.W. Hawker, and Hugh L. Bennett, "A Soil Survey of Bell County, Texas," *Report, Bureau of Soils, of the U.S. Department of Agriculture, 1918* (Washington: Government Printing Office, 1919). See also George W. Tyler, *History of Bell County*, ed. by Charles W. Ramsdell (Belton, TX: Dayton Kelley, 1966, facsimile of 1936 original), xii-xviii; Zelma Scott, *A History of Coryell County, Texas* (Austin: Texas State Historical Association, 1965), 3-8.

2. Tyler, *History of Bell County*, xvi-xvii. See also Walter P. Webb, *The Handbook of Texas* (2 vols., Austin: Texas State Historical Association, 1952), I, 142, 418.

3. For details about the prehistory of this region, see S. Alan Skinner, Frederick L. Briuer, George B. Thomas, Ivan Shaw, and Eli Mishuck, *Initial Archaeological Survey, Fort Hood, Texas, Fiscal Year 1978* (Report Submitted to U.S. Army Corps of Engineers by Science Applications, Inc., 1981). See also Scott, *History of Coryell County*, viii.

4. *Ibid.*, 18.

5. *Ibid.*, 19-25; Frank E. Simmons, *History of Coryell County* (Belton, TX: Dayton Kelley, 1965, facsimile of 1936 original), 11-13.

6. Mildred W. Mears, "The Three Forts in Coryell County," *Southwestern Historical Quarterly*, LXVII (July 1963), 2-6; Tyler, *History of Bell County*, 102.

7. Scott, *History of Coryell County*, 9-15.

8. A copy of this act is in Tyler, *History of Bell County*, 107-109.

9. Details of the act creating this county are quoted in Scott, *History of Coryell County*, 34-35.

10. *Ibid.*, 60-62. See also Tyler, *History of Bell County*, 273-178.

11. *Armored Sentinel*, September 21, 1967, p. 15; *Killeen Daily Herald*, September 21, 1967, Section 2, p. 2.

12. *Ibid.*

13. Jim D. Bowmer and Daurice Bowmer, *Folklore of Bell County* (Belton, TX: Privately printed, 1980), Chapter 7.

14. Letter, Jim L. Shirah to Chief, Historical Services Division, Center for Military History, August 12, 1974, in Fort Hood File, Center For Military History, Washington, D.C.

15. Bowmer and Bowmer, *Folklore of Bell County*, Chapter 10.

16. Tyler, *History of Bell County*, 301-304.

17. E.A. Limmer, Jr., ed. and comp., *Story of Bell County, Texas* (2 vols., Austin: Eakin Press, 1988), I, 52-53.

18. Scott, *History of Coryell County*, 155.

19. Limmer, ed., *Story of Bell County*, 42; Tyler, *History of Bell County*, 340.

20. Limmer, ed., *Story of Bell County*, 140-141, 191; Tyler, *History of Bell County*, 340.

21. Coryell County Genealogical Society, *Coryell County, Texas Families, 1854-1985* (Dallas: Taylor Publishing Co., 1986), 45; Scott, *History of Coryell County*, 155.

22. Coryell County Genealogical Society, *Coryell County*, 45, 53-54; Limmer, ed., *Story of Bell County*, 142, 197; Simmons, *History of Coryell County*, 82; Webb, ed., *Handbook of Texas*, I, 418, 676, 957.

23. Scott, *History of Coryell County*, 181-185.

24. For details about this era in Temple and Bell County, see Odie B. Faulk and Laura E. Faulk, *Frank W. Mayborn: A Man Who Made a Difference* (Belton, TX: University of Mary Hardin-Baylor Press, 1989), Chapter Three.

## Chapter Two: *Creation of the Post*

1. Established in 1917, Camp Bullis for a time was the target range and a place for maneuvers for troops from Fort Sam Houston and Camp Travis, both at San Antonio. In 1922 it became part of Fort Sam Houston, although that part of the post continued to be referred to as Camp Bullis. See Walter Prescott Webb, ed., *The Handbook of Texas* (2 vols., Austin: Texas State Historical Association, 1952), I, 279.

2. Interview, Beverley E. Powell with OBF, October 2, 1989, FMC.

3. Russell F. Weigley, *History of the United States Army* (New York: Macmillan Company, 1967), 424-425; R. Ernest Dupuy, *The Compact History of the United States Army* (New York: Hawthorne Books, 1956), 241-251..

4. *Ibid.*, 428-429.

5. Key Personnel Files, History Section, Headquarters, III Corps and Fort Hood, Killeen, Texas; *Killeen Daily Herald*, September 21, 1967, Section 2, p. 13.

6. Emory A. Dunham, *The Tank Destroyer History* (Headquarters, Army Ground Forces, Study No. 29, 1946), 1.

7. *Ibid.*; Christopher R. Gabel, *Seek, Strike, and Destroy: U.S. Army Tank Destroyer Doctrine in World War II* (Fort Leavenworth, KS: Combat Studies Institute, Leavenworth Papers No. 12, 1985), 9; O.F. Marston, "Fast Moving Targets," *Field Artillery Journal*, X (July-August 1940), 264-267.

8. Gabel, *Seek, Strike, and Destroy*, 10-11.

9. *Ibid.*, 6-7; Dunham, *The Tank Destroyer History*, 2-3; John Weeks, *Men Against Tanks: A History of Antitank Warfare* (New York: Mason/Charter, 1975), 96.

10. Gable, *Seek, Strike, and Destroy*, 22; Dunham, *The Tank Destroyer History*, 2-3.

11. *The Armored Sentinel*, September 21, 1967, 17-B; Weigley, *History of the United States Army*, 429.

12. *Killeen Daily Herald*, September 21, 1967, Section 2, p. 13; *The Armored Sentinel*, September 21, 1967, 17-B.

13. *Ibid.*; Dunham, *The Tank Destroyer History*, 4-5.

14. *Ibid.*, 6; Key Personnel Files, History Section, Headquarters, III Corps and Fort Hood, Killeen, Texas.

15. Weigley, *History of the United States Army*, 333-334.

16. *Ibid.*, 419.

17. *Killeen Daily Herald*, September 21, 1967, Section 2, p. 13; *The Armored Sentinel*, September 21, 1967, 13-B; and Weigley, *History of the United States Army*, 431.

18. "Camp Hood, 1940-47" File, History Section, Headquarters, III Corps and Fort Hood, Killeen.

19. For details about Mayborn's life, see Faulk and Faulk, *Frank W. Mayborn*.

20. See "Temple Chamber of Commerce, Industrial Committee, 1940-1941" File, FMC; and "Temple Chamber of Commerce: Magnesium Plant, 1941" File, FMC.

21. *Ibid.*; Frank W. Mayborn, undated oral interview, Tapes 2, FMC; and *Temple Daily Telegram*, June 20, 1981.

22. Frank W. Mayborn, undated oral interview, Tapes 2 and 6, FMC. For details about Oveta Culp Hobby's background and her marriage to William P. Hobby, see *Temple Daily Telegram*, February 24, 1931.

23. Some copies of this bulletin are in "Temple Chamber of Commerce: NATIONAL DEFENSE–GENERAL, 1941-1942" File, Frank W. Mayborn Collection, Mayborn Foundation, Temple, Texas; hereafter cited as FMC.

24. Letter, Frank Mayborn to W.R. Poage, February 14, 1941, in *ibid*.

25. A copy of the brochure prepared for Brownwood is in "TEMPLE

CHAMBER OF COMMERCE: NATIONAL DEFENSE–ARMY CAMP, 1941" File, FMC. See also *Killeen Daily Herald*, September 14, 1942.

26. Letter, A.C. Ater to Frank W. Mayborn, February 15, 1941, in "TEMPLE CHAMBER OF COMMERCE: NATIONAL DEFENSE–ARMY CAMP, 1941" File, FMC.

27. Letter, Frank W. Mayborn to A.C. Ater, March 1, 1941, *Ibid.*

28. See Letter, Frank W. Mayborn to Joe Woods "Re: Army Cantonment South of Gatesville, TX," April 29, 1941, in *ibid.*

29. Letter, W.R. Poage to Frank W. Mayborn, June 7, 1941, in "Temple Chamber of Commerce: NATIONAL DEFENSE–GENERAL, 1941-1942" File, FMC.

30. Letter, Frank W. Mayborn to Don McClellan, June 17, 1941, "TEMPLE CHAMBER OF COMMERCE: NATIONAL DEFENSE–ARMY CAMP, 1941" File, FMC.

31. Letter, Frank W. Mayborn to Mrs. Tom R. Mears [Secretary, Gatesville Chamber of Commerce], July 9, 1941, *ibid.*

32. Scott, *History of Coryell County*, 201.

33. See letter, Will C. Grant to Frank W. Mayborn, October 2, 1941; and letter, Frank W. Mayborn to Clyde A. Northington [Lampasas Chamber of Commerce], October 4, 1941, "TEMPLE CHAMBER OF COMMERCE: NATIONAL DEFENSE–ARMY CAMP, 1941" File, FMC.

34. Frank W. Mayborn, undated oral interview, Tapes 2 and 14, FMC; letter, Frank W. Mayborn to Senator Morris Sheppard, November 27, 1940, in "Temple Chamber of Commerce, National Defense, *Army Camp*" File, FMC; and "Poage Recalls Camp Planning," in Duncan, *Killeen: Tale of Two Cities*, 108.

35. Mayborn later would say, "We in Central Texas wanted to offer what we had to the country, and the notable results of that offer are due in large part to the work of Jim Reinhold." See *Temple Daily Telegram*, December 16, 1950.

36. See *ibid.*, June 20, 1981; *Killeen Daily Herald*, September 21, 1967, Section 2, p. 3, and November 9, 1973. For the history of Killeen, see Gra'Delle Duncan, *Killeen: Tale of Two Cities, 1882-1982* (Austin: Eakin Publications, 1984), and Gra'Delle Duncan and Joe Buckler, *Killeen Area Bicentennial Sketchbook* (Killeen: Commercial Printing Company, 1985).

37. A copy of this telegram is in "Temple Chamber of Commerce: Industrial Committee, 1940-1941" File, FMC. See also Frank W. Mayborn, undated oral interview, Tape 15, FMC.

38. *Temple Daily Telegram*, January 7, 1942, and June 21, 1950. See also "Temple Chamber of Commerce, National Defense, *Hospital*" File, FMC.

39. Frank W. Mayborn, undated oral interview, Tape 15, FMC; *Temple*

*Daily Telegram*, January 14, 1942, June 21, 1950, and November 10, 1972. Letters and telegrams concerning this are in "Temple Chamber of Commerce: Industrial Committee, 1940-1941" File, FMC. See also *Killeen Herald*, January 16, 1942.

## Chapter Three: *Acquiring the Land*

1. Bell County Historical Commission, *Story of Bell County, Texas*," I, 258.

2. Walter R. Humphrey, "Sugar Loaf in Heart of Camp Hood Firing Area, Could Tell Many an Interesting Tale," *Temple Daily Telegram*, March 3, 1942, p. 2.

3. *Killeen Daily Herald*, September 21, 1967, Section 2, p. 2.

4. *Ibid.*; Sylvia A. Edwards, "Land Acquisition in Coryell County, Texas, for the Formation of Camp Hood, 1942-45: A Civilian Perspective" (M.A. thesis, Baylor University, 1988), xiv; *Second War Powers Act, 1942, Statutes At Large*, 56, title II (1942), 177.

5. Richard Morehead, *Dewitt C. Greer: King of the Highway Builders* (Austin: Eakin Press, 1984), 43-49; *Killeen Daily Herald*, September 21, 1967, Section 2, p. 8.

6. War Department General Orders Number 12, March 6, 1942, copy in Fort Hood File, Center for Military History, Washington, D.C. The quarters maintained for visiting dignitaries at Food Hood today is called the John Bell Hood House.

7. Dumas Malone, ed., *Dictionary of American Biography* (11 vols., New York: Charles Scribners' Sons, 1932-1937), V, 193-194. See also *Killeen Daily Herald*, September 16, 1982.

8. J. Aikens, "History of Fort Hood and Local Area" File, History Section, Headquarters, III Corps and Fort Hood, Killeen, Texas, p. 9.

9. Letter, W.R. Poage to Frank Mayborn, February 27, 1942, in "TEMPLE CHAMBER OF COMMERCE: NATIONAL DEFENSE–GENERAL, 1942" File, FMC. Apparently Poage later changed his mind about the impact of the Army's land acquisitions in Central Texas, commenting that he received many complaints on this score, "many of them justified, and that the construction of Camp Hood was the most important event in his district during World War II"; see Edwards, "Land Acquisition in Coryell County, Texas," 9-10, 18.

10. Duncan, *Killeen: A Tale of Two Cities*, 103-104; Oscar Lewis, *On the Edge of the Black Waxy: A Cultural Survey of Bell County, Texas* (St. Louis: Washington University Studies, 1948), 19-20.

11. Aikens, "History of Fort Hood and Local Area," 17. Sylvia A. Edwards, in "Land Acquisition in Coryell County, Texas," claimed there were three suicides as a result of the land acquisitions.

12. Aikens, "History of Fort Hood and Local Area," 17; *Killeen Daily Herald*, September 14, 1962, Section 3, p. 5, and Section 6, p. 6; September 21, 1967; November 9, 1972.

13. Aikens, "History of Fort Hood and Local Area," 17-18; *Killeen Daily Herald*, September 21, 1967, Section 4, p. 6, and September 16, 1982; and "Project FORT HOOD, Central Texas Cattlemen's Association, 1953-1956," Poage Projects, Fort Hood Miscellaneous File, The Congressional Collection, Baylor University, Waco.

14. *Killeen Daily Herald*, September 21, 1967, Section 2, p. 9.

15. *Armored Daily Sentinel*, September 21, 1967, 9-B.

16. Aikens, "History of Fort Hood and Local Area," 27-31; Coryell County Genealogical Society, *Coryell County, Texas, Families*, 25-27.

17. "Camp Hood, 1941-47" File, History Section, Headquarters, III Corps and Fort Hood, Killeen, Texas.

18. Aikens, "History of Fort Hood and Local Area," 9-10; *Killeen Daily Herald*, September 16, 1982.

19. Duncan, *Killeen: A Tale of Two Cities*, 96.

20. *Ibid.*, 96-97; *Killeen Daily Herald*, November 9, 1972, February 27, 1986.

21. For conditions in Killeen during this period, see Duncan, *Killeen: A Tale of Two Cities*," 93-110, and *Killeen Daily Herald*, September 14, 1962, Section 5, p. 7.

22. Scott, *History of Coryell County*, 189; Edwards, "Land Acquisition in Coryell County, Texas," 17.

23. *Temple Daily Telegram*, March 13, 1942; Duncan, *Killeen: A Tale of Two Cities*,97; and *Killeen Daily Herald*, September 21,1967, Section 3, p.14.

24. "Camp Hood, 1941-47" File, History Section, Headquarters, III Corps and Fort Hood, Killeen; *Temple Daily Telegram*, February 20, 1944; *Killeen Daily Herald*, September 16, 1982; and Clifford J. Hughes, "A Study of Temple, Texas During World War II" (Master's Thesis, Southwest Texas State University, 1972), 88, copy in FMC.

25. *Temple Daily Telegram*, February 17, 1942.

26. Letter, Colonel Stanley J. Grogan to Brigadier General A.D. Bruce, April 20, 1942, copy in "TEMPLE CHAMBER OF COMMERCE: NATIONAL DEFENSE—ARMY CAMP, 1941-1942" File, FMC.

27. Hughes, "A Study of Temple, Texas During World War II," 25-43; "Camp Hood, 1941-47" File, History Section, Headquarters, III Corps and Fort Hood, Killeen, Texas.

28. *Ibid.*; and *Killeen Daily Herald*, September 16, 1982; "Camp Hood, 1941-47" File, History Section, Headquarters, III Corps and Fort Hood, Killeen.

29. *Temple Daily Telegram*, January 15, June 10, 1942.

30. *Killeen Daily Herald*, September 16, 1942; "Project CAMP HOOD, 1942," Poage Projects, Camp Hood File, The Congressional Collection, Baylor University, Waco.

31. *Killeen Daily Herald*, September 21, 1967, Section 2, p. 4.

32. Dunham, *Tank Destroyer History*, 14.

33. "Camp Hood, 1941-47" File, History Section, Headquarters, III Corps and Fort Hood, Killeen.

34. *Ibid.*

35. For the story of these two prisoners of war, see "Special Historic Supplement," *Fort Hood Sentinel*, September 7, 1989, 3. See also Duncan, *Killeen: A Tale of Two Cities*, 101-102.

36. Duncan, *Killeen: A Tale of Two Cities*, 101-102; *Killeen Daily Herald*, September 21, 1967, Section 2, p. 19. See also Post War Utilization Studies, "Camp Hood," War Department, Office of the Chief of Engineers, September 1945, copy in "Organizational History Files (1945)," History Section, Headquarters, III Corps and Fort Hood, Killeen, Texas.

37. Duncan, *Killeen: A Tale of Two Cities*, 101-102; and Gra'Delle Duncan, *Central Texas Diary* (Killeen: Killeen Centennial Commission, 1982), 13-14.

38. *Ibid.*

39. Camp Hood General Orders No. 10, August 20, 1942, "U.S. Army Commands 1942-, Camp Hood, Texas," RG 338, Washington National Records Center, National Archives and Records Administration, Washington, D.C.

40. Aikens, "History of Fort Hood and Local Area" File, 11-12.

41. *The Killeen Herald and Messenger*, September 25, 1942, headlined this event, "Estimated 25,000 Visitors At Camp Hood Opening," commenting that "the Tank Destroyer Center was dedicated to a relentless war to an uncompromised victory." See also *Temple Daily Telegram*, September 19, 1942; *Killeen Daily Herald*, September 21, 1967, Section 2, p. 5; *Armored Sentinel*, September 21, 1967, B-19.

## Chapter Four: *Camp Hood—The Tank Destroyer School*

1. Dunham, *Tank Destroyer History*, 6; Gabel, *Seek, Strike, and Destroy*, 17-18.

2. Dunham, *Tank Destroyer History*, 7-9; Gabel, *Seek, Strike, and Destroy*, 19-20.

3. Dunham, *Tank Destroyer History*, 8-9; Gabel, *Seek, Strike, and Destroy*, 20.

4. *Temple Daily Telegram*, June 10, 1942; Key Personnel Files, History

Section, Headquarters, III Corps and Fort Hood, Killeen; Dunham, *Tank Destroyer History*, 11.

5. J.A. Warren, Jr., "Soldier-Teacher Couldn't Even Find Camp Hood," *Killeen Daily Herald*, September 21, 1967, Section 2, p.1.

6. "Camp Hood, 1941-47" File, History Section, Headquarters, III Corps and Fort Hood, Killeen.

7. *Killeen Daily Herald* September 21, 1967, Section 2, p.1; Dunham, *Tank Destroyer History*, 18; "Camp Hood, 1941-47" File, History Section, Headquarters, III Corps and Fort Hood, Killeen.

8. *Killeen Daily Herald*, September 14, 1962, Section 2, p. 2, and Section 4, p. 2.

9. *Ibid.*, Section 4, p. 7.

10. The activation of the post was ordered effective "this date" at the staging area of Temple, Texas, in Camp Hood General Orders No. 1, April 13, 1942; Camp Hood General Orders No. 2, May 28, 1942, activated a Military Police unit for Camp Hood; provisions for guards and guardhouses were stipulated in Camp Hood General Orders No. 12, August 21, 1942; and a Chemical Warfare Service Detachment was activated in Camp Hood General Orders No. 3, May 28, 1942; all in RG 338,"U.S. Army Commands, 1942-, Camp Hood, Texas," Washington National Records Center, National Archives and Records Administration, Washington, D.C.

11. Camp Hood General Orders No. 6, July 21, 1942, *ibid.*; *Armored Sentinel*, September 21, 1967, 13-B; *Killeen Daily Herald*, September 14, 1962, Section 5, p. 7, and September 21, 1967, Section 2, p. 6; "Organizational History Files (1942)," and "Camp Hood, 1941-47" File, History Section, Headquarters, III Corps and Fort Hood, Killeen.

12. Dunham, *Tank Destroyer History*, 17; Stephen Elliott, "Sameness Impresses Heistand," *Armored Sentinel*, September 21, 1967, 15-B; Gabel, *Seek, Strike, and Destroy*, 29-30; *Temple Daily Telegram*, September 5, 1982; and interview, Stewart Meyer with OBF, August 14, 1989. See also War Department FM 18-5, *Tank Destroyer Field Manual: Organization and Tactics of Tank Destroyer Units* (Washington: Government Printing Office, 1942).

13. FM 18-5, *Tank Destroyer Field Manual*; Dunham, *Tank Destroyer History*, 15-22; Gabel, *Seek, Strike, and Destroy*, 29.

14. *Killeen Daily Herald*, September 21, 1967, Section 4, p. 5.

15. *Ibid.*, Section 2, pp. 1-2; Gabel, *Seek, Strike, and Destroy*, 15, 22, 28.

16. Frank Mayborn, undated oral interview, Tape 6, FMC; *Temple Daily Telegram*, October 6, 1942.

17. "Report of Physical Examination, October 30, 1942," in "Mayborn, Frank W.–Military–ORDERS" File, FMC; "TANK DESTROYER SCHOOL–January 28, 1943, Officer Candidate Class 15" File, FMC; "Frank

W. Mayborn Military Service and Association" Scrapbook, FMC, contains his commission as well as related military papers; for his experiences in the Tank Destroyer OCS, see "Mayborn, Frank W.–Military–TANK DE-STROYER SCHOOL" File, FMC. For his reminiscences about this part of his life, see Frank Mayborn, undated oral interview, Tape 6, FMC.

18. Letter, Quintus C. Atkinson to Mrs. Frank W. Mayborn, September 19, 1983, in "Chamber of Commerce: TANK DESTROYER ASSN.– Miscellaneous" File, FMC. For details about Mayborn's service during World War II, see Odie B. Faulk and Laura E. Faulk, *Frank W. Mayborn: A Man Who Made a Difference* (Belton, TX: University of Mary Hardin-Baylor Press, 1989), Chapter Five.

19. *Killeen Daily Herald*, September 21, 1967, Section 2, p. 10.

20. Dunham, *Tank Destroyer History*, 24. See also Basic Training Program General Orders No. 1, November 20, 1943; Basic Training Program General orders No. 2, November 23, 1943; and Basic Training Program General orders No. 6, December 3, 1943; all in "U.S. Army Commands, 1942-, Camp Hood, Texas," RG 338, Washington National Records Center, National Archives and Records Administration, Washington, D.C.

21. Dunham, *Tank Destroyer History*, 24.

22. *Ibid.*, 31; *Armored Sentinel*, September 21, 1967, 13-B.

23. "Organizational History Files (1943)," History Section, Headquarters, III Corps and Fort Hood, Killeen; *Armored Sentinel*, September 21, 1967, 12-B; Dunham, *Tank Destroyer History*, 33.

24. Dunham, *Tank Destroyer History*, 24-28.

25. Quoted in *ibid.*, 26.

26. *Ibid.*, 26, 52.

27. *Ibid.*, 52-61; Gabel, *Seek, Strike, and Destroy*, 27-28; "Tank Destroyer History" (4 vols., vol. I is missing), III, 1 March 1944 to 31 October 1944, in Fort Hood Files, Center for Military History, Washington, D.C.; *Armored Sentinel*, September 21, 1967, 5-B. The British version of the M-10 was known as the Achilles; it carried a 17-pound gun and proved very satisfactory.

28. Frank Mayborn, undated oral interview, Tape 6, FMC.

29. Mary Lee Stubbs and Stanley Russell Connor, *Armor-Cavalry* (2 vols, Washington: Office of Chief of Military History, Army Lineage Series, 1972, 1984), II, 69.

30. Dunham, *Tank Destroyer History*, 31.

31. *Temple Daily Telegram*, September 5, 1982.

32. *Armored Sentinel*, September 21, 1967, 17-B; *Killeen Daily Herald*, September 14, 1962, Section 5, p. 7.

33. "Tank Destroyer History" (4 vols., vol. I is missing), III, 1 March 1944 to 31 October 1944, Fort Hood File, Center for Military History, Washington, D.C.; Dunham, *Tank Destroyer History*, 35.

34. Dunham, *Tank Destroyer History*, 36; "Organizational History Files (1943)," History Section, Headquarters, III Corps and Fort Hood, Killeen; *Killeen Daily Herald*, September 21, 1967, Section 4, p. 1.

35. Dunham, *Tank Destroyer History*, 36.

36. Camp Hood General Orders No. 1, January 23, 1944; Camp Hood General Orders No. 26, April 5, 1944; Camp Hood General Orders No. 39, August 1, 1944; all in "U.S. Army Commands, 1942-, Camp Hood, Texas," RG 338, Washington National Records Center, National Archives and Records Administration, Washington, D.C.

37. Camp Hood General Orders No. 7, February 17, 1944, *ibid.*

38. Camp Hood General Orders No. 10, February 19, 1944, *ibid.*

39. Camp Hood General Orders No. 9, February 19, 1944, *ibid.*

40. "Tank Destroyer History" (4 vols., vol. I is missing), III, 1 March 1944 to 31 October 1944, Fort Hood File, Center for Military History, Washington, D.C.; *Killeen Daily Herald*, September 21, 1967, Section 2, P. 5; Gabel, *Seek, Strike, and Destroy*, 54.

41. Gabel, *Seek, Strike, and Destroy*, 54; Dunham, *Tank Destroyer History*, 38; "Tank Destroyer History" (4 vols., vol. I is missing), III, 1 March 1944 to 31 October 1944, Fort Hood File, Center for Military History.

42. "Organizational History Files (1944)," History Section, Headquarters, III Corps and Fort Hood, Killeen.

43. *Ibid.*; Camp Hood General Orders No. 1, January 23, 1944; Camp Hood General Orders No. 14, March 5, 1944; Camp Hood General Orders No. 37, July 1, 1944; all in "U.S. Army Commands, 1942-, Camp Hood, Texas," RG 338, Washington National Records Center, National Archives and Records Administration, Washington, D.C.

44. Infantry Replacement Training Center General Orders No. 1, March 10, 1944; Infantry Replacement Training Center General Orders No. 3, March 30, 1944; both in "U.S. Army Commands, 1942-, Camp Hood," RG 338, Washington National Records Center, National Archives and Records Administration, Washington, D.C.

45. "Organizational History Files (1944)," History Section, Headquarters, III Corps and Fort Hood, Killeen.

46. Southern Branch, United States Disciplinary Barracks, North Camp Hood, *Annual Report*, 1945, "U.S. Army Commands, 1942-, Camp Hood, Texas," RG 338, Washington National Records Center, National Archives and Records Administration, Washington, D.C.

47. *Armored Sentinel*, September 21, 1967, 5-B.

48. Basic Training Program General Orders No. 6, December 3, 1943, "U.S. Army Commands, 1942, Camp Hood, Texas," RG 338, Washington National Records Center, National Archives and Records Administration, Washington, D.C.

49. "Tank Destroyer History" (4 vols., vol. I is missing), IV, 1 November 1944 to 8 May 1945, Fort Hood File, Center for Military History, Washington, D.C.; Camp Hood General Orders No. 30, April 14, 1944, "U.S. Army Commands, 1942-, Camp Hood, Texas," RG 338, Washington National Records Center, National Archives and Records Administration, Washington, D.C.

50. "Organizational History Files (1945)," History Section, Headquarters, III Corps and Fort Hood, Killeen.

51. Dunham, *Tank Destroyer History*, 39.

52. *Ibid.*, 45-49.

53. *Killeen Daily Herald*, September 21, 1967, Section 2, p. 4.

54. Dunham, *Tank Destroyer History*, 50.

55. *Killeen Daily Herald*, September 14, 1962, Section 6, p. 1, and September 21, 1967, Section 2, p. 5.

56. "Organizational History Files (1945)" and "Fort Hood, 1941-47" File, History Section, Headquarters, III Corps and Fort Hood, Killeen.

57. *Killeen Daily Herald*, September 14, 1962, Section 7, p. 7; Infantry Replacement Training Center General Orders No. 22, October 2, 1945, "U.S. Army Commands, 1942-, Camp Hood, Texas," RG 338, Washington National Records Center, National Archives and Records Administration, Washington, D.C.

58. "Camp Hood, Texas," *Post War Utilization Studies*, Office of the Chief of Engineers, War Department, September 1945, copy in Fort Hood Files, Center For Military History, Washington, D.C.

59. *Killeen Daily Herald*, September 21, 1967, Section 4, p. 3.

60. Southern Branch, United States Disciplinary Barracks, North Camp Hood, Texas, *Annual Report, 1945*, and *Annual Report, 1946*, both in "U.S. Army Commands, 1942-, Camp Hood, Texas," RG 338, Washington National Records Center, National Archives and Records Administration, Washington, D.C.

61. *Killeen Daily Herald*, Section 2, pp. 5 and 16, and Section 4, p. 7; Duncan, *Killeen: Tale of Two Cities*, 106-107.

62. "Organizational History Files (1946)," History Section, Headquarters, III Corps and Fort Hood, Killeen.

63. *Killeen Daily Herald*, September 21, 1967, Section 3, p. 6.

64. "Organizational History Files (1946), (1947)," History Section, Headquarters, III Corps and Fort Hood, Killeen.

65. Francis T. Julia, *Army Staff Reorganization, 1903-1985* (Washington: Analysis Branch, U.S. Army Center for Military History, 1987), 12-13. See also *Killeen Daily Herald*, September 21, 1967, Section 3, p. 13.

66. "Organizational History Files (1946), (1947)," History Section, Headquarters, III Corps and Fort Hood, Killeen.

## Chapter Five: *A Permanent Two Division Post*

1. "Building For the Future," in Organizational History Files, FY-54 and FY-56, History Section, Headquarters, III Corps and Fort Hood, Killeen. See also "What's Happening at Hood," Rotogravure Magazine, *Houston Chronicle*, November 2, 1947.

2. *Ibid.*

3. *Ibid.*; George Marker, "Fort Hood: Ideal Armor Center," *Army Times*, 1959, copy in History Section, Headquarters, III Corps and Fort Hood, Killeen.

4. *Ibid.*; *Killeen Daily Herald*, September 21, 1967, Section 2, p. 10.

5. *Killeen Daily Herald*, September 21, 1967, Section 2, p. 14; Duncan, *Killeen*, 114.

6. Duncan, *Killeen*, 109.

7. *Ibid.*; "Analysis of Existing Facilities, Killeen Base, Texas," Revised January 1968, attached to "Real Property Evaluation Report," March 1976, copy in FY-68 File, History Section, Headquarters, III Corps and Fort Hood, Killeen. See also *Temple Daily Telegram*, October 5, 1969; "Hood's Atomic Storage: Original Purpose of 'Killeen Base,'" *Fort Hood Sentinel*, Supplement, September 7, 1989, p. 39; and interview, Richard Cavazos with OBF, September 15, 1989, FMC.

8. Weigley, *History of the United States Army*, 498-501.

9. "Camp Hood, 1 January to 31 December 1948," History Section, Headquarters, III Corps and Fort Hood, Killeen.

10. Letter, Frank W. Mayborn to Tom Connally, August 17, 1945, "C of C–Military Affairs–Misc. Correspondence 1945 through 1952" File, FMC.

11. Letter, Jim Reinhold to Frank Mayborn, September 20, 1945, *ibid.*

12. *Temple Daily Telegram*, November 6, 1945.

13. Frank W. Mayborn, "Hood Permanent Home of Second Armored," *ibid.*. See also Harry Blanding, "Every Indication At Hood Is That Giant Camp Will Be Permanent," *ibid.*, January 17, 1946.

14. *Ibid.*, February 9, 1946; Gatesville Chamber of Commerce to Camp Site Locating Board of the War Department of the United States Government, the Representative of the 11th Congressional District of Texas, and the U.S. Senators from Texas, "Applications for the Right to File a Brief When the Question as to the Final Disposition of Camp Hood Arises," in Poage Projects, Camp Hood File, The Congressional Collection, Baylor University, Waco; accompanying this is a letter, Frank C. Higginbotham to W.R. Poage, September 20, 1945, *ibid.*. Also accompanying the effort by the Gatesville Chamber of Commerce is the brochure from the St. Louis Southwestern Railway Lines to the Camp Site Locating Board, War Department, Washington, D.C.,

in *ibid..* See also "Post War Planning Board of Coryell County in Assembly with Citizens of Coryell County," January 29, 1946, sent to Congressman Poage and to Texas Senators Tom Connally and W. Lee O'Daniel, in *ibid.*

15. Letter, L.S. Hobbs to Commanding General, Army Ground Forces, June 2, 1947, "U.S. Army Commands, 1942-, Camp Hood, Texas," RG 338, Washington National Records Center, National Archives and Records Administration, Washington, D.C.

16. Letter, J.M. Wainwright to commanding general, Army Ground Forces, June 2, 1947, *ibid.*

17. Letter, Charles L. Bolte to Adjutant General, June 23, 1947; letter, Edward F. Witsell to commanding general, Army Ground Forces, February 11, 1948; both in *ibid.*

18. For details, see Faulk and Faulk, *Frank W. Mayborn,* Chapter Seven. For information about Mayborn's crucial role in getting Lyndon Johnson elected to the United States Senate in 1948, see *ibid.,* Chapter Ten.

19. Letter, W. Guy Draper to Frank W. Mayborn, December 10, 1949, in "C of C–Military Affairs–Misc. Correspondence 1945 through 1952" File, FMC; *Temple Daily Telegram,* October 21, 1950.

20. Mayborn's acceptance of appointment to the Army Advisory Commission is in letter, Frank W. Mayborn to General J.M. Wainwright, March 15, 1947. The members of this commission are noted in letter, Mayborn to Lieutenant Colonel Henry W. Allard, May 5, 1947, "Army Advisory Commission" File, FMC. See also Scrapbook 10, "Temple and Bell County Affairs," FMC.

21. Telegram, Sarah McClendon to Harry Blanding, editor of the *Temple Daily Telegram,* April 13, 1950. The story was in the next day's paper.

22. *Ibid.,* May 9, 1950.

23. *Ibid.,* April 15, 1950.

24. For background, see Roy E. Appleman, *South to the Naktong, North to the Yalu: the United States Army in the Korean War* (Washington: Department of the Army, 1960); John Miller, Jr., Owen J. Carroll, and Margaret E. Tackley, *Korea, 1951-1953* (Washington: Department of the Army, 1956); and T.R. Fehrenbach, *This Kind of War: A Study in Unpreparedness* (New York: Macmillan, 1963).

25. *Killeen Daily Herald,* September 21, 1967, Section 2, p. 4.

26. Fourth Army General Orders No. 46, March 5, 1951, "Army AG Command Reports, 1949-1954," RG 319, Washington National Records Center, National Archives and Records Administration, Washington, D.C.; "Command Report for 1951, 1st Armored Division," *ibid.;* Organizational History Files, History Section, Headquarters, III Corps and Fort Hood, Killeen. See also *Killeen Daily Herald,* September 21, 1967, Section 3, p. 3.

FORT HOOD

27. 1st Armored Division General Orders No. 1, March 10, 1951, "Army AG Command Reports, 1949-1954," RG 319, Washington National Records Center, National Archives and Records Administration, Washington, D.C.; Key Personnel Files, History Section, Headquarters, III Corps and Fort Hood, Killeen; *Killeen Daily Herald*, September 21, 1967, Section 2, p. 11.

28. Command Report, 1st Armored Division, 1951, "Army AG Command Reports, 1949-1954," RG 319, Washington National Records Center, National Archives and Records Administration, Washington, D.C.

29. John H. Thompson, *This Is Your Army* (Chicago: *Chicago Tribune*, 1952), 66-74; this is from a series of articles about major Army posts done in the *Tribune* in 1951.

30. Organizational History Files, History Section, Headquarters, III Corps and Fort Hood, Killeen; *Killeen Daily Herald*, September 21, 1967, Section 3, p. 6.

31. Command Report, 1st Armored Division, 1951, "Army AG Command Reports, 1949-1954," RG 319, Washington National Records Center, National Archives and Records Administration, Washington, D.C.; Organizational History Files, History Section, Headquarters, III Corps and Fort Hood, Killeen; Thompson, *This Is Your Army*, 66-74; *Killeen Daily Herald*, September 21, 1967, Section 3, p. 3.

32. Records Pertaining to Exercise Longhorn, 1951-1952, "U.S. Army Commands, 1942-, Camp Hood, Texas," RG 338; Fort Hood Command Report, 1952, Part I, May 1, 1953, "Army AG Command Reports, 1949-1954," RG 319; both in Washington National Records Center, National Archives and Records Administration, Washington, D.C. See also III Corps and Fort Hood, "Fort Hood Welcomes You," June 1, 1971, Pam 360-28, copy in III Corps File, Unit Files, Center for Military History, Washington, D.C.

33. Fort Hood Command Report, 1952, Part I, Narrative, "Army AG Command Reports, 1949-1954," RG 319, Washington National Records Center, National Archives and Records Administration, Washington, D.C.

34. Organizational History Files, History Section, Headquarters, III Corps and Fort Hood, Killeen; Thompson, *This Is Your Army*, 66-74; *Killeen Daily Herald*, September 14, 1962, Section 3, p. 3; "Project FORT HOOD, 1952," Poage Projects, Fort Hood 1952-1953 File, The Congressional Collection, Baylor University, Waco.

35. Fort Hood Command Report, 1952, Part I, Narrative, "Army AG Command Reports, 1949-1954," RG 319, Washington National Records Center, National Archives and Records Administration, Washington, D.C.

36. Letter and Petition, James H. Russell to W.R. Poage, General Bruce Clarke, and Army General Staff, June 6, 1952, in "Fort Hood, 1950-1961" File, FMC. Mayborn had his Washington correspondent, Sarah McClendon,

get these copies for use in stories that appeared in the *Daily Telegram*.

37. Letter, W.R. Poage to James H. Russell, June 17, 1952, copy in *ibid*. See also "Project FORT HOOD, 1953," Poage Projects, Fort Hood 1953-1954 File, The Congressional Collection, Baylor University.

38. "Property Utilization Report, March 1976," copy in FY-68 File, History Section, Headquarters, III Corps and Fort Hood, Killeen; "Project FORT HOOD, Expansion 1953," Poage Projects, Fort Hood 1953-61 File, The Congressional Collection, Baylor University, Waco; *Killeen Daily Herald*, September 21, 1967, Section 2, p. 12.

39. Duncan, *Killeen*, 112; "Assigned Fort Hood Strength, August 25, 1952," History Section, Headquarters, III Corps and Fort Hood, Killeen.

40. Duncan, *Killeen*, 112; Thomas Turner, "Killeen...The Town that Boomed by Blue Print," *Texas Parade Magazine* (June 1954), offprint in Killeen Public Library.

41. Fort Hood Command Report, 1952, Part I, Narrative, "Army AG Command Reports, 1949-1954," RG 319, Washington National Records Center, National Archives and Records Administration, Washington, D.C.

42. Duncan, *Killeen*, 112.

43. "1953 Was Busy Year at Fort Hood," *Temple Daily Telegram*, January 1, 14, 1954.

44. Fort Hood Command Report, 1952, Part I, May 1, 1953, "Army AG Command Reports, 1949-1954," RG 319, Washington National Records Center, National Archives and Records Administration, Washington, D.C.

45. *Ibid*.

46. *Armored Sentinel*, September 21, 1967, B-5.

47. *Temple Daily Telegram*, February 11, 12, 16, 1954.

48. *Ibid*., February 18, 1954.

49. *Ibid*., March 6, April 8, 1954.

50. *Ibid*., March 9, 1954; "Project FORT HOOD 1954," Poage Projects, Fort Hood 1953-1954 File, The Congressional Collection, Baylor University, Waco.

51. Organizational History Files, History Section, Headquarters, III Corps and Fort Hood; *Killeen Daily Herald*, September 21, 1967, Section 4, p. 4.

52. Some commanding generals of III Corps have tried to have its history traced to a Civil War corps bearing the same number, but the Center for Military History in Washington, D.C., which traces lineage and honors for all units in the Army, has steadfastly denied such linkage. See memorandum, Janice E. McKenney to Captain Moody, August 19, 1986, and Brigadier General William A. Stoft to Lieutenant General Crosbie E. Saint, December 5, 1986, both in Fort Hood File, Center for Military History, Washington, D.C.

53. III Corp's role in World War II was recounted in *The Phantom Corps*, a pamphlet issued at the orders of Major General James A. Van Fleet, III Corps commander from March 1945 to February 1946; a copy is in III Corps File, Unit Files, Center for Military History, Washington, D.C.

54. Organizational History Files, History Section, Headquarters, III Corps and Fort Hood; Fort Hood, Unit Files, Center for Military History, Washington, D.C.; *Killeen Daily Herald*, Section 3, p. 8.

55. Key Personnel Files, History Section, Headquarters, III Corps and Fort Hood, Killeen; *Temple Daily Telegram*, April 13, 1954.

56. Duncan, *Killeen*, 112.

## Chapter Six: *Fort Hood–Biggest Army Post in the Free World*

1. *Temple Daily Telegram*, May 22, 1954.

2. "Building For the Future," in Organizational History Files, FY-54 and FY-56, History Section, Headquarters, III Corps and Fort Hood, Killeen.

3. *Killeen Daily Herald*, September 21, 1967, Section 4, pp. 1-2.

4. *Armored Sentinel*, September 21, 1967, B-5 and B-7.

5. *Ibid.*, B-7; *Killeen Daily Herald*, September 21, 1967, Section II, p. 12, and Section 4, p. 7.

6. See "Memorandum" of meeting between Secretary Stevens, members of the Texas congressional delegation, and concerned citizens in the office of the Majority Leader, Room G-14, U.S. Capitol, June 9, 1955, copy in "C of C: Military Affairs–Re Sagebrush, Camp Polk Move" File, FMC. Also in this file are clippings of related stories in the *Temple Daily Telegram* and numerous letters written by a concerned Frank Mayborn, who was in Washington for this meeting with Secretary Stevens.

7. See numerous letters, telegrams, and new stories in *ibid.* and clippings for the period in "Fort Hood 1950-1961" File, FMC.

8. Telegrams between Frank Mayborn and Sarah McClendon, the Washington correspondent for the *Daily Telegram*, concerning appointments for Mayborn on this trip are in *ibid.*

9. Details are in *ibid.* See also Organizational History Files, History Section, Headquarters, III Corps and Fort Hood, Killeen. See also "Project FORT HOOD, Maneuvers, 1955," Poage Projects, Fort Hood Miscellaneous File, The Congressional Collection, Baylor University, Waco.

10. Key Personnel Files, History Section, Headquarters, III Corps and Fort Hood, Killeen.

11. Organizational History Files, History Section, Headquarters, III Corps and Fort Hood, Killeen, and *Temple Daily Telegram*, February 2, 1957.

12. *Temple Daily Telegram*, March 11 and 13, 1955; *Armored Sentinel*,

September 21, 1967, B-19.

13. *Temple Daily Telegram*, March 1, 1957.

14. *Killeen Daily Herald*, September 21, 1967, Section 2, p. 7; *Armored Sentinel*, September 21, 1967, B-19; and Organizational History Files, History Section, Headquarters, III Corps and Fort Hood, Killeen.

15. *Temple Daily Telegram*, August 1, 1957.

16. Organizational History Files, History Section, Headquarters, III Corps and Fort Hood, Killeen; *Killeen Daily Herald*, September 14, 1962, Section 3, p. 6, and September 21, 1967, Section 2, p. 19; *Armored Sentinel*, September 21, 1967, B-11.

17. Key Personnel Files, History Section, Headquarters, III Corps and Fort Hood, Killeen; *Temple Daily Telegram*, February 12, 1959; *Killeen Daily Herald*, September 21, 1967, Section 2, p. 8.

18. Organizational History Files, History Section, Headquarters, III Corps and Fort Hood, Killeen; *Temple Daily Telegram*, March 16, 1959.

19. Organizational History Files, History Section, Headquarters, III Corps and Fort Hood, Killeen; *Killeen Daily Herald*, September 21, 1967, Section 4, p. 1.

20. *Killeen Daily Herald*, September 14, 1962, Section 4, p. 5.

21. Fort Hood General Orders No. 74, April 23, 1959, states that III Corps would become inactive effective May 5, 1959; copy in III Corps File, Unit Files, Center for Military History, Washington, D.C. See also Organizational History Files, History Section, Headquarters, III Corps and Fort Hood, Killeen; *Armored Sentinel*, September 21, 1967, B-3.

22. Fact Sheet, "Army Combat Arms...in 1959," January 4, 1960, Public Information Division, 4th Army Headquarters, Fort Sam Houston, Texas, copy in "Fort Hood 1950-1961" File, *Temple Daily Telegram* offices.

23. *Temple Daily Telegram*, April 26, 1961.

24. *Killeen Daily Herald*, September 14, 1962, Section 3, p. 4.

25. Fourth Army General Orders No. 87, August 30, 1961, orders the reactivation of III Corps effective September 26, 1961; copy in "Historical Report, 1 September-31 December 1961, III Corps File, Unit Files, Center for Military History, Washington, D.C.

26. "III Corps STRAC Historical Report, 1 January 1962-31 March 1962," in III Corps File, Unit Files, Center for Military History, Washington, D.C.

27. *Killeen Daily Herald*, September 14, 1962, Section 2, p. 6, and Section 6, p. 1; Organizational History Files and Key Personnel Files, History Section, Headquarters, III Corps and Fort Hood, Killeen.

28. *Temple Daily Telegram*, September 7, 11, 30, 1961.

29. *Ibid*., December 15, 1961, January 4, 1962; Organizational History Files, History Section, III Corps and Fort Hood, Killeen.

30. Interview, Ralph E. Haines, Jr., with OBF, August 22, 1989, FMC; Key Personnel Files, History Section, III Corps and Fort Hood, Killeen; Gary L. Harvey and David R. King, "Evolving the Army of the 21st Century," *Military Review*, LXVIII (August 1988), 3.

31. *Ibid.*; interview, Frank Norvell with OBF, August 14, 1989, FMC.

32. Interview, Ralph E. Haines, Jr., with OBF, August 22, 1989, FMC; interview, Frank Norvell with OBF, August 14, 1989, FMC.

33. *Killeen Daily Herald*, September 21, 1967, Section 3, p. 14.

34. *Ibid.*, Section 2, p. 6; *Temple Daily Telegram*, September 19, 30, 1962; interview, Ralph E. Haines, Jr., with OBF, August 22, 1989, FMC; News Release, September 18, 1962, Madill Air Force Base, Florida, copy in "Fort Hood '62" File, *Temple Daily Telegram* offices. See also "MILITARY AFFAIRS–Proposed Maneuvers in Central Texas, October 1962" File, FMC.

35. Interview, Ralph E. Haines, Jr., with OBF, August 22, 1989, FMC; Organizational History Files, History Section, Headquarters, III Corps and Fort Hood, Killeen; clippings in "Fort Hood '62" File, *Temple Daily Telegram* offices; and *Killeen Daily Herald*, September 21, 1967, Section 2, p. 8.

36. *Killeen Daily Herald*, September 21, 1967, Section 2, p. 10; and related clippings in "Fort Hood '63" File, *Temple Daily Telegram* offices.

37. *Temple Daily Telegram*, May 18-June 2, 1964; and *Killeen Daily Herald*, September 21, 1967, Section 2, pp. 6, 8.

38. *Temple Daily Telegram*, December 9, 1964; letter, H.H. Fischer to Sue Mayborn, August 26, 1989, FMC.

39. *Ibid.*, January 21, February 2, 1965.

40. Letter, H.H. Fischer to Sue Mayborn, August 26, 1989, FMC.

## Chapter Seven: *No Other Post Like It*

1. *Killeen Daily Herald*, September 21, 1967, Section 4, p. 8.

2. "Fort Hood 1965" and "Fort Hood 1966" Files, *Temple Daily Telegram* offices; *Killeen Daily Herald*, September 21, 1967, Section 2, p. 4; Section 3, p. 1. See also *Old Ironsides 1969* (n.p., n.d.), a publication similar to a yearbook which obviously was made available to the men of the 1st Armored; a copy of this is in the FMC and in the History Section, Headquarters, III Corps and Fort Hood, Killeen.

3. For an example, see *Temple Daily Telegram*, May 16, 1971.

4. Interview, Ralph E. Haines, Jr., with OBF, August 22, 1989, FMC; *Waco Tribune-Herald*, February 6, 1988, Section C, p. 1; *Waco Times-Herald*, April 1, 1966; and *Armored Sentinel*, September 21, 1967, B-1.

5. Key Personnel Files, History Section, Headquarters, III Corps and Fort Hood, Killeen; *Armored Sentinel*, September 21, 1967, B-8; and *Killeen Daily*

*Herald*, September 21, 1967, Section 4, p. 1.

6. See *Temple Daily Telegram*, May 28, October 20, 1967, and January 22, 1967.

7. Various clippings, "Fort Hood 1967" File, *Temple Daily Telegram* offices; *Killeen Daily Herald*, September 17, 1982, 9-A.

8. Interview, Beverley E. Powell with OBF, October 2, 1989, FMC; Legal Services, "Local Laws Affecting Fort Hood Personnel" (PAM 27-15), Headquarters, III Corps and Fort Hood, October 7, 1970, copy in Fort Hood File, Center for Military History, Washington, D.C.

9. Interview, Beverley E. Powell with OBF, October 2, 1989, FMC.

10. Lieutenant Colonel Carl W. Warren, Annual Historical Summary, January 7, 1970, in Fort Hood File, Center for Military History, Washington, D.C.; "Information Brief, 2 June 1969," Fort Hood File, Center for Military History, Washington, D.C.

11. Interview, Beverley E. Powell with OBF, October 2, 1989, FMC.

12. *Ibid.*; interview, Stewart Meyer with OBF, August 14, 1989, FMC.

13. Organizational History Files, History Section, Headquarters, III Corps and Fort Hood, Killeen; *Temple Daily Telegram*, January 14, 1971, March 13, 1978.

14. *Ibid.*, March 25, 1971.

15. Organizational History Files, History Section, Headquarters, III Corps and Fort Hood, Killeen; *ibid.*, April 10, May 6, 1971; *Killeen Daily Herald*, September 17, 1982, Section 2, p. 4.

16. III Corps File, Unit Files, Center for Military History, Washington, D.C.; Organizational History Files, History Section, Headquarters, III Corps and Fort Hood, Killeen; III Corps and Fort Hood, "Fort Hood Welcomes You," June 1, 1971, Pam 360-28, copy in III Corps File, Unit Files, Center for Military History, Washington, D.C.; "Special Historic Supplement," *Fort Hood Sentinel*, September 7, 1989, 3.

17. *Time*, May 17, 1971; Organizational History Files, History Section, Headquarters, III Corps and Fort Hood, Killeen; *Temple Daily Telegram*, April 10, May 5, 6, 1971.

18. Key Personnel Files, History Section, Headquarters, III Corps and Fort Hood, Killeen; *Temple Daily Telegram*, June 30, May 6, July 31, 1971.

19. Excellent studies have been done on each of the REFORGER exercises. See, for example, Historical Branch, Office of the Deputy Chief of Staff for Military Operations and Reserve Forces, USCONARC, *Selected Chronology of Actions–REFORGER I*, March 1969, copy in Center for Military History, Washington, D.C.

20. Interview, Jack Hemingway with OBF, August 28, 1989, FMC.

21. Organizational History Files, History Section, Headquarters, III Corps

and Fort Hood, Killeen; *Temple Daily Telegram*, February 5, 8, 20, 1975.

22. Key Personnel Files, History Section, Headquarters, III Corps and Fort Hood, Killeen; *Temple Daily Telegram*, September 23, 1973.

23. *Temple Daily Telegram*, February 12, March 12, 1975.

24. *Ibid.*, March 4, 6, 1975; and numerous letters from individuals in Coryell County and local and national politicians to Frank W. Mayborn in "FORT HOOD LAND ACQUISITION–Miscellaneous Correspondence" File, FMC. Some information also came from a Public Service program held on Channel 6, KCEN-TV, in which General Robert M. Shoemaker discussed the proposed acquisition with Jim Hamm, News Director at KCEN, and Harry Provence, News Chief of the *Waco Tribune-Herald*; a videotape of this program is in the possession of Robert Shoemaker.

25. Letter, Fontaine Erskine to Frank W. Mayborn, March 14, 1975, in "FORT HOOD LAND ACQUISITION–Miscellaneous Correspondence" File, FMC; and Resolution of the Temple Chamber of Commerce, April 8, 1975, in *ibid.*

26. Letter, Frank W. Mayborn to Senator John Tower, February 26, 1976, *ibid.*; interview, Robert M. Shoemaker with OBF, August 23, 1989, FMC.

27. For newspaper clippings about this, see "FORT HOOD LAND ACQUISITION–Clips" File, FMC; see particularly *Temple Daily Telegram*, December 1, 1976, and February 4, 1977; and *Killeen Daily Herald*, September 17, 1982, 10-A. See also the videotape cited above, footnote 24.

28. Organizational History Files, History Section, Headquarters, III Corps and Fort Hood, Killeen; "Fort Hood 1979" and "Fort Hood 1980" Files, *Temple Daily Telegram* offices; *Temple Daily Telegram*, December 20, 1980; and *Killeen Daily Herald*, September 17, 1982, 11-A.

29. Interview, Robert M. Shoemaker with OBF, August 23, 1989, FMC.

30. Key Personnel Files, History Section, Headquarters, III Corps and Fort Hood, Killeen; *Temple Daily Telegram*, November 30, 1978.

31. Organizational History Files, History Section, Headquarters, III Corps and Fort Hood, Killeen; *Temple Daily Telegram*, February 17, September 17, 29, 1978.

32. Organizational History Files, History Section, Headquarters, III Corps and Fort Hood, Killeen; *Temple Daily Telegram*, August 11, 20, 1978.

33. Letter, Marvin D. Fuller to Sue Mayborn, August 6, 1989, FMC.

34. Interview, Richard Cavazos with OBF, September 15, 1989, FMC.

35. *Temple Daily Telegram*, June 25, 1978; *Killeen Daily Herald*, September 17, 1982, 10-A.

36. *Temple Daily Telegram*, May 15, 1980; *Killeen Daily Herald*, September 17, 1982, 11-A; "Fort Hood 1980" and "Fort Hood 1981" Files, *Temple Daily Telegram* offices; *Waco Tribune-Herald*, May 21, 1989, 13A, 14A;

letter, Mrs. Charles A. Jackson to Sue Mayborn, August 5, 1989, FMC (this letter contained the insights of her husband, Brigadier General Jackson, whose health prevented his writing).

37. John A. Adams, "Balancing Strategic Mobility and Tactical Capability," *Military Review*, LXVIII (August 1988), 9-23.

38. *Temple Daily Telegram*, January 13, February 1, 1980; Key Personnel Files, History Section, Headquarters, III Corps and Fort Hood, Killeen; *Fort Hood Sentinel*, March 23, 1989, Section C, p. 1.

39. *Temple Daily Telegram*, February 9, 1978.

40. *Ibid.*, December 7, 1972. See also *Waco Tribune-Herald*, May 30, 1989. For one analyst's view of what the increased number of women in the Army means, see Brian Mitchell, *Weak Link: The Feminization of the American Military* (Chicago: Regnery Gateway, 1988).

41. *Temple Daily Telegram*, January 9, 22, February 7, May 25, 1980; Ralph Peters, "The Age of Fatal Visibility," *Military Review*, LXVIII (August 1988), 49-59.

42. Key Personnel Files, History Section, III Corps and Fort Hood, Killeen; interview, Richard Cavazos with OBF, September 15, 1989, FMC.

43. Organizational History Files, History Section, III Corps and Fort Hood, Killeen; interview, Richard Cavazos with OBF, September 15, 1989, FMC.

44. Organizational History Files, History Section, III Corps and Fort Hood, Killeen; "Special Historic Supplement," *Fort Hood Sentinel*, 52.

45. Key Personnel Files, History Section, Headquarters, III Corps and Fort Hood, Killeen; *Temple Daily Telegram*, January 29, February 20, 26, 1982.

46. Interview, Richard Cavazos with OBF, September 15, 1989, FMC; *Temple Daily Telegram*, March 16,1980; *Waco Tribune-Herald*, Section B, p.1.

47. "Notes on Fort Hood Events 1983-1985," and "Fort Hood Leadership Study" (Final Report, February 28, 1986, Contract No. MDA903-85-C-0341), copy in Letter, Walter F. Ulmer, Jr., to Sue Mayborn, August 16, 1989, FMC; "Fort Hood Statistics As of September 30, 1985" in "Historical Review FY-85" File, and Fact Sheet, 1988, both in History Section, Headquarters, III Corps and Fort Hood, Killeen. See also "FORT HOOD–Personnel–Officers & Miscellaneous Data File," FMC; and *Temple Daily Telegram*, March 7, 1966, and June 23, 1984. For information about the M-1 tank, see Orr Kelly, *King of the Killing Zone: The Story of the M-1, America's Super Tank* (New York: W.W. Norton & Company, 1989).

48. Key Personnel Files, History Section, Headquarters, III Corps and Fort Hood, Killeen; *Temple Daily Telegram*, October 12, 1986.

49. Interview, Crosbie E. Saint with OBF, August 28, 1989, FMC.

50. Key Personnel Files, History Section, Headquarters, III Corps and Fort Hood, Killeen; *Temple Daily Telegram*, June 18, 1988; interview, Richard

FORT HOOD

Graves with OBF; August 28, 1989, FMC.

51. Organizational History Files, History Section, Headquarters, III Corps and Fort Hood, Killeen.

52. For an example see *Temple Daily Telegram*, May 4, 1988.

53. Interview, Richard Graves with OBF, August 28, 1989, FMC.

54. *Ibid.*

## Chapter Eight: *The Changing Nature of "R and R"*

1. *Killeen Daily Herald*, September 18, 1942; Duncan, *Killeen*, 94.

2. Duncan, *Killeen*, 96.

3. *Ibid.*, 97; *Killeen Daily Herald*, September 21, 1967, Section 3, p. 16; Hughes, "A Study of Temple, Texas During World War II," 32-34.

4. Hughes, "A Study of Temple, Texas During World War II," 34-35.

5. Camp Hood General Orders No. 4, June 12, 1942; Camp Hood General Orders No. 16, March 7, 1944; Camp Hood General Orders No. 18, March 10, 1944; all in "U.S. Army Commands, 1942-, Camp Hood, Texas," RG 338, Washington National Records Center, National Archives, Washington, D.C.

6. *Killeen Daily Herald*, September 14, 1962, Section 4, p. 4.

7. Organizational History Files (FY-42), History Section, Headquarters, III Corps and Fort Hood, Killeen.

8. *Armored Sentinel*, September 21, 1967, 15.

9. *Ibid.*, B-19.

10. *Ibid.*, B-20.

11. Camp Hood General Orders No. 13, September 14, 1942, "U.S. Army Commands, 1942-," RG 338, Washington National Records Center, National Archives and Records Administration, Washington, D.C.; *Armored Sentinel*, B-4; *Killeen Daily Herald*, September 21, 1967, Section 3, p. 4, and Section 4, p. 4.

12. *Armored Sentinel*, September 21, 1967, B-5 and B-20.

13. *Killeen Daily Herald*, September 21, 1967, Section 2, p. 2.

14. *Ibid.*, Section 2, p. 6.

15. *Ibid.*, Section 2, pp. 9, 16.

16. *Ibid.*, Section 2, p. 2.

17. *Ibid.*, September 14, 1962, Section 5, p. 5.

18. Jules Tygiel, *Baseball's Great Experiment: Jackie Robinson and His Legacy* (New York: Oxford University Press, 1983), 59-62; *Killeen Daily Herald*, September 21, 1967, Section 2, p. 7; Duncan, *Killeen*, 97.

19. Letter, John M. Devine to Frank W. Mayborn, September 23, 1946, in "C of C–Military Affairs–Misc.–Correspondence 1945 thru 1952" File,

FMC; *Killeen Daily Herald*, September 21, 1967, Section 2, p. 9.

20. *Temple Daily Telegram*, September 21, 28, October 5, 12, 19, 26, November 2, 9, 1946.

21. *Killeen Daily Herald*, September 21, 1967, Section 2, p. 8.

22. "What's Happening at Hood?" Rotogravure Magazine, *Houston Chronicle*, November 2, 1947; "Building for the Future," in Organizational History Files (FY-54 and FY-56), History Section, Headquarters, III Corps and Fort Hood, Killeen.

23. *Armored Sentinel*, September 21, 1967, B-10.

24. *Ibid.*, B-4; *Fort Hood: A Center for Advanced Armor Technology and Training* (El Cajon, CA: National Military Publications, 1981), 29-32.

25. *Killeen Daily Herald*, September 21, 1967, Section 3, p. 4.

26. *Temple Daily Telegram*, November 25, 1982.

27. *Killeen Daily Herald*, September 21, 1967, Section 3, p. 4.

28. *Armored Sentinel*, September 21, 1967, B-10.

29. *Killeen Daily Herald*, September 21, 1967, Section 3, pp. 10, 14; *Temple Daily Telegram*, July 5, 1983; and *Fort Hood*, 33-35.

30. *Temple Daily Telegram*, November 16, 1978; *Fort Hood*, 36.

31. Camp Hood General Orders No. 11, August 25, 1943, and Camp Hood General Orders No. 13, August 28, 1943, "U.S. Army Commands, 1942-, Camp Hood, Texas," RG 338, Washington National Records Center, National Archives and Records Administration, Washington, D.C.; *Killeen Daily Herald*, September 21, 1967, Section 4, p. 10; *Fort Hood*, 36-37.

32. *Fort Hood*, 34.

33. *Killeen Daily Herald*, September 21, 1967, Section 3, p. 15.

34. *Ibid.*, Section 3, p. 10; *Fort Hood*, 37.

35. *Killeen Daily Herald*, September 21, 1967, Section 4, p. 5, March 7, 1971, and July 9, 1978.

36. *Ibid.*, September 21, 1967, Section 4, p. 5.

37. *Ibid.*, Section 3, p. 14.

38. *Ibid.*, Section 4, p. 4; *Armored Sentinel*, September 21, 1967, B-10; and interview, Ralph E. Haines, Jr., with OBF, August 22, 1989, FMC.

39. *Armored Sentinel*, September 21, 1967, B-20.

40. *Armored Sentinel*, September 21, 1967, B-2, B-11; *Temple Daily Telegram*, August 28, October 23, 1988.

41. *Killeen Daily Herald*, September 21, 1967, Section 4, p. 6; *Fort Hood*, 22-23.

42. *Fort Hood*, 23.

43. *Killeen Daily Herald*, September 21, 1967, Section 4, pp. 7, 9; *Temple Daily Telegram*, January 30, 1971.

44. *Temple Daily Telegram*, March 29, 1958; *Killeen Daily Herald*, March

29, 1958, and September 21, 1967, Section 2, p. 12.

45. *Ibid.*

46. Interview, Roy Smith with OBF, August 6, 1989, FMC; Duncan, *Killeen*, 126-127.

47. *Killeen Daily Herald*, September 21, 1967, Section 2, p. 12. For additional details about Presley's training at Fort Hood, see Albert H. Goldman, *Elvis* (New York: McGraw-Hill, 1981).

48. *Temple Daily Telegram*, February 14, 1971.

49. *Armored Sentinel*, September 21, 1967, B-9; *Fort Hood*, 41.

50. "Memorandum For Record: 1st Cavalry Horse Platoon," in Organizational Unit Files (FY-73), History Section, Headquarters, III Corps and Fort Hood, Killeen.

51. *Fort Hood*, 41-42.

52. *Armored Sentinel*, September 21, 1967, B-4.

53. *Temple Daily Telegram*, September 6, 8, 15, 1985.

## Chapter Nine: *Friendship and Mutual Support*

1. Duncan, *Killeen*, 94-97.

2. The Census Bureau's estimated population for Killeen, which was revised on June 1, 1984 (the latest figures available), was 55,666. See Mike Kingston, editor, *1988-1989 Texas Almanac and State Industrial Guide* (Dallas: Dallas Morning News, 1987), 139. Estimates of Killeen's population by 1989 were approximately 60,000.

3. The *Temple Daily Telegram* of October 5, 1980, lists many of these problems. See also *ibid.*, September 14, 1962, Section 6, p. 7; and Duncan, *Killeen*, 146.

4. *Temple Daily Telegram*, September 17, 18, 1982; Duncan, *Killeen*, 146-153; Bell County Historical Commission, *Story of Bell County*, I, 143-146.

5. Kingston, ed., *1988-1989 Texas Almanac*, 139. See also Bell County Historical Commission, *Story of Bell County*, I, 129-130.

6. Kingston, ed., *1988-1989 Texas Almanac*, 139; Bell County Historical Commission, *Story of Bell County*, I, 159-161.

7. For details, see Faulk and Faulk, *Frank W. Mayborn*, Chapter 7.

8. Duncan, *Killeen*, 146.

9. Kingston, ed., *1988-1989 Texas Almanac*, 139.

10. *Ibid.*, 158.

11. Interview, Beverley E. Powell with OBF, October 2, 1989; Coryell County Genealogical Society, *Coryell County*, 53-56.

12. AG 000.7 AKAIN, "Coordination in Organization of Army Advisory Committees," copy in "ARMY ADVISORY COMMITTEE" File, FMC. See

also letter, Frank W. Mayborn to General J.M. Wainwright, March 15, 1947, copy in *ibid.*, in which Mayborn agreed to serve on the Army Advisory Committee for Fort Hood.

13. *Army Advisory Committee, Fourth Army* (pamphlet issued by the 4th Army), copy in "ARMY ADVISORY COMMITTEE" File, FMC.

14. See various letters in *ibid.*, and interview, Roy Smith with OBF, August 6, 1989, FMC.

15. General Bruce Clarke presented Mayborn a certificate of appreciation "For Community Service to Fort Hood, Texas, During the Year 1952," Scrapbook 10, "Military Affairs (1)," FMC.

16. For details of the Committee during these years, see numerous letters, clippings, and documents in "MILITARY AFFAIRS–Civilian Advisory Committee–1963-1967" File, FMC.

17. This agenda was contained in a letter calling the Army Advisory Committee to meet on September 19, 1963; see letter, General T.W. Dunn to Frank W. Mayborn, August 29, 1963, *ibid.*

18. See letters, documents, and clippings in *ibid.*

19. See "MILITARY AFFAIRS–Civilian Advisory Committee, 1967–" File, FMC, and Scrapbook 11, "Military Affairs (2)," FMC; interview, Crosbie E. Saint with OBF, August 28, 1989, FMC; interview, Richard Graves with OBF, August 28, 1989, FMC.

20. See "C of C–MILITARY AFFAIRS–Re Sagebrush–Camp Polk Move" File, FMC; "C of C–MILITARY RELATIONS COMMITTEE" File, FMC; *Killeen Daily Herald*, September 14, 1962, and September 21, 1967, Section 4, p. 11.

21. Interview, Richard Cavazos with OBF, September 15, 1989, FMC.

22. Interview, Beverley E. Powell with OBF, October 2, 1989, FMC; interview, Frank Norvell with OBF, August 14, 1989, FMC.

23. *Killeen Daily Herald*, September 21, 1967, Section 4, p. 7.

24. "AUSA's Primary Aim Is To Support U.S. Army," *ibid.*, Section 3, p. 15.

25. *Temple Daily Telegram*, October 16, 1969; Scrapbook 11, "Military Affairs (2)," FMC.

26. Scrapbook 11, "Military Affairs (2)," FMC; *Temple Daily Telegram*, October 17, 1979; *Killeen Daily Herald*, October 17, 1979; *Waco Tribune-Herald*, October 17, 1979.

27. *Killeen Daily Herald*, September 14, 1962.

28. *Ibid.*, September 21, 1967.

29. *Ibid.*, September 21, 1967, Section 2, p. 18.

30. *Armored Sentinel*, September 21, 1967, B-13.

31. *Killeen Daily Herald*, September 21, 1967, Section 2, p. 18.

32. *Ibid.* See also *Temple Daily Telegram*, February 12, 27, 1973.

33. *Killeen Daily Herald*, September 21, 1967, Section 2, p. 18.

34. *Ibid.*

35. *Ibid.*

36. *Ibid.*

37. *Temple Daily Telegram*, July 2, 1975.

38. *Ibid.*, September 23, 1973.

39. *Ibid.*, February 9, 10, 14, 1978.

40. *Ibid.*, September 1, 1988.

41. *Ibid.*, June 9, 1973.

42. See "FORT HOOD–Personnel–Officers–& Miscellaneous Data" File, FMC.

43. *Temple Daily Telegram*, October 20, 1965.

## Chapter Ten: *Toward the 21st Century*

1. Interview, Roy Smith with OBF, August 6, 1989, FMC.

2. "III Corps and Fort Hood Facts," June 30, 1989, copy in authors' possession.

3. Quoted in Harvey and King, *Evolving the Army of the 21st Century*, 3.

4. *Ibid.*, 4-8.

5. *Killeen Daily Herald*, September 21, 1967, II-13.

6. 1st Armored Division Command Report, 1951, "Army AG Command Reports, 1949-1954," RG 319, Washington National Records Center, National Archives and Records Administration, Washington, D.C.

7. Interview, Robert M. Shoemaker with OBF, August 23, 1989, FMC. See also interview, Richard Cavazos with OBF, September 15, 1989, FMC.

8. Interview, Robert M. Shoemaker with OBF, August 23, 1989, FMC.

9. General Vuono's plan, "A Strategic Force for the 1990s and Beyond," was analyzed by Michael R. Gordon and Bernard E. Trainor of the New York Times News Service; see "Army Proposes Changing Mission," *Waco Tribune-Herald*, December 12, 1989, 13-B.

# Index

167, 171, 177
Grazing, at Fort Hood, 43-44
Greer, Dewitt C., 39
Grogan, Stanley J., 50
Groves, James R., 157
Gulf, Colorado and Santa Fe Railroad. See Santa Fe Railroad

Haines, Ralph E., Jr., 134-136, 137-139, 147, 197, 215, 227
Halley, Robert B., 9
Hamilton County, 136
Hardin, John Wesley, 7
Harker Heights, TX, 121, 146, 159, 209-211, 217, 222, 223, 226
Harrold, Thomas L., 127
H.B. Zachary Company, 51, 52
Helicopters, 155, 170-171
"Hell on Wheels." See Second Armored Division
Hester, John H., 77-80
Hiestand, Harry H., 67-68
Higginbotham, Frank C., 102
Highways, around Fort Hood, 10-11, 38-39, 52, 55, 134, 191, 206
Hillandale Hospital, 220
Hobbs, L.S., 91, 103-104
Hobby, Oveta Culp, 25, 73
Hobby, Will, 25
Honest John Rocket, 128-129
Hood, John Bell, 39, 58
Hood Village, 55, 92, 97
Hoover, A.J., 96
Hope, Bob, 186
Horse Platoon, 204
Hospital, at Fort Hood, 117, 148, 198, 200. See also Darnall Army Hospital
Hospital Branch Library, 198
Housing, at Fort Hood, 93-96, 115-116, 174, 190-191, 214, 217. See

also names of individual housing areas
Houston, TX, 144, 222
*Houston Post*, 25
Houston, O.P., 90
Hudson Hotel, Killeen, 47
Humphrey, Walter R., 35-36
Hunt and Saddle Club, 194

Indians, in Central Texas, 3-5
Individual Tank Training Course, 110
Industrial Electric Company, 52
Infantry Replacement Training Center, 81-86
Insects, at Fort Hood, 65-66
"Iron Deuce." See Second Armored Division

Jack Mountain, 132
James, Frank, 7
James, Jesse, 7
Jeep-Mounted Band, 1st AD, 136
Jethro, Gilbert, 76
Johnson, Lyndon B., 104, 106, 126, 145
Jones, Jesse, 16, 25-26
J.W. France Company, 52

KCEN-TV, 159
Kennedy, John F., 132-133, 134, 137, 139, 145
Kennon, Robert, 126
Kern, Harvey, 209
Killeen, 9, 30, 31, 32, 33, 35, 49, 50, 51, 52, 60, 63, 73, 76, 77, 88, 96; impact of Fort Hood on, 46-48, 53; dance at, 57; schools at, 97-98; business in, 98, 107, 115-116, 121, 207-209, 210-211; and *passim*

Whittle, 52
McNair, Lesley J., 16-17, 19, 20, 72, 78, 103, 104
McNamara, Robert S., 133
Medical Department Activity (MEDDAC), 176
Medieval Fair, 205-206
Meredith, Burgess, 186
Meyer, Stewart, 152-153
Milam County, 3, 4
Military Assistance to Safety and Traffic (MAST), 223
Military Operations in Urban Terrain, 172-173
Military Police, 67, 84-85, 176
Miller, Charles S., 32
Mills County, 136
Minor, T.H., 47, 180
Missiles, 132
Mobile Army Sensor System, Test and Evaluation Resources. See MASSTER
Mobilization and Training Equipment Site (MATES), 166
Montague Riding Club, 194
Moore, Ray, 97
Morale Support Activities Division, 204-206
Murphy, A., 63
Museums, at Fort Hood, 198-200
Musical groups, at Fort Hood, 196

National Aeronautics and Space Administration, 144
National Defense Act, 1920, 13
National Guard, 87, 100, 105, 108, 133, 165-166, 178, 211
National Housing Act, 1949, 115
National Security Act, 1947, 100-101
Nazi Town, 68

New Hope, TX, 8, 44
Nichols, W.R., 80
Nolan Creek, 219, 221-222
Nolanville, TX, 4, 9, 159, 210, 222
Non-Commissioned Officers, 110, 157, 162, 192-193, 232
Non-Commissioned Officer Academy, 110, 157
Non-Commissioned Officers Open Mess, 192-193
North Camp Hood, construction of, 45, 54-55, 58, 65, 72, 78; status at end of World War II, 86-87; National Guard at, 100, 102-103, 105, 165-166, 178, 184
North Village, 55
Norvell, Frank, 135, 217

Officer Candidate School Regiment, 70-71
Officers' clubs, 184-185, 192
Officers' quarters, 93-94. See also Housing
Oglesby, TX, 30
"Old Ironsides." See First Armored Division
Old Ironsides Sports Arena, 183
Old Killeen. See Palo Alto
Operation Big Lift, 140-141
Operation Gyroscope, 129-130
Operation Longhorn, 111-112, 125, 152
Operation Sage Brush, 127, 216
Operation Seminole, 91
Organization of Retired Military, 218
Oswalt, G.C., Jr., 96
Our Land, Our Lives, 158-161, 212
Outlaws, in Central Texas, 5-9
Owl Creek, 1, 7, 9